AFTER HEGEMONY

AFTER HEGEMONY

Cooperation and Discord in the

World Political Economy

With a new preface by the author

ROBERT O. KEOHANE

Princeton University Press
Princeton and Oxford

Published by Princeton University Press, 41 William Street,
Princeton, New Jersey 08540
In the United Kingdom: Princeton University Press,
3 Market Place, Woodstock, Oxfordshire OX20 1SY

First edition, 1984

First Princeton Classic Edition, with a new preface by the author, 2005

Library of Congress Control Number 2004116492

ISBN 0-691-12248-2

British Library Cataloging-in-Publication Data is available

This book has been composed in Linotron Sabon

Printed on acid-free paper. ∞

pup.princeton.edu

Printed in the United States of America

3   5   7   9   10   8   6   4

ISBN-13: 978-0-691-12248-9 (pbk.)

ISBN-10: 0-691-12248-2 (pbk.)

To Nannerl Overholser Keohane

CONTENTS

PREFACE TO THE 2005 EDITION

It is a source of great satisfaction to any author that his book is still read and cited after more than twenty years. But to an author of a book about contemporary world politics, in this era of rapid change, such longevity is also a source of amazement. Since the publication of *After Hegemony*, the Soviet Union has collapsed; the United States has maintained its economic advantage over other industrialized democracies and has risen to a position of unparalleled military dominance; and terrorism has replaced fear of interstate nuclear war as the principal threat to the security of the American people.

"After hegemony," indeed! The title of my book seems quaintly out of touch with contemporary reality. Relationships among the major capitalist countries had been remarkably cooperative between 1945 and 1984, a fact attributed by many theorists (e.g., Gilpin, 1975; Krasner, 1976) to American hegemony. Yet hegemony in the world political economy seemed to be in decline: in fact, the U.S. share of world GDP had fallen quite markedly in the previous twenty years (see table 9.1, p. 197). I did not expect a precipitous decline in the future, but I thought that we were entering a post-hegemonic era. The conjunction of what I called hegemonic cooperation and the apparent decline of hegemony framed the key issue for my book: "How can cooperation take place in world politics in the absence of hegemony?" (p. 14). This question seemed to have urgent policy relevance, since many voices were claiming that the continuing decline of American hegemony signaled a return to much greater conflict, and the collapse of international institutions that had promoted cooperation.

This framing of my argument soon proved too limited. My friend and collaborator Joseph S. Nye told me when he saw drafts of *After Hegemony* that it was misleading to exclude the analysis of military-security relationships. But I found that I needed to limit the scope of the argument in order to develop and seek to evaluate (if not really test) a coherent line of thought. So I settled for a paragraph (pp. 136-37) explaining that I would set security issues aside. Nye, who continued to connect economic and security issues in his work, argued as early as 1990 that the United States was more powerful than the con-

I am indebted for comments on an earlier draft of this preface to Stephen D. Krasner, Lisa L. Martin, Helen V. Milner, Chuck Myers, Joseph S. Nye, Jr., and Beth Simmons—exemplary colleagues and friends.

ventional wisdom suggested—that it was "bound to lead" (Nye, 1990). The collapse of the Soviet Union and the technological revolution in warfare combined to render his analysis even more correct, perhaps, than he had anticipated.

Furthermore, although since 1984 economic growth has been much faster in China, India, and other rapidly developing countries than in the United States, both of America's then-rivals, Europe and Japan, have grown more slowly (World Bank, 2004). By the turn of the millennium, the United States had achieved a preponderance of military capabilities that was unrivaled in modern history, and had extended its economic advantage over other advanced industrialized states (Wohlforth, 2002, p. 105). As a result, we have not really seen a test of whether institutions will last "after hegemony." Indeed, the contemporary issue is whether these institutions can survive the ex-treme degree of unipolarity that has emerged, particularly after Sep-tember 11 prompted radical changes in American foreign policy.

THE THEORETICAL ARGUMENT

So why is *After Hegemony* not simply gathering dust on library shelves, ignored when not being ridiculed for its errors? In my view, because the central theoretical argument of the book is largely unaf-fected by its anachronistic framing. Part II of the book conceptualizes cooperation not as harmony but as an intensely political process of mutual adjustment in a situation of actual and potential discord (p. 52). I agree with Kenneth N. Waltz that "in anarchy there is no auto-matic harmony" (Waltz, 1959, p. 182), and go on to ask how coop-eration is possible under these conditions.

My answer builds deliberately and explicitly both on Realism, par-ticularly Waltz's neorealism, and rational choice theory. States do not typically cooperate out of altruism or empathy with the plight of oth-ers, nor for the sake of pursuing what they conceive as "international interests." They seek wealth and security for their own people, and search for power as a means to these ends. The units of action (states) and the motivations ascribed to states in *After Hegemony* would be familiar to a reader of Hans J. Morgenthau (1948) or Arnold Wolfers (1962). As I say in chapter 1, "we need to go beyond Realism, not discard it" (p. 16).

On this Realist foundation, however, I build an institutionalist edi-fice. The key to my argument is the "functional theory of interna-tional regimes," which appears in chapter 6 and was foreshadowed two years earlier in my article "The demand for international regimes"

(Keohane, 1982). According to my argument, states build international regimes in order to promote mutually beneficial cooperation. The international trade regime of the General Agreement on Tariffs and Trade (GATT) is an institution to which I often refer; indeed, it could be argued that my theory generalizes the experience of GATT. International regimes—clusters of principles, norms, rules, and decision-making procedures—reduce transaction costs for states, alleviate problems of asymmetrical information, and limit the degree of uncertainty that members of the regime face in evaluating each others' policies. Like other political institutions, international regimes can be explained in terms of self-interest. Furthermore, they exert an impact on state policies largely by changing the costs and benefits of various alternatives. They do not override self-interest but rather affect calculations of self-interest.

A crucial argument, which foreshadows later arguments in game-theoretic treatments of world politics, is that information is a *variable*. It is not just that world politics is uncertain; institutionalization can provide information, increase credibility, and generate focal points, thus reducing uncertainty.

In my judgment, the central arguments of *After Hegemony* have held up well. Indeed, some of my severest critics seem to have accepted substantial elements of it. Joseph Grieco declares at the end of *Cooperation among Nations* (1990) that Realist theory holds that "international institutions do matter for states as they attempt to cooperate" (pp. 233-34). Lloyd Gruber (2000) writes that "rather than seeking to destroy neoliberalism's theoretical edifice, realists are now themselves actively building on it" (p. 29).

The 1990s were supportive of the theory of cooperation and institutions developed in *After Hegemony*. Realists imagined that the end of the Cold War would lead to the decline or collapse of international institutions, which they saw as reflections of superpower conflict rather than as devices by which states could achieve mutually beneficial cooperation in functionally defined issue-areas (Mearsheimer, 1990, 1994-95). But during the 1990s the European Union expanded and strengthened its institutions, NATO expanded both its membership and its range of activities, and the World Trade Organization (WTO) broadened its tasks and was given substantial new powers to settle disputes. Some observers worried that international institutions were co-opted by a revived version of American hegemony. But in general, it appeared to many of us that cooperation could be sustained by the prospect of mutual benefit, apart from superpower rivalry.

Since September 11, we have moved into a new era, characterized by the vigorous exercise of America's unprecedented political and military power. The military dominance of the United States encouraged the Bush administration to persuade itself that its need for allies had radically diminished. President Bush decided to invade Iraq in 2003, in part with the ambitious objective of instituting democratic governance in the Middle East. In view of the radical shifts in American policy, it is hardly surprising that America's allies in Europe and Asia have sought to constrain American actions. Conflicts of interest between the United States and its allies have increased.

The extent to which such conflicts of interest are inherent in the structure of contemporary world politics is not clear. Certainly in 1984 I did not anticipate sharp increases in geopolitical conflicts of interest to appear between the United States and other major capitalist countries. On the contrary, I expected an increasing demand for cooperation. Like most observers, however, I believed that the struggle between Western liberal democracy and Soviet communism would last indefinitely. On security issues, the collapse of the adversary certainly made discord between Europe and the United States more likely, and it is natural that such discord should have had effects on non-security issues as well. Yet in my view, the turn taken by the United States in 2002 and 2003 was profoundly affected by the ideological orientations of the people in power in the U.S. government. Had the election of 2000 turned out differently, it is very difficult to imagine that the United States would have attacked Iraq in the absence of either authorization from the United Nations or support from its traditional European allies.

Nothing in *After Hegemony* would have enabled one to anticipate the degree of conflict that now exists, in the fall of 2004, between the United States and its European allies. The book's argument would lead one, however, to expect that the United States could not successfully attain its political objectives through military power, while scorning the United Nations. The failure of unilateralism to achieve American objectives in Iraq supports this position. If the argument of *After Hegemony* is correct, future American administrations will have to rely to a considerable extent on international institutions to attain their objectives in a variety of issue areas.

The argument of *After Hegemony,* that cooperation can take place without hegemony, also implies that international cooperation does not necessarily require American participation. The coming into force of the Kyoto Protocol on climate change, and the creation of the International Criminal Court without U.S. membership, indicate that new global institutions can exist without the United States. The possibility of global cooperation without the United States comes at a time of increasing differences in values between Europe (and to some extent other industrialized democracies) and America. One thinks of issues such as state regulation of the economy, provision of welfare benefits, the death penalty, and respect for international law. Hence the substance of the rules created will be different in new institutions created without the United States, than it would be with the United States fully engaged.

Major Shortcomings

Only a very rigid thinker or a fool would fail to change his views on some important points over the course of twenty-one years. One of the joys, furthermore, of writing a work that attracts attention is that younger scholars find contradictions or anomalies, or otherwise identify weaknesses in the argument. Let me discuss some of the weaknesses that I think have been identified in *After Hegemony*.

The most obvious weakness was deliberate: the theoretical discussion of *After Hegemony* treats states as units, without taking into account variations in domestic politics or in the ideas prevailing within them. The historical accounts of American hegemonic policy in chapters 8 and 9 are replete with references to the importance of domestic politics; but domestic politics plays no role in my theory. The reason for the inconsistency was simple: I did not know how to incorporate a sophisticated domestic politics theory into my analysis in a cogent and parsimonious way. As a result, *After Hegemony* lacks a theory of how domestic politics and international institutions connect. A number of efforts have been made to rectify this omission. Since many scholars have made important contributions to this line of work, I hesitate to mention names; but it should be noted that Helen Milner's efforts to link domestic and international politics have been particularly noteworthy and influential (Milner, 1997, 1998).

After Hegemony has probably been most severely criticized for de-emphasizing the issue of the *distribution* of gains from institutionalized cooperation. *After Hegemony* adopts what Alexander Wendt (1999) later referred to as a Lockean culture of anarchy, in which actors are neither enemies nor friends, but rivals. They all seek their own advantage, without particular animosity, or empathy, toward others. In this context, my argument stresses what could be called the "efficiency gains" from cooperation. I recognized that distributional issues are important in world politics, but I did not emphasize these issues and my theory did not account for how the benefits of agreements would be distributed (Krasner, 1991).

In the late 1980s and early 1990s a lively debate occurred about distributional issues related to international cooperation (Grieco, 1988; Keohane, 1993). In my view, that debate concluded with an acknowledgement that distributional issues deserve more emphasis than I gave them, but that they can be understood within a standard utility and bargaining framework (Powell, 1993, p. 228; Powell, 1999, p. 76). Under some conditions distributional issues can have important effects on cooperation, although they do not render such cooperation impossible in the real world.

The distributional issues are undoubtedly more complex than the argument in *After Hegemony* indicates. I emphasized correctly that agreements in world politics have to be self-enforcing. Therefore, actors will comply with such agreements only if they benefit as much from the agreement as from the reversion point—what they could achieve without the agreement. What I did not sufficiently appreciate are the implications of the fact that states or coalitions of states may be able, through international agreement, to change the status quo, and therefore reduce the value of the reversion point for other states. The latter states may then face an unpleasant choice: between accepting an agreement that is worse than the previous status quo, on the one hand, and remaining independent of commitments under conditions that are also worse than the previous status quo, on the other (Gruber, 2000).

This criticism has implications for our ethical evaluations of international regimes: we should be even more skeptical than I was in 1984. I warned that international regimes would not necessarily increase welfare, since states could be excluded and regimes could be directed against them. I criticized the International Monetary Fund (IMF), GATT, and other international institutions quite specifically for reflecting the ideologies and interests of powerful, wealthy states, and therefore falling far short of what would be demanded by cosmopolitan ethical standards (p. 256). However, I retained the faith that these institutions would not worsen the situation of poor countries relative to a situation in which no such institutions existed. But the WTO negotiations on intellectual property rights (TRIPs) provide a specific illustration of the problem that Lloyd Gruber highlighted. The agreement establishing the WTO required states to accept all provisions of the Uruguay Round if they wished to benefit from any of them. Such provisions can worsen the situation of poor countries, particularly if negotiations are complex and they are poorly staffed relative to their richer bargaining partners (Steinberg, 2002).

Unresolved Questions and Directions for Research

After Hegemony claims that international institutions have significant impacts on important outcomes in world politics. The fundamental theoretical problem here, which is not recognized in the book, is that of endogeneity. Institutions are explained, in my theory, by power and interest—one could add the ideas, or worldviews, of participants and the nature of domestic political regimes. That is, they are endogenous to these other factors. What, then, happens to the impact of institutions? "Insofar as the theory of institutional origins and functions is accepted, the independent explanatory power of institutions seems to disappear" (Keohane and Martin, 2003, p. 98).

However, it turns out that for three reasons it does not really disappear. The existence of multiple equilibria in game-theoretic outcomes means that there is no unique institutional outcome dictated by power and interests, whether combined with ideational and domestic political factors or not. Hence the characteristics of institutions can affect the nature of the equilibria that result—even though institutions do not specify a unique equilibrium any more than do power and interest. Secondly, organizations persist over time, exerting effects even after the configurations of power, interests, and ideas existing at their formation have changed. Finally, agency theory shows how agents (such as international organizations) can exert effects within constraints—sometimes broad ones—imposed by principals (Keohane and Martin, 2003).

Each of these three reasons for institutional impact suggests a deficiency in the analysis of *After Hegemony*, and some directions for further research.

First, the existence of multiple equilibria in game theory means that *After Hegemony* falls far short of explaining cooperation and discord. It provides a framework for the analysis of these phenomena, but not a testable theory. Such a theory would require the specification of conditional hypotheses with clear observable implications, and strategies for measurement and empirical assessment, that would enable scholars to test the hypotheses. Social science is not yet at the point at which such a theory, about such a complex and multifaceted phenomenon as cooperation in world politics, can be devised and tested.

Second, even at a less ambitious level, *After Hegemony* does not pay enough attention to organizations and their dynamics (Barnett and Finnemore, 1998). The framework of my book—useful as far as it goes but incomplete—was designed to understand how states interact to create international regimes, conceptualized as institutionalized structures of rules. The organizational characteristics of regimes are largely ignored. Hence my framework is less helpful for studying the World Bank or IMF than for analyzing the WTO, because the World Bank and IMF are large organizations whose bureaucracies engage in strategic action, which is not entirely rule-bound.

Third, *After Hegemony* lacks a theory of delegation. Ironically, my functional theory, focused on the interaction of states, may have given too much credit to the Realist anarchy paradigm that it sought to criticize. I was aware in 1984 that the problem of incomplete contracts and asymmetric information was fundamental, as works, which I had cited, by such scholars as Akerlof, Coase, and Williamson had argued. Yet to assure credibility and reduce uncertainty, incomplete contracts require authoritative interpretation, which in international law entails delegation—often to courts (Goldstein et al., 2001). Within complex organizations, interpretation of rules and their effective implementation require delegation. But delegation to agents implies potential shifts in power, and problems of control. Agency theory has recently been used, in promising ways, to explore these implications with respect to international organizations (Nielson and Tierney, 2003).

Another important direction for research involves issues of compliance. In *After Hegemony* I relied heavily on reputation as a motivation for compliance with international commitments (pp. 105-6). Indeed, my next research project was an attempt to demonstrate the importance of reputation for compliance. Research, however, has an interesting way of revealing the unexpected, and what I found did not match my expectations. In examining U.S. compliance, or lack thereof, with its international commitments, I found more noncompliance than I had expected (extending over the history of the United States between 1776 and 1989). Reputational concerns, although genuine, seemed to have less impact on policy than I had expected. Since I have not yet invented a theory that would compellingly account for the great variations in compliance that I found, much of this research has not led to publication. But it has made me wiser, and more cautious, about reputation as an incentive for compliance.

Some excellent recent work on this subject (Simmons, 2000; Hathaway, 2002) suggests both that reputation is important in states' calculations and that concerns about it are not a guarantee of compliance with international commitments.

CONCLUSION

When *After Hegemony* was written, the word "globalization" was not part of our lexicon. The Internet was little more than a gleam in the eye of some scientists affiliated with the Defense Department. The number of transnational non-governmental networks was probably at least an order of magnitude less than it is today. Nye and I had already discussed what we called transgovernmental relations (Keohane and Nye, 1974), but these networks were miniscule compared to the situation at present (Slaughter, 2004). Scholars had not yet identified "issue-advocacy networks" (Keck and Sikkink, 1998) or "global civil society" (Keene, 2003) as important subjects for analysis. Hence *After Hegemony* appears too state-centric for the twenty-first century.

Were a new volume on "cooperation and discord in the world political economy" to be written today, it would have to integrate three forms of analysis. Like *After Hegemony,* it would have to investigate how states form international regimes and comply or not with their rules. But it would also have to discuss how the decisions of states and intergovernmental organizations are affected by the activities of non-governmental organizations (NGOs) and the transnational and transgovernmental networks in which they are embedded. And it would have to link the analysis of both state and transnational action to domestic politics, making use of contemporary theory and research in comparative politics.

In an autobiographical context, one way of making this point is to say that a rewriting of *After Hegemony* today would need to return to some themes that Nye and I pursued in the 1970s, in *Transnational Relations and World Politics* (1972) and *Power and Interdependence* (1977/2001). In 1984 I did not reject the arguments we had made during the previous decade. But I put some of these complexities aside in order to develop a clearer conceptualization for understanding cooperation among states. Some of my recent work—as in *Power and Governance in a Partially Globalized World* (2002)—can be taken as the beginning of an attempt to understand cooperation in the context of globalization, which I view as the intensification and transformation of patterns of interdependence. But the best new scholarship on global political economy all relies heavily on sophisticated models and quantitative as well as qualitative evidence about domestic politics—areas missing from my résumé.

Once published, a book is open to interpretation by all readers. The author has no privileged status in this enterprise, and his interpretation may even be partially impaired by self-interest and the tricks of memory. Others' reflections are at least equally valuable. My hope is that *After Hegemony* will continue not only to provide fuel for argument, but to stimulate new thinking and more rigorous research during the next phase of its shelf life.

REFERENCES

Baldwin, David A., ed., 1993. *Neorealism and Neoliberalism: The Contemporary Debate* (New York: Columbia University Press).

Barnett, Michael, and Martha Finnemore, 1999. The politics, power, and pathologies of international organizations. *International Organization*, vol. 53, no. 4 (Autumn), pp. 699-732.

Elman, Colin, and Miriam Fendius Elman, eds., 2003. *Progress in International Relations Theory: Appraising the Field* (Cambridge: MIT Press).

Gilpin, Robert, 1975. *U.S. Power and the Multinational Corporation* (New York: Basic Books).

Goldstein, Judith, et al., 2001. *Legalization and World Politics* (Cambridge: MIT Press).

Grieco, Joseph, 1988. Anarchy and the limits of cooperation: a realist critique of the newest liberal institutionalism. *International Organization*, vol. 42, no. 3 (Summer), pp. 485-507. Reprinted in Baldwin, 1993, pp. 116-40.

Grieco, Joseph, 1990. *Cooperation among Nations* (Ithaca: Cornell University Press).

Gruber, Lloyd, 2000. *Ruling the World: Power Politics and the Rise of Supranational Institutions* (Princeton: Princeton University Press).

Hathaway, Oona A., 2002. Do human rights treaties make a difference? *Yale Law Journal*, vol. 111, no. 8 (June), pp. 1935-2042.

Ikenberry, G. John, ed., 2002. *America Unrivaled* (Ithaca: Cornell University Press).

Katzenstein, Peter J., Robert O. Keohane, and Stephen D. Krasner, 1999. *Exploration and Contestation in World Politics* (Cambridge: MIT Press).

Keck, Margaret, and Kathryn Sikkink, 1998. *Activists beyond Borders: Advocacy Networks in International Politics* (Ithaca: Cornell University Press).

Keene, John, 2003. *Global Civil Society?* (Cambridge: Cambridge University Press).

Keohane, Robert O., 1982. The demand for international regimes. *Interna-*

tional Organization, vol. 36, no. 2 (Spring), pp. 325-55. Reprinted in Krasner, 1983, pp. 141-71.

Keohane, Robert O., 1993. Institutional theory and the Realist challenge after the Cold War. In Baldwin, 1993, pp. 269-300.

Keohane, Robert O., 2002. *Power and Governance in a Partially Globalized World* (London: Routledge).

Keohane, Robert O., and Joseph S. Nye, Jr., eds., 1972. *Transnational Relations and World Politics* (Cambridge: Cambridge University Press).

Keohane, Robert O., and Joseph S. Nye, Jr., 1974. Transgovernmental relations and international organizations. *World Politics*, vol. 27, no. 1 (October), pp. 39-62.

Keohane, Robert O., and Joseph S. Nye, Jr., 1977/2001. *Power and Interdependence* (New York: Addison Wesley Longman).

Keohane, Robert O., and Lisa L. Martin, 2003. Institutional theory as a research program. In Elman and Elman, 2003, pp. 71-108.

Krasner, Stephen D., 1976. State power and the structure of international trade. *World Politics*, vol. 28, no. 3 (April), pp. 317-43.

Krasner, Stephen D., ed., 1983. *International Regimes* (Ithaca: Cornell University Press).

Krasner, Stephen D., 1991. Global communications and national power: life on the Pareto frontier. *World Politics*, vol. 43, no. 3 (April), pp. 336-66. Reprinted in Baldwin, 1993, pp. 234-49.

Mearsheimer, John J., 1990. Back to the future: instability in Europe after the Cold War. *International Security*, vol. 15, no. 1 (Summer), pp. 5-56.

Mearsheimer, John J., 1994-95. The false promise of international institutions. *International Security*, vol. 19, no. 3 (Winter), pp. 5-49.

Milner, Helen V., 1997. *Interests, Institutions, and Information: Domestic Politics and International Relations* (Princeton: Princeton University Press).

Milner, Helen V., 1998. Rationalizing politics: the emerging synthesis of international, American, and comparative politics. *International Organization*, vol. 52, no. 4 (Autumn), pp. 759-86. Reprinted in Katzenstein et al., 1999, pp. 119-46.

Morgenthau, Hans J., 1948. *Politics among Nations* (New York: Knopf).

Nielsen, Daniel, and Michael Tierney, 2003. Delegation to international organizations: agency theory and World Bank environmental reform. *International Organization*, vol. 57, no. 2 (Spring), pp. 241-76.

Nye, Joseph S., Jr., 1990. *Bound to Lead: The Changing Nature of American Power* (New York: Basic Books).

Powell, Robert, 1993. Absolute and relative gains in international relations theory. In Baldwin, 1993, pp. 209-33. Reprinted from the *American Political Science Review*, vol. 85, no. 4 (December 1991), pp. 1303-20.

Powell, Robert, 1999. *In the Shadow of Power: States and Strategies in World Politics* (Princeton: Princeton University Press).

Simmons, Beth A., 2000. International law and state behavior: commitment and compliance in international monetary affairs. *American Political Science Review*, vol. 94, no. 4 (December), pp. 819-38.

Slaughter, Anne-Marie, 2004. *The New World Order* (Princeton: Princeton University Press).

Steinberg, Richard H., 2002. In the shadow of law or power? Consensus-based bargaining and outcomes in the GATT/WTO. *International Organization*, vol. 56, no. 2 (Spring), pp. 339-74.

Waltz, Kenneth, 1959. *Man, the State, and War* (New York: Columbia University Press).

Wendt, Alexander, 1999. *Social Theory of International Politics* (Cambridge: Cambridge University Press).

Wohlforth, William, 2002. U.S. strategy in a unipolar world. In Ikenberry, 2002, pp. 98-120.

Wolfers, Arnold, 1962. *Discord and Collaboration: Essays in International Politics* (Baltimore: Johns Hopkins University Press).

World Bank, 2004. *World Development Indicators* (Washington, D.C.: The World Bank).

PREFACE

In its genesis and support, this is an old-fashioned book. It is essentially the work of an individual scholar, unaided by a research team or large-scale funding. Nevertheless, I have accumulated a number of institutional debts of gratitude during the seven years of research and writing. I benefited, during the early stages of reflection and reading, from being a Fellow of the Center for Advanced Study in the Behavioral Sciences during 1977-78, under a grant from the German Marshall Fund of the United States. Most of the research was done while I was teaching at Stanford University until the spring of 1981 and at Brandeis University since then. Stanford helped me to finance research assistance and a trip to the International Energy Agency in Paris in 1981. The Mazur Fund for Faculty Research at Brandeis supplied funds for photocopying the manuscript and circulating it to colleagues. Thanks to a sabbatical leave generously provided by Brandeis University for the academic year 1983-84, I was able to devote myself wholeheartedly, between June 1983 and January 1984, to preparing the final manuscript. Wellesley College permitted me to use its convenient and well-organized library and to take advantage of its computer system for word-processing, which greatly expedited my work. Staff members of both the library and the computer center were most helpful. For all of this support I am most grateful.

The overall argument of this book has never appeared in print before, although "The demand for international regimes," published in *International Organization*, Spring 1982, contains early versions of some of the core ideas of chapters 5-6. The theme of Part III—the complementarity of hegemony and cooperation in practice—is also first presented here, but some of the case material has been published before. Chapter 8 builds on "Hegemonic leadership and U.S. foreign economic policy in the 'Long Decade' of the 1950s," published in William P. Avery and David P. Rapkin, eds., *America in a Changing World Political Economy* (New York: Longman, 1982). Chapter 9 is in part based on "The theory of hegemonic stability and changes in international economic regimes, 1967-1977." Sections of this chapter that reproduce parts of the earlier article, in modified form, are reprinted by permission of Westview Press from Ole R. Holsti, Randolph M. Siverson, and Alexander L. George, eds., *Change in the International System* (copyright 1980 by Westview Press, Boulder, Colorado). Some of chapter 10 also appeared in "International agencies and the art of the possible: the case of the IEA," *Journal of Policy Analysis and Management*, vol. 1, no. 4 (Summer 1982), copyright 1982 by John Wiley & Sons.

This book on cooperation also benefited from the noninstitutional cooperation of scores of friends, students, and colleagues—so many, indeed, that I refrain from trying to list them all, lest some inadvertently be excluded. Earlier versions of several chapters, in draft or as previously published articles, were circulated to quite a few political scientists and economists, and I received many helpful observations, all of which I seriously considered and many of which led to changes. The willingness of scholars to devote time and intelligence to helping each other improve the quality of their work is one of the most rewarding features of contemporary academic life. Fortunately for me, the field of international political economy contains a large number of very talented and generous people.

I do want to mention by name a small number of people who have made special contributions. Karen Bernstein and Shannon Salmon served ably as research assistants, gathering material used in chapters 8-10. I shared many early, otherwise uncirculated drafts with Helen Milner. I am grateful to her both for offering trenchant criticisms and for not giving up on the project even when my preliminary arguments may have seemed hopelessly contorted and confused. Joseph Nye, my close friend and former co-author, has been a valuable source of both intellectual perspective and moral support. Vinod Aggarwal, Robert Axelrod, James Caporaso, Benjamin Cohen, Robert Gilpin, Peter Gourevitch, Leah Haus, Harold Jacobson, Peter Katzenstein, Nannerl Keohane, David Laitin, Helen Milner, Joseph Nye, Susan Moller Okin, Robert Putnam, and Howard Silverman read all or large parts of the penultimate draft and gave me valuable comments.

Equally important are the senior scholars whom I have sought to emulate: creative people who respect and care about younger thinkers, and who refuse to hide self-protectively behind reputations and titles. These intellectuals are willing to propose new ideas and to submit them to scrutiny. Knowing that social science advances not so much by the cumulative grubbing of facts as by the dialectical confrontation of ideas, they are not afraid to be criticized or even proven wrong. Among these mentors I include particularly Alexander George, Ernst Haas, Albert Hirschman, Stanley Hoffmann, Charles Kindleberger, Robert North, Raymond Vernon, and Kenneth Waltz—a diverse set of scholars united only by their fertile imaginations, intellectual honesty, and vigor of mind and spirit.

Two men who were inspirations to me are no longer alive. One is

Fred Hirsch, an imaginative political economist, author of *Social Limits to Growth*, and a great person who died too young. The other is Robert E. Keohane, my father. Although he had a powerful intellect, he never produced major works of scholarship; but my memory of the range and richness of his knowledge and his utter integrity still serve to warn me against superficiality and opportunism.

The remaining members of my immediate family have made major contributions to this enterprise. My mother, Mary P. Keohane, has for over forty years provided me with a synergistic combination of maternal love, moral precepts, and intellectual stimulation. She continues to be supporter, critic, and exemplar to me. Concern for my children's futures reinforces my belief in the urgency of understanding cooperation in world politics; but they themselves have more often reminded me that sometimes scholarship should be subordinated to fun. Nannerl Overholser Keohane, my wife, has played such an enormously important and multifaceted role that it is difficult for me to convey its significance. Her own writings set a high standard for depth of research, clarity of expression, and grace of style. Her accomplishments as college president both fill me with admiration and bolster my determination to make the most of the happy life of scholarship that dedicated people in such positions make possible. Her criticisms of my works and her high expectations for them impel me to greater levels of effort. In addition to everything else, she has been a source of love, moral support, and domestic contentment.

Wellesley, Massachusetts
January 1984

AFTER HEGEMONY

PART I

Questions and Concepts

· 1 ·

REALISM, INSTITUTIONALISM,
AND COOPERATION

Since the repeal of the "iron law of wages," economics has ceased to be the "dismal science." Economists no longer believe that most people must exist at the subsistence level, but argue, on the contrary, that gradual improvement in the material conditions of human life is possible. Yet while economics has become more cheerful, politics has become gloomier. The twentieth century has seen an enormous expansion of real and potential international violence. In the world political economy, opportunities for conflict among governments have increased as the scope of state action has widened. The greatest dangers for the world economy, as well as for world peace, have their sources in political conflicts among nations.

In the study of politics, perhaps nothing seems so dismal as writing about international cooperation. Indeed, when I told a friend and former teacher of mine that I was writing a book on this subject, she replied that it would have to be a short book. Was I planning extra-large type and wide margins to justify hard covers?

I could have retorted that my book would also discuss discord, a much more common feature of world politics. Yet the issue goes deeper than that. International cooperation among the advanced industrialized countries since the end of World War II has probably been more extensive than international cooperation among major states during any period of comparable length in history. Certainly the extent and complexity of efforts to coordinate state economic policies have been greater than they were between the two world wars, or in the century before 1914. Yet cooperation remains scarce relative to discord because the rapid growth of international economic interdependence since 1945, and the increasing involvement of governments in the operation of modern capitalist economies, have created more points of potential friction. Interdependence can transmit bad influences as well as good ones: unemployment or inflation can be exported as well as growth and prosperity. American steel workers may lose their jobs because of subsidies to European steel producers by the European Economic Community and European governments; high interest rates in the United States may constrain economic activity abroad.

Interdependence leads democratic governments to expand state ac-

5

tivity in order to protect their citizens from fluctuations in the world economy (Cameron, 1978). When this state activity takes the form of seeking to force the costs of adjustment onto foreigners, international discord results. Thus even a rising absolute level of cooperation may be overwhelmed by discord, as increased interdependence and governmental intervention create more opportunities for policy conflict. As in *Alice in Wonderland*, it may be necessary to keep running faster in order to stand still. Scholars should not wait for cooperation to become the rule rather than the exception before studying it, for ignorance of how to promote cooperation can lead to discord, conflict, and economic disaster before cooperation ever has a chance to prevail.

This book is about how cooperation has been, and can be, organized in the world political economy when common interests exist. It does not concentrate on the question of how fundamental common interests can be created among states. Thus two topics that could legitimately be treated in a book on international economic cooperation are not systematically considered: I neither explore how economic conditions affect patterns of interests, nor do I investigate the effects of ideas and ideals on state behavior. The theory that I develop takes the existence of mutual interests as given and examines the conditions under which they will lead to cooperation. I begin with the premise that even where common interests exist, cooperation often fails. My purpose is to diagnose the reasons for such failure, and for the occasional successes, in the hope of improving our ability to prescribe remedies.

Because I begin with acknowledged common interests, my study focuses on relations among the advanced market-economy countries, where such interests are manifold. These countries hold views about the proper operation of their economies that are relatively similar— at least in comparison with the differences that exist between them and most less developed countries, or the nonmarket planned economies. They are engaged in extensive relationships of interdependence with one another; in general, their governments' policies reflect the belief that they benefit from these ties. Furthermore, they are on friendly political terms; thus political-military conflicts between them complicate the politics of economic transactions less than they do in East–West relations.

The arguments of this book surely apply to some relationships between the advanced market-economy countries and less developed countries. These states have interests in common, which can only be realized through cooperation. To perhaps a more limited extent, my analysis should also be relevant to those areas of East–West relations where common interests exist. The focus of this book on cooperation among the advanced industrialized countries by no means implies that cooperation is impossible, or unnecessary, between North and South or East and West. To illustrate and test my ideas about cooperation and discord, however, I focus first on the area where common interests are greatest and where the benefits of international cooperation may be easiest to realize. Careful extension of this argument into East–West and North–South relations, including security as well as economic issues, would be most welcome.

REALISM, INSTITUTIONALISM, AND COOPERATION

Impressed with the difficulties of cooperation, observers have often compared world politics to a "state of war." In this conception, international politics is "a competition of units in the kind of state of nature that knows no restraints other than those which the changing necessities of the game and the shallow conveniences of the players impose" (Hoffmann, 1965, p. vii). It is anarchic in the sense that it lacks an authoritative government that can enact and enforce rules of behavior. States must rely on "the means they can generate and the arrangements they can make for themselves" (Waltz, 1979, p. 111). Conflict and war result, since each state is judge in its own cause and can use force to carry out its judgments (Waltz, 1959, p. 159). The discord that prevails is accounted for by fundamental conflicts of interest (Waltz, 1959; Tucker, 1977).

Were this portrayal of world politics correct, any cooperation that occurs would be derivative from overall patterns of conflict. Alliance cooperation would be easy to explain as a result of the operation of a balance of power, but system-wide patterns of cooperation that benefit many countries without being tied to an alliance system directed against an adversary would not. If international politics were a state of war, institutionalized patterns of cooperation on the basis of shared purposes should not exist except as part of a larger struggle for power. The extensive patterns of international agreement that we observe on issues as diverse as trade, financial relations, health, telecommunications, and environmental protection would be absent.

At the other extreme from these "Realists" are writers who see cooperation as essential in a world of economic interdependence, and who argue that shared economic interests create a demand for international institutions and rules (Mitrany, 1975). Such an approach, which I refer to as "Institutionalist" because of its adherents' emphasis on the functions performed by international institutions, runs the risk of being naive about power and conflict. Too often its proponents

7

incorporate in their theories excessively optimistic assumptions about the role of ideals in world politics, or about the ability of statesmen to learn what the theorist considers the "right lessons." But sophisticated students of institutions and rules have a good deal to teach us. They view institutions not simply as formal organizations with headquarters buildings and specialized staffs, but more broadly as "recognized patterns of practice around which expectations converge" (Young, 1980, p. 337). They regard these patterns of practice as significant because they affect state behavior. Sophisticated institutionalists do not expect cooperation always to prevail, but they are aware of the malleability of interests and they argue that interdependence creates interests in cooperation.[1]

During the first twenty years or so after World War II, these views, though very different in their intellectual origins and their broader implications about human society, made similar predictions about the world political economy, and particularly about the subject of this book, the political economy of the advanced market-economy countries. Institutionalists expected successful cooperation in one field to "spill over" into others (Haas, 1958). Realists anticipated a relatively stable international economic order as a result of the dominance of the United States. Neither set of observers was surprised by what happened, although they interpreted events differently.

Institutionalists could interpret the liberal international arrangements for trade and international finance as responses to the need for policy coordination created by the fact of interdependence. These arrangements, which we will call "international regimes," contained rules, norms, principles, and decisionmaking procedures. Realists could reply that these regimes were constructed on the basis of principles espoused by the United States, and that American power was essential

---

[1] In a preliminary draft I referred to "Functionalists" rather than "Institutionalists," since the scholars to whom I am alluding often adopted the former label or some variant of it, for themselves. On the suggestion of a reader, however, I altered the terminology in order to avoid confusion between "Functionalism" and the functional theory of international regimes presented in chapter 6. It should be emphasized that, as noted in the text, I employ a stylized contrast between Realism and Institutionalism to focus sharply on the issues addressed by this book, not to identify any given author with a simplistic variant of either position. For instance, although Stanley Hoffmann writes of international relations as "a state of war," his highly nuanced view of world politics would not normally be considered representative of Realism. Among the Institutionalists as well, there is substantial variation. Ernst Haas, for instance, has taken state power more seriously, and has been more cautious about the growth of international institutions, than David Mitrany.

for their construction and maintenance. For Realists, in other words, the early postwar regimes rested on the *political hegemony* of the United States. Thus Realists and Institutionalists could both regard early postwar developments as supporting their theories.

After the mid-1960s, however, U.S. dominance in the world political economy was challenged by the economic recovery and increasing unity of Europe and by the rapid economic growth of Japan. Yet economic interdependence continued to grow, and the pace of increased U.S. involvement in the world economy even accelerated after 1970. At this point, therefore, the Institutionalist and Realist predictions began to diverge. From a strict Institutionalist standpoint, the increasing need for coordination of policy, created by interdependence, should have led to more cooperation. From a Realist perspective, by contrast, the diffusion of power should have undermined the ability of anyone to create order.

On the surface, the Realists would seem to have made the better forecast. Since the late 1960s there have been signs of decline in the extent and efficacy of efforts to cooperate in the world political economy. As American power eroded, so did international regimes. The erosion of these regimes after World War II certainly refutes a naive version of the Institutionalist faith in interdependence as a solvent of conflict and a creator of cooperation. But it does not prove that only the Realist emphasis on power as a creator of order is valid. It might be possible, after the decline of hegemonic regimes, for more symmetrical patterns of cooperation to evolve after a transitional period of discord. Indeed, the persistence of attempts at cooperation during the 1970s suggests that the decline of hegemony does not necessarily sound cooperation's death knell.

International cooperation and discord thus remain puzzling. Under what conditions can independent countries cooperate in the world political economy? In particular, can cooperation take place without hegemony and, if so, how? This book is designed to help us find answers to these questions. I begin with Realist insights about the role of power and the effects of hegemony. But my central arguments draw more on the Institutionalist tradition, arguing that cooperation can under some conditions develop on the basis of complementary interests, and that institutions, broadly defined, affect the patterns of cooperation that emerge.

Hegemonic leadership is unlikely to be revived in this century for the United States or any other country. Hegemonic powers have historically only emerged after world wars; during peacetime, weaker countries have tended to gain on the hegemon rather than vice versa

9

(Gilpin, 1981). It is difficult to believe that world civilization, much less a complex international economy, would survive such a war in the nuclear age. Certainly no prosperous hegemonic power is likely to emerge from such a cataclysm. As long as a world political economy persists, therefore, its central political dilemma will be how to organize cooperation without hegemony.

COOPERATION AND VALUES

Cooperation is elusive enough, and its sources are sufficiently multi-faceted and intertwined, that it constitutes a difficult subject to study. It is particularly hard, perhaps impossible, to investigate with scientific rigor. No sensible person would choose it as a topic of investigation on the grounds that its puzzles could readily be "solved." I study it, despite the lack of rich, multi-case data suitable for the testing of hypotheses and despite the relative paucity of relevant theory, because of its normative significance.

This choice poses problems both for the author and for the reader. My values necessarily affect my argument; yet I am sufficiently pos-itivistic to attempt to distinguish between my empirical and normative assertions. Except for this chapter and chapter 11, *After Hegemony* represents an attempt at theoretical, historical, and interpretive anal-ysis rather than an exercise in applied ethics. I seek to increase our understanding of cooperation, in the belief that increased understand-ing can help to improve political amity and economic welfare, though not with the naive supposition that knowledge necessarily increases either amity or welfare. I try to provide an account of cooperation that can be analyzed, if not tested in a strict sense, by others who do not share my normative views, even as I recognize that, except for my own values, I would never have decided to write this book. Yet since I can surely not keep my analysis entirely distinct from my values, it seems fair to the reader for me to indicate briefly my thoughts about whether, or under what conditions, international cooperation is a "good" that we should strive to increase.

Cooperation is viewed by policymakers less as an end in itself than a means to a variety of other objectives. To inquire about the moral value of cooperation is partly to ask about the ends for which it is pursued. Along with many others, I would disapprove of cooperation among the governments of wealthy, powerful states to exploit poorer, weaker countries. Even if the goals sought through cooperation were judged desirable in principle, particular attempts to achieve them could have perverse effects. That is, the consequences of cooperation could be adverse, either for certain countries not fully represented in decision-making or for overall world welfare. When the conventional international economic wisdom is misguided, cooperation can be worse than doing nothing. So the economic orthodoxy of 1933 appeared to Franklin Delano Roosevelt when he wrecked the London Economic Conference of that year (Feis, 1966); and so does the internationally oriented Keynesianism of the Carter Administration now appear to economic theorists of rational expectations who put their trust in markets (Saxonhouse, 1982). Under conditions of interdependence, some cooperation is a necessary condition for achieving optimal levels of welfare; but it is not sufficient, and more cooperation may not necessarily be better than less.

Although it would be naive to believe that increased cooperation, among any group of states for whatever purposes, will necessarily foster humane values in world politics, it seems clear that more effective coordination of policy among governments would often help. Internationally minded Keynesians recommend extensive harmonization of macroeconomic policies (Whitman, 1979). Even proponents of international laissez-faire, who reject these proposals, have to recognize that free markets depend on the prior establishment of property rights (North and Thomas, 1973; Field, 1981; Conybeare, 1980; North, 1981). People may disagree on what forms of international cooperation are desirable and what purposes they should serve, but we can all agree that a world without any cooperation would be dismal indeed.

In the conclusion, I return explicitly to the problem of moral evaluation. Is it good that the international regimes discussed in this book exist? In what ways are they deficient when evaluated by appropriate moral standards? Would it have been better had they never come into being? No comprehensive or definitive answers to these questions are offered, but the importance of the problem of ethical evaluation demands that they be raised.

THE PLAN OF THIS BOOK

I hope that *After Hegemony* will be read not only by students of world politics but also by economists interested in the political underpinnings of the international economy and by citizens concerned about international cooperation. To encourage readers outside of political science, I have tried to eliminate professional jargon wherever possible and to define my terms clearly using ordinary language. Yet since this book is meant for people with different disciplinary backgrounds, and since it draws on disparate traditions to do so, its key concepts may be easily misunderstood. I hope that readers will be careful not to seize on words and phrases out of context as clues to pigeonholing my argument. Is it "liberal" because I discuss cooperation, or "mercantilist" because I emphasize the role of power and the impact of hegemony? Am I a "radical" because I take Marxian concepts seriously, or a "conservative" because I talk about order? The simplemindedness of such inferences should be obvious.

Since I use concepts from economics to develop a political theory about cooperation and discord in the world economy, I need to be particularly clear about my definitions of economics and politics and my conception of theory. Chapter 2 discusses these questions, as a necessary prologue to the development of my theory in Part II. Chapter 3 then prepares the ground for a serious analysis of cooperation, and the effects of institutions on it, by examining the "theory of hegemonic stability," which holds that order, in the Realist lexicon, depends on the preponderance of a single state. Chapter 3 argues that although hegemony can facilitate cooperation, it is neither a necessary nor a sufficient condition for it. We will see later that hegemony is less important for the continuation of cooperation, once begun, than for its creation.

Part II, which constitutes the theoretical core of this book, begins by defining two key terms, "cooperation" and "international regimes." Since these terms are used in chapter 3 before their full elaboration in chapter 4, it is important to note here that cooperation is defined in a deliberately unconventional way. Cooperation is contrasted with discord; but is also distinguished from harmony. Cooperation, as compared to harmony, requires active attempts to adjust policies to meet the demands of others. That is, not only does it depend on shared interests, but it emerges from a pattern of discord or potential discord. Without discord, there would be no cooperation, only harmony.

It is important to define cooperation as mutual adjustment rather than to view it simply as reflecting a situation in which common interests outweigh conflicting ones. In other words, we need to distinguish between cooperation and the mere fact of common interests. We require this distinction because discord sometimes prevails even when common interests exist. Since common interests are sometimes associated with cooperation but sometimes with discord, cooperation is evidently not a simple function of interests. Especially where uncertainty is great and actors have different access to information, obstacles to collective action and strategic calculations may prevent them from realizing their mutual interests. The mere existence of common

12

interests is not enough: institutions that reduce uncertainty and limit asymmetries in information must also exist.

Using chapter 4's definitions of cooperation and international regimes, chapters 5-7 present my functional theory of international regimes. Chapter 5 employs game theory and collective goods theory to argue that "the emergence of cooperation among egoists" (Axelrod, 1981, 1984) is possible, even in the absence of common government, but that the extent of such cooperation will depend on the existence of international institutions, or international regimes, with particular characteristics. Rational-choice theory enables us to demonstrate that the pessimistic conclusions about cooperation often associated with Realism are not necessarily valid, even if we accept the assumption of rational egoism. Chapter 6 then uses theories of market failure in economics, as well as more conventional rational-choice theory, to develop a functional theory of international regimes that shows why governments may construct regimes and even abide by their rules. According to this argument, regimes contribute to cooperation not by implementing rules that states must follow, but by changing the context within which states make decisions based on self-interests. International regimes are valuable to governments not because they enforce binding rules on others (they do not), but because they render it possible for governments to enter into mutually beneficial agreements with one another. They *empower* governments rather than shackling them.

Chapter 7 relaxes our earlier assumptions of rationality and narrow egoism. First it explores the implications of deviating from the premise of classic rationality by assuming, more realistically, that decisions are costly for governments to make. That is, governments operate under the constraints of "bounded rationality" (Simon, 1955), rather than as classically rational actors. On this assumption, regimes do not substitute for continuous calculations of self-interest (which are impossible), but rather provide rules of thumb to which other governments also adhere. These rules may provide opportunities for governments to bind their successors, as well as to make other governments' policies more predictable. Cooperation fostered by awareness of bounded rationality does not require that states accept common ideals or renounce fundamental principles of sovereignty. Even egoistic actors may agree to accept obligations that preclude making calculations about advantage in particular situations, if they believe that doing so will have better consequences in the long run than failure to accept any rules or acceptance of any other politically feasible set of rules.

Chapters 5-6 and the first two sections of chapter 7 adopt the premise of egoism. The last two sections of chapter 7 relax this assumption by distinguishing between egoistic self-interest and conceptions of self-interest in which empathy plays a role. Actors that interpret their interests as empathetically interdependent, in our terminology, may find it easier to form international regimes than those whose definitions of self-interest are more constricted. I explore the strengths and limitations of egoist and empathetic interpretations of state behavior by analyzing two features of the world political economy that may appear puzzling from an egoistic standpoint: the facts that regime rules and principles are sometimes treated as having morally obligatory status and that unbalanced exchanges of resources often persist over a considerable period of time.

The argument of Part II, taken as a whole, constitutes both a critique and modification of Realism. Realist theories that seek to predict international behavior on the basis of interests and power alone are important but insufficient for an understanding of world politics. They need to be supplemented, though not replaced, by theories stressing the importance of international institutions. Even if we fully understand patterns of power and interests, the behavior of states (and of transnational actors as well) may not be fully explicable without understanding the institutional context of action.

This institutionalist modification of Realism provides some rather abstract answers to the major puzzle addressed by this book: namely, how can cooperation take place in world politics in the absence of hegemony? We understand the creation of regimes as a result of a combination of the distribution of power, shared interests, and prevailing expectations and practices. Regimes arise against the background of earlier attempts, successful or not, at cooperation. Furthermore, the theory of Part II explains the continuation of existing regimes even after the conditions that facilitated their creation have disappeared: regimes acquire value for states because they perform important functions and because they are difficult to create or reconstruct. In order to realize fully the significance of this theoretical argument for understanding contemporary international regimes, we need to combine it with a historical understanding of the creation of contemporary international regimes and of their evolution since the end of World War II. This is the task of Part III.

Part III argues that the creation of contemporary international regimes can largely be explained by postwar U.S. policy, implemented through the exercise of American power. As American economic preponderance eroded between the 1950s and the 1970s, major international economic regimes came under pressure. Thus far Realist expectations are met. Yet the changes in these regimes did not always correspond to the shifts in power, and the decline of American hegemony did not lead uniformly to the collapse of regimes. Cooperation persists and, on some issues, has increased. Current patterns of discord and cooperation reflect interacting forces: the remaining elements of American hegemony as well as the effects of its erosion, the current mixture of shared and conflicting interests, and the international economic regimes that represent an institutional legacy of hegemony.

The first step in the empirical analysis of Part III is to examine how American hegemony actually operated. Chapter 8 therefore discusses American hegemony during the two decades of U.S. dominance, spanning the years from the Truman Doctrine and Marshall Plan (1947) to the late 1960s, when the United States began to show signs of seeking to protect itself from the impact of economic interdependence. The sources and practices of hegemonic cooperation are the focus of attention here. The episodes studied in this chapter illustrate the intimate connection between discord and cooperation pointed out in chapter 4, and they also reveal that inequalities of power can be quite consistent with mutual adjustment, policy coordination, and the formation of international regimes. Hegemony and international regimes may be complementary, or even to some extent substitute for each other: both serve to make agreements possible and to facilitate compliance with rules.

This period of hegemonic cooperation was short: Henry Luce's "American Century" was under severe pressure after less than twenty years. No system-level theory accounts for this, since—as chapter 8 shows—one of the most important reasons for the brevity of U.S. dominance was the pluralistic nature of American politics.[2] Given a decline in American power, however, believers in the theory of hegemonic stability would predict a decline in cooperation. Chapter 9 evaluates the applicability of this theory to the evolution of international regimes for money, trade, and oil between the mid-1960s and the early 1980s. Did international regimes embodying patterns of hegemonic cooperation become less effective because of the erosion of American power? Chapter 9 shows that the pattern of regime change varied a great deal from one issue-area to another, and that shifts in American power were of different significance in international finance, trade, and oil. The decline of American hegemony provides only part

---

[2] The question of the causes of the decline of American hegemony, not addressed systematically in this volume, is dealt with in an original and provocative way by Robert Gilpin (1975, 1981).

of the explanation for the decline of postwar international regimes. Chapter 9 reaches this conclusion without itself attempting to provide a complete explanation for this phenomenon, since to do so would require close examination of the effects of changes in macroeconomic conditions and international economic competitiveness, the role of ideas and learning, and the impact of domestic politics on foreign economic policies in the United States and elsewhere.

Chapter 9 also points out that although international regimes came under pressure in the 1970s, the advanced industrialized countries continue to coordinate their policies, albeit imperfectly, on international economic issues. Contemporary attempts to cooperate reflect not only the erosion of hegemony but the continued existence of international regimes, most of which had their origins in American hegemony. Old patterns of cooperation work less well than they did, partly because U.S. hegemony has declined; but the survival of patterns of mutual policy adjustment, and even their extension, can be facilitated by international regimes that had their origins in the period of hegemony. From chapter 9 we can see that both Realist concepts of power and self-interest and the arguments developed here about the significance of international regimes provide valuable insights into the nature of the contemporary world political economy. We need to go beyond Realism, not discard it. By documenting the erosion of American hegemony, furthermore, chapter 9 shows that our key puzzle—how cooperation can take place in the absence of hegemony—is not merely hypothetical but highly topical. It thus suggests the relevance for our own era of the theories of international cooperation put forward in Part II. Shared interests and existing institutions make it possible to cooperate, but the erosion of American hegemony makes it necessary to do so in new ways.

Chapter 10 further explores how regimes affect patterns of cooperation by investigating in detail the most significant international economic regime established among the advanced industrialized countries since 1971: the energy arrangements, revolving around the International Energy Agency (IEA), set up under U.S. leadership after the oil crisis of 1973-74. This regime was not global, but was limited to oil-consuming countries and competed with another partial regime formed by oil producers. We will see in chapter 10 that regime-oriented efforts at cooperation do not always succeed, as the fiasco of IEA actions in 1979 illustrates, but that they can have a positive impact under relatively favorable conditions, as the events of 1980 suggest. Chapter 10 also lends some support to the general proposition that successful attempts to use international regimes to facilitate cooperation depend on efforts to reduce the costs of transactions involved in policy coordination and on measures to provide information to governments, rather than on enforcement of rules.

The final chapter reviews the argument as a whole, assesses the moral value of cooperation, and examines implications for policy. My discussion of ethics concludes that, despite some defects in their principles, contemporary international regimes are morally acceptable, at least conditionally. They are easy to justify on the basis of criteria that stress the importance of the autonomy of states, although evaluation is more difficult when cosmopolitan and egalitarian standards are employed. The policy implications of the book stem most directly from my emphasis on the value of information produced and distributed by international regimes. Providers as well as recipients of information benefit from its availability. It can therefore make sense to accept obligations that restrain one's own freedom of action in unknown future situations if others also accept responsibilities, since the effect of these reciprocal actions is to reduce uncertainty. Assumptions about the value of "keeping one's options open" therefore need to be rethought. The pursuit of flexibility can be self-defeating: like Ulysses, it may be better, on occasion, to have oneself tied to the mast.

· 2 ·

POLITICS, ECONOMICS, AND
THE INTERNATIONAL
SYSTEM

Robert Gilpin has offered a helpful working definition of the phrase "world political economy" (1975, p. 43):

> In brief, political economy in this study means the reciprocal and dynamic interaction in international relations of the pursuit of wealth and the pursuit of power.

Causality is reciprocal rather than unidirectional: on the one hand, the distribution of power creates patterns of property rights within which wealth is produced and distributed; on the other hand, changes in productive efficiency and access to resources affect relations of power in the long term. The interaction between wealth and power is dynamic because both wealth and power are continually altered, as are the connections between them.

Wealth and power are linked in international relations through the activities of independent actors, the most important of which are states, not subordinated to a worldwide governmental hierarchy. There is no authoritative allocator of resources: we cannot talk about a "world society" making decisions about economic outcomes. No consistent and enforceable set of comprehensive rules exists. If actors are to improve their welfare through coordinating their policies, they must do so through bargaining rather than by invoking central direction. In world politics, uncertainty is rife, making agreements is difficult, and no secure barriers prevent military and security questions from impinging on economic affairs. In addition, disagreements about how benefits should be distributed permeate the relations among actors and persist because bargains are never permanently valid. Actors are continually tempted to try imposing burdens on others rather than absorbing costs of adjustment themselves. Furthermore, this struggle to make others adjust is played repeatedly. Apparent victory can be illusory or defeat ephemeral, for political bargaining and maneuver result not in definitive choices conferring power on some people rather than others, but in agreements that may in the future be reversed or in discord that signals a continuation of bargaining and maneuver.

All of this is understood by students of international relations. More

18

difficult to grasp are the meanings of the basic and misleadingly familiar terms "wealth" and "power." Gilpin (1975, p.23) defines wealth as "anything (capital, land, or labor) that can generate future income; it is composed of physical assets and human capital (including embodied knowledge)." The problem with this definition is that it seems to limit wealth to investment goods, excluding assets that merely provide value in consumption. Edible foodstuffs, ample quantities of gasoline for pleasure driving, and decorous jewelry are all, in ordinary language, considered to be wealth; but they would be excluded by Gilpin's definition. Adam Smith's definition of wealth as "the annual produce of the land and labour of a society" (1776/1976, p. 4) avoids this difficulty, but creates another one, since it refers to a *flow* of income rather than a *stock* of assets. Our ordinary contemporary usage of "wealth" refers to a stock rather than a flow concept. Taking this into account, we could follow Karl Polanyi, regarding wealth as "the means of material want satisfaction" (1957/1971, p. 243). Polanyi's definition, however, is also subject to telling objections. Lionel Robbins (1932, p. 9) pointed out a half-century ago that if economics refers to the satisfaction of material wants alone, it includes the services of the cook but not of the dancer. Yet although the cook produces a material product, the ultimate end (the pleasure of eating tasty food) may be quite as immaterial as the ultimate purpose of attending the ballet or the opera.

Considering this objection, we could define wealth simply as the "means of want satisfaction," or anything that yields utility, whether in the form of investment or consumption. This definition has the virtue of viewing wealth as a stock of resources, without arbitrarily excluding either consumption goods or nonmaterial sources of satisfaction. Yet it remains excessively broad in two ways. First, it omits reference to scarcity. In neoclassical economic analysis, value is derivative from market relationships: wealth can only be assessed after markets have evaluated different products or services. What is not scarce has no market value. Pure water, for instance, might be considered a "produce of the land," but in an ecologically pristine society, it would not constitute wealth because it would be free. In neoclassical value theory, "exchange value" rather than "use value" is decisive. Second, even if we take scarcity into account, we still need to distinguish between valued experiences that cannot be exchanged for money without altering their intrinsic nature (such as love, acts of pure friendship, and the ability to make others feel that they are in a state of grace) and those that can be so exchanged (such as sexual acts with strangers, favors done for business associates, and the ability to produce "that Pepsi feeling"). This is done by limiting "wealth" to means of want satisfaction that are not only scarce but also *marketable*: they can be bought and sold on a market. Thus "the pursuit of wealth" in the world political economy refers to the pursuit of marketable means of want satisfaction, whether these are to be used for investment or consumed by their possessors.

Gilpin asserts that "the nature of power is even more elusive than that of wealth." Rather than enter the "intradisciplinary squabble" about it, however, he follows Hans J. Morgenthau's definition of power as "man's control over the minds and actions of other men." Power, for Gilpin, refers to a causal relationship and varies according to the context in which it is exercised: "there is no single hierarchy of power in international relations" (1975, p. 24).

To define power in terms of control is plausible enough, but it does not address the question of the value of the concept in the study of politics. To use the concept of power to explain behavior, one needs to be able to measure power prior to the actions being explained and to construct models in which different amounts or types of power lead to different outcomes. What James G. March has called "basic force models" are designed to achieve this purpose by using tangible measures of power resources—such as numbers of people, quality of weapons, or wealth—to predict outcomes of political contention. Yet the predictions of these models are inaccurate, partly because some actors care more about particular outcomes than others and are therefore willing to use greater proportions of their resources to attain them (March, 1966; Harsanyi, 1962/1971). Thus basic force models, such as the "crude" theory of hegemonic stability discussed in chapter 3, are only useful as first approximations. These models can be qualified by adding auxiliary hypotheses that refer to the role of intangible factors such as will, intensity of motivation, or—in the "refined" version of the theory of hegemonic stability—leadership. Unfortunately, however, these factors can only be measured after the event. Power is no longer used to account for behavior; rather, it provides a language for describing political action.

We saw above that, in the neoclassical economic theory of value, wealth is not used as a primary category to explain demand or prices; on the contrary, value (hence wealth) is inferred from demand and supply, as reflected in price movements on markets. Thus the concepts of power and wealth have a common deficiency as the basis for explanations of behavior: to estimate the power of actors, or whether a given product, service, or raw material constitutes wealth, one has to observe behavior—in power relationships or in markets. To use the

Figure 2.1. Politics and Economics: A Schematization

Wealth

(To what extent are wants satisfied through
production and exchange of marketable goods and services?)

		High	Medium	Low
Power (What role does control over other actors play in the process of want satisfaction?)	**High**		Political	"pure politics"
	Medium		Economy	
	Low	"pure economics"		(pure love?) (mysticism?)

concepts of power and wealth to account for the behavior that allows us to identify their presence would be to engage in circular reasoning. Thus the insight expressed by Gilpin, that the world political economy revolves around power and wealth, does not enable us to construct strong explanations of the behavior that we observe.

Nevertheless, defining international political economy as the reciprocal and dynamic interaction of the pursuit of wealth and the pursuit of power is useful from a descriptive standpoint. We can view international political economy as the intersection of the substantive area studied by economics—production and exchange of marketable means of want satisfaction—with the process by which power is exercised that is central to politics. Wherever, in the economy, actors exert power over one another, the economy is political. This area of intersection can be contrasted with "pure economics," in which no actor has any control over others but faces an externally determined environment. One can also imagine a situation, also an "ideal type," in which noneconomic resources were used solely in pursuit of values that could not be exchanged on a market, such as status, or power itself. Such a situation would be one of "pure politics." Figure 2.1 makes these points schematically.

As figure 2.1 illustrates, attempts to separate a sphere of real activity, called "economics," from another sphere of real activity, called "politics," are doomed to frustration and failure. Very little of the polity in modern societies is untouched by the economy, and vice versa; even apart from questions of governmental intervention, much of the modern economy is political because firms, unions, and other organizations seek to exert control over one another. Defined in purely economic or political terms, the world economy and the international political sys-

21

tem are both abstractions. In the real world of international relations, most significant issues are simultaneously political and economic.

We have seen that thinking about international political economy in terms of wealth and power does not enable us to construct strong explanatory models of behavior. Yet focusing on the *pursuit* of wealth and power does contribute to insightful interpretation, since it provides us with working hypotheses about the motivations of actors that emphasize specific interests rather than ideology or rhetoric. To remind ourselves about wealth and power is a useful antidote to a onesided emphasis on interdependence and the problem of realizing common interests. In reflecting on the later discussion in this volume of international regimes, the reader should keep in mind that these regimes are rarely if ever instituted by disinterested idealists for the sake of the common good. Instead, they are constructed principally by governments whose officials seek to further the interests of their states (as they interpret them) and of themselves. They seek wealth and power, and perhaps other values as well, no matter how much they may indulge in rhetoric about global welfare or a world "safe for interdependence."

THE COMPLEMENTARITY OF WEALTH AND POWER

Reflection on wealth and power as state objectives soon yields the conclusion that they are complementary. For contemporary statesmen, as for the mercantilists of the seventeenth and eighteenth centuries, power is a necessary condition for plenty, and vice versa. Two examples, considered in more detail in later chapters, illustrate the point. In the late 1940s American power was used to build international economic arrangements consistent with the structure of American capitalism; conversely, U.S. military strength depended in the long run on close economic as well as political ties between the United States on the one hand and Western Europe and Japan on the other. To say that American economic or political goals were primary, as historians involved in controversies over the Cold War often do, is to miss the point, which is that U.S. economic interests abroad depended on establishing a political environment in which capitalism could flourish, and that American political and security interests depended on economic recovery in Europe and Japan. The two sets of objectives were inextricably linked, and similar policies were required to achieve them. Likewise, when the United States proposed the establishment of an international energy agency in 1974 to help cope with the shift of power over oil to producing countries, it did so both to deal with the economic consequences of higher oil prices and to reinforce its own political influence. Effective international action to alleviate economic distress seemed impossible without American leadership; conversely, U.S. influence and prestige were likely to be enhanced by leading a successful collective effort to ensure energy security.

The complementarity of wealth and power provides a thread of continuity between the world political economy of the seventeenth century and that of today. Most governments still appear to adhere to the propositions that Jacob Viner ascribes to seventeenth-century mercantilists (1948, p. 10):

> 1) Wealth is an absolutely essential means to power, whether for security or for aggression; 2) power is essential or valuable as a means to the acquisition or retention of wealth; 3) wealth and power are each proper ultimate ends of national policy; 4) there is a long-run harmony between these ends, although in particular circumstances it may be necessary for a time to make economic sacrifices in the interest of military security and therefore also of long-run prosperity.

The qualification Viner offers to his fourth point is important. In the short run, tradeoffs exist between the pursuit of power and the pursuit of wealth. One of the tasks of students of international political economy is to analyze these tradeoffs, without forgetting the long-run complementarity underlying them.

The key tradeoffs for the United States in the 1980s, as for mercantilist statesmen in the seventeenth century and American leaders in the late 1940s, are not between power and wealth but between the long-term power/wealth interests of the state and the partial interests of individual merchants, workers, or manufacturers on the one hand or short-term interests of the society on the other. The United States is not the only country that has been unable to formulate long-term goals without making concessions to partial economic interests. Viner observes that in Holland during the seventeenth and eighteenth centuries, "where the merchants to a large extent shared directly in government, major political considerations, including the very safety of the country or its success in wars in which it was actually participating, had repeatedly to give way to the cupidity of the merchants and their reluctance to contribute adequately to military finance" (1948, p. 20). In Britain also, "the autonomy of business connections and traditions," according to Viner, hindered the pursuit of state interests. During the Marshall Plan years, American administrators had to deal with "the special demands of the American business and agricultural community that expected direct and early profit from the program—and who were well-represented in Congress. . . . The general goals of multilateral trade were certainly in the interests of all these constituencies; yet they, unlike the State Department, were willing to undermine the achievement of the general aim for even the smallest immediate gain" (Kolko and Kolko, 1972, pp. 444-45).

The conflict between short-run and long-run objectives arises largely in the form of choices between consumption on the one hand and savings or investment on the other. When the economy underinvests, it is favoring the present over the future. One can use similar concepts in discussing power. A state invests in power resources when it binds allies to itself or creates international regimes in which it plays a central role. During the 1930s Germany followed a "power approach" to trade questions, changing the structure of foreign trade so that its partners would be vulnerable to its own actions (Hirschman, 1945/1980). After World War II American policy had a broader geographical focus and was less coercive, but it also stressed power investment. The United States absorbed short-run economic costs, such as those imposed by discrimination in the early 1950s against American goods in Europe, for the sake of political influence that could lead to longer-term gains. It established international regimes that revolved around Washington, and on which its allies were highly dependent.

Power disinvestment may also take place; power can be consumed and not replaced. Governments may be able to maintain levels of consumption in the present by running current account deficits, borrowing abroad to compensate for low levels of saving at home, as the United States did during the first few years of the 1980s. In the long run, however, such policies are unsustainable and erode the bases of influence, or creditworthiness, on which they depend.

Whether to invest in additional power resources or to consume some of those that have been accumulated is a perennial issue of foreign policy. Many of the most important choices governments face have to do with the relative weight given to consumption (of wealth or power) versus investment, and with devising strategies for action that are both viable in the short run and capable of achieving wealth and power objectives in the long run. Any analysis of the world political economy must keep in mind the extent to which investments, in power as well as production, are being made or dissipated. Some of these investments will be reflected in international regimes and the leadership strategies that help to construct and maintain them. Defining international political economy in terms of the pursuit of wealth and power leads us to analyze cooperation in the world political economy less as an effort to implement high ideals than as a means of attaining self-interested economic and political goals.

SYSTEMIC ANALYSIS OF INTERNATIONAL POLITICS

Wealth and power are sought by a variety of actors in world politics, including nonstate organizations such as multinational business corporations (Keohane and Nye, 1972). But states are crucial actors, not only seeking wealth and power directly but striving to construct frameworks of rules and practices that will enable them to secure these objectives, among others, in the future. Our analysis of international cooperation and regimes therefore focuses principally on states.

State behavior can be studied from the "inside-out" or from the "outside-in" (Waltz, 1979, p. 63). "Inside-out," or unit-level, explanations locate the sources of behavior within the actor—for instance, in a country's political or economic system, the attributes of its leaders, or its domestic political culture. "Outside-in," or systemic, explanations account for state behavior on the basis of attributes of the system as a whole. Any theory will, of course, take into account the distinctive characteristics of actors as well as of the system itself. But a systemic theory regards these internal attributes as constants rather than as variables. The variables of a systemic theory are *situational*: they refer to the location of each actor relative to others (Waltz, 1979, pp. 67-73; Keohane, 1983, p. 508). Systemic analysis of the international political economy begins by locating actors along the dimension of relative power on the one hand and wealth on the other.

Kenneth Waltz has convincingly shown the error of theorizing at the unit level without first reflecting on the effects of the international system as a whole. There are two principal reasons for this. First, causal analysis is difficult at the unit level because of the apparent importance of idiosyncratic factors, ranging from the personality of a leader to the peculiarities of a given country's institutions. Parsimonious theory, even as a partial "first cut," becomes impossible if one starts analysis here, amidst a confusing plethora of seemingly relevant facts. Second, analyzing state behavior from "inside-out" alone leads observers to ignore the context of action: the pressures exerted on all states by the competition among them. Practices such as seeking to balance the power of potential adversaries may be accounted for on the basis of distinctive characteristics of the governments in question when they could be explained more satisfactorily on the basis of enduring features of world politics. Without prior systemic theory, unit-level analysis of world politics floats in an empirical and conceptual vacuum (Waltz, 1979, chs. 4-5).

For these reasons, the analysis of this book begins at the systemic level. I focus on the effects of system characteristics because I believe that the behavior of states, as well as of other actors, is strongly affected by the constraints and incentives provided by the international environment. When the international system changes, so will incentives and behavior. My "outside-in" perspective is therefore similar to that of systemic forms of Realist theory, or "structural Realism" (Krasner, 1983). What distinguishes my argument from structural Realism is my emphasis on the effects of international institutions and practices on state behavior. The distribution of power, stressed by Realists, is surely important. So is the distribution of wealth. But human activity at the international level also exerts significant effects. International regimes alter the information available to governments and the opportunities open to them; commitments made to support such institutions can only be broken at a cost to reputation. International regimes therefore change the calculations of advantage that governments make. To try to understand state behavior simply by combining the structural Realist theory based on distribution of power and wealth with the foreign policy analyst's stress on choice, without understanding international regimes, would be like trying to account for competition and collusion among oligopolistic business firms without bothering to ascertain whether their leaders met together regularly, whether they belonged to the same trade associations, or whether they had developed informal means of coordinating behavior without direct communication. International regimes not only deserve systematic study; they virtually cry out for it.

Yet no systemic analysis can be complete. When we come to our discussion of the postwar international political economy in Part III, we will have to look beyond the system toward accounts of state behavior that emphasize the effects of domestic institutions and leadership on patterns of state behavior. That is, we will have to introduce some unit-level analysis as well. In doing so, we will pay special attention to the most powerful actor in the world political economy, the United States. Since the United States shaped the system as much as the system shaped it, and since it retained greater leeway for autonomous action than other countries throughout the thirty-five years after World War II, we have to look at the United States from the inside-out as well as from the outside-in.

LIMITATIONS OF SYSTEMIC ANALYSIS

My choice of systemic theory as a place to begin analysis does not imply that I regard it as completely satisfactory even as a "first cut." Before going on to the systemic analysis of Part II, therefore, it is necessary to indicate some of its limitations.

The prevailing model for systemic analysis in politics comes from economics—in particular, from microeconomic theory. Such theory posits the existence of firms, with given utility functions (such as profit maximization), and attempts to explain their behavior on the basis of environmental factors such as the competitiveness of markets. It is systemic rather than unit-level theory because its propositions depend on variations in attributes of the system, not of the units (Waltz, 1979, pp. 89-91, 93-95, 98). Firms are assumed to act as rational egoists. Rationality means that they have consistent, ordered preferences, and that they calculate costs and benefits of alternative courses of action in order to maximize their utility in view of those preferences. Egoism means that their utility functions are independent of one another: they do not gain or lose utility simply because of the gains or losses of others. Making these assumptions means that rationality and conceptions of self-interest are constants rather than variables in systemic theory. Variations in firms' behavior are accounted for not by variations in their values, or in the efficiency of their internal organizational arrangements, but by variations in characteristics of the economic system—for instance, whether its market structure is competitive, oligopolistic, or monopolistic. Without the assumptions of egoism and rationality, variations in firms' behavior might have to be accounted for by differences in values or in their calculating, choice-making abilities. In that case, analysis would revert to the unit level, and the parsimony of systemic theory—resting on only a small number of variables—would be lost.[1]

Systemic theories based on rational-egoist assumptions work best when there is one uniquely superior course of action. Arnold Wolfers pointed out this feature of such theories long ago, in arguing that they provide the best predictions when there is extreme "compulsion," as in the case of a fire breaking out in a house that has only one exit. For such a situation, "decision-making analysis would be useful only in regard to individuals who decided to remain where they were rather than join the general and expected rush" (1962, p. 14). Spiro J. Latsis (1976) has more recently argued, in similar terms, that microeconomic

---

[1] For a fully developed version of this argument, see Keohane, 1983.

theory based on rational-choice assumptions performs best when applied to "single-exit" situations. Under these conditions, what Latsis calls the research program of "situational determinism" works very well. We do not need to understand the idiosyncracies of the actors to explain their behavior, since the situation they face mandates that they must act in a particular way. They will do so if they are rational; if they fail to do so, they may (if the environmental conditions are stringent) cease to exist.

This research program has had great success in situations of pure competition or pure monopoly—and, by extension, in situations that approximate these ideal types. Situational determinism works under these circumstances because there is *no power competition* in pure competition or pure monopoly. Either economic actors adjust their behavior to signals from an impersonal market (in competition), or they dominate the market (in monopoly). In neither case do they have to react to the actions of others. As Latsis puts it (1976, pp. 25-26):

> Under perfect competition entrepreneurs do not really *compete* with *each other*. The situation may be compared to that of a player in an *n*-person game where *n* is very large. Such games are reducible to one-person games against nature where the opponent has no objectives and no known strategy. The "nature" of perfect competition is unusually strict in allowing a choice between following a single strategy or going under.
>
> Pure monopoly, usually regarded as the exact opposite of perfect competition is in fact its heuristic twin. . . . The monopolist maximizes on the basis of his knowledge of the market conditions and the application of the simple optimizing rule. As with perfect competition, so with monopoly the "rational" decision-maker will arrive at the uniquely determined optimal decision by a simple calculation.

Difficulties arise for this research program under conditions of oligopoly, or "monopolistic competition." Under these conditions, the situation can be treated as a variable-sum game, played repeatedly over an indefinite period of time, with a small number of players. This type of game does not have a determinate solution for any actor, independent of the behavior of others. It is a "multiple-exit" situation, and arbitrary assumptions are required to reach unique solutions to it (Latsis, 1976, pp. 26-39). As we will see in chapters 5 and 6, rational-egoist calculations of whether to cooperate with one another under these conditions will depend heavily on the expectations of actors about others' behavior—and therefore on the nature of institutions.

28

Microeconomic theory does not generate precise, accurate predictions about behavior in situations of strategic interdependence (Simon, 1976). And as we have seen, strategic interdependence, which bedevils only part of economics, afflicts the entire study of international politics.

Conclusions

Systemic analysis will not yield determinate predictions about states' pursuit of wealth and power. Even if it did, these predictions would be subject to inaccuracy insofar as great variations in state behavior resulted from variations in their internal characteristics. Nevertheless, systemic theory can help us understand how the constraints under which governments act in the world political economy affect their behavior. As in Cournot models of oligopoly, however, we also need to be able to specify something about actors' "reaction functions"—how they will respond to others' behavior (Fellner, 1949). To do this on the basis of empirical information, rather than arbitrarily, we must investigate the institutional context, including the "cues" provided to actors by rules, practices, and informal patterns of action. That is, we are led from strictly power-based, game-theoretic analysis toward the study of international regimes.

Admittedly, accepting rational-egoist assumptions involves taking seriously a purely hypothetical notion of rationality that does not accurately model actual processes of human choice (McKeown, 1983b). Yet beginning with assumptions of egoism and rationality has three important virtues. First, it simplifies our premises, making deductions clearer. Second, it directs our attention toward the constraints imposed by a system on its actors, since it holds the internal determinants of choice constant. This helps to retain our focus on systemic constraints—whether the result of unequal distributions of power or wealth in the world or of international institutions and practices—rather than on domestic politics. Finally, adopting the assumption of rational egoism places the argument of this book on the same foundation as that of Realist theories. The argument here for the importance of international regimes does not depend on smuggling in assumptions about altruism or irrationality. Starting with similar premises about motivations, I seek to show that Realism's pessimism about welfare-increasing cooperation is exaggerated. Having done this, in chapter 7 I relax the assumption of classical rationality and the assumption of egoistic, independent utility maximization, to see how the theory of regime functions developed earlier on rational-egoist grounds is affected by these changes in premises.

29

My interest in both the structure of world power and the institutions and practices devised by human beings reflects a concern with constraints and choices in world politics. The constraints imposed by distributions of wealth and power are often severe. As Marx said, we make our own history not just as we please, but "under circumstances directly found, given, and transmitted from the past" (1852/1972, p. 437). Yet since we do make our own history, there is some room for choice at any point in time, and over a period of time some of the constraints can themselves be altered. The limitations of deterministic theory along the lines of nineteenth-century physics may be disturbing for social scientists who still carry obsolete images of natural science in their heads ("weighing like a nightmare on the brains of the living," to use another Marxian phrase). But they offer hope for policy. They suggest that human beings may be able to learn: to develop institutions and practices that will enable them to cooperate more effectively without renouncing the pursuit of self-interest. The weakness of theory, but the hope for policy, lies in the fact that people adapt their strategies to reality. This book seeks to show how adaptive strategies of institution-building can also change reality, thereby fostering mutually beneficial cooperation.

· 3 ·

HEGEMONY IN THE WORLD
POLITICAL ECONOMY

It is common today for troubled supporters of liberal capitalism to
look back with nostalgia on British preponderance in the nineteenth
century and American dominance after World War II. Those eras are
imagined to be simpler ones in which a single power, possessing superiority of economic and military resources, implemented a plan for
international order based on its interests and its vision of the world.
As Robert Gilpin has expressed it, "the *Pax Britannica* and *Pax Americana*, like the *Pax Romana*, ensured an international system of relative
peace and security. Great Britain and the United States created and
enforced the rules of a liberal international economic order" (1981,
p. 144).

Underlying this statement is one of the two central propositions of
the theory of hegemonic stability (Keohane, 1980): that order in world
politics is typically created by a single dominant power. Since regimes
constitute elements of an international order, this implies that the
formation of international regimes normally depends on hegemony.
The other major tenet of the theory of hegemonic stability is that the
maintenance of order requires continued hegemony. As Charles P.
Kindleberger has said, "for the world economy to be stabilized, there
has to be a stabilizer, one stabilizer" (1973, p. 305). This implies that
cooperation, which we define in the next chapter as mutual adjustment
of state policies to one another, also depends on the perpetuation of
hegemony.

I discuss hegemony before elaborating my definitions of cooperation
and regimes because my emphasis on how international institutions
such as regimes facilitate cooperation only makes sense if cooperation
and discord are not determined simply by interests and power. In this
chapter I argue that a deterministic version of the theory of hegemonic
stability, relying only on the Realist concepts of interests and power,
is indeed incorrect. There is some validity in a modest version of the
first proposition of the theory of hegemonic stability—that hegemony
can facilitate a certain type of cooperation—but there is little reason
to believe that hegemony is either a necessary or a sufficient condition
for the emergence of cooperative relationships. Furthermore, and even
more important for the argument presented here, the second major

31

proposition of the theory is erroneous: cooperation does not necessarily require the existence of a hegemonic leader after international regimes have been established. Post-hegemonic cooperation is also possible.

A detailed analysis of how hegemony and cooperation have been related to one another in the postwar international political economy is deferred to chapters 8 and 9, after my theories about cooperation and the functions of international regimes have been presented. The task of the present chapter is to explore in a preliminary way the value and limitations of the concept of hegemony for the study of cooperation. The first section analyzes the claims of the theory of hegemonic stability; the second section briefly addresses the relationship between military power and hegemony in the world political economy; and the final section seeks to enrich our understanding of the concept by considering Marxian insights. Many Marxian interpretations of hegemony turn out to bear an uncanny resemblance to Realist ideas, using different language to make similar points. Antonio Gramsci's conception of ideological hegemony, however, does provide an insightful supplement to purely materialist arguments, whether Realist or Marxist.

Evaluating the Theory of Hegemonic Stability

The theory of hegemonic stability, as applied to the world political economy, defines hegemony as preponderance of material resources. Four sets of resources are especially important. Hegemonic powers must have control over raw materials, control over sources of capital, control over markets, and competitive advantages in the production of highly valued goods.

The importance of controlling sources of raw materials has provided a traditional justification for territorial expansion and imperialism, as well as for the extension of informal influence. We will see in chapter 9 how shifts in the locus of control over oil affected the power of states and the evolution of international regimes. Guaranteed access to capital, though less obvious as a source of power, may be equally important. Countries with well-functioning capital markets can borrow cheaply and may be able to provide credit to friends or even deny it to adversaries. Holland derived political and economic power from the quality of its capital markets in the seventeenth century; Britain did so in the eighteenth and nineteenth centuries; and the United States has similarly benefited during the last fifty years (De Cecco, 1975; Feis, 1930; Ford, 1962; Kindleberger, 1978c; Lindert, 1969; Wallerstein, 1980).

Potential power may also be derived from the size of one's market for imports. The threat to cut off a particular state's access to one's own market, while allowing other countries continued access, is a "potent and historically relevant weapon of economic 'power'" (McKeown, 1983a, p. 78). Conversely, the offer to open up one's own huge market to other exporters, in return for concessions or deference, can be an effective means of influence. The bigger one's own market, and the greater the government's discretion in opening it up or closing it off, the greater one's potential economic power.[1]

The final dimension of economic preponderance is competitive superiority in the production of goods. Immanuel Wallerstein has defined hegemony in economic terms as "a situation wherein the products of a given core state are produced so efficiently that they are by and large competitive even in other core states, and therefore the given core state will be the primary beneficiary of a maximally free world market" (1980, p. 38). As a definition of economic preponderance this is interesting but poorly worked out, since under conditions of overall balance of payments equilibrium each unit—even the poorest and least developed—will have some comparative advantage. The fact that in 1960 the United States had a trade deficit in textiles and apparel and in basic manufactured goods (established products not, on the whole, involving the use of complex or new technology) did not indicate that it had lost predominant economic status (Krasner, 1978b, pp. 68-69). Indeed, one should expect the economically preponderant state to import products that are labor-intensive or that are produced with well-known production techniques. Competitive advantage does not mean that the leading economy exports *everything*, but that it produces and exports the most profitable products and those that will provide the basis for producing even more advanced goods and services in the future. In general, this ability will be based on the technological superiority of the leading country, although it may also rest on its political control over valuable resources yielding significant rents.

To be considered hegemonic in the world political economy, therefore, a country must have access to crucial raw materials, control major sources of capital, maintain a large market for imports, and hold comparative advantages in goods with high value added, yielding

---

[1] The classic statement of this point is by Hirschman (1945/1980). For a recent discussion of the same issue with reference to textiles, see Aggarwal, 1983, p. 622. Aggarwal notes that a large importer of goods may exercise influence not merely over sellers but also over other buyers, who fear diversion of imports into their markets if a large market is closed.

relatively high wages and profits. It must also be stronger, on these dimensions taken as a whole, than any other country. The theory of hegemonic stability predicts that the more one such power dominates the world political economy, the more cooperative will interstate relations be. This is a parsimonious theory that relies on what was referred to in chapter 2 as a "basic force model," in which outcomes reflect the tangible capabilities of actors.

Yet, like many such basic force models, this crude theory of hegemonic stability makes imperfect predictions. In the twentieth century it correctly anticipates the relative cooperativeness of the twenty years after World War II. It is at least partially mistaken, however, about trends of cooperation when hegemony erodes. Between 1900 and 1913 a decline in British power coincided with a decrease rather than an increase in conflict over commercial issues.[2] As we will see in chapter 9, recent changes in international regimes can only partially be attributed to a decline in American power. How to interpret the prevalence of discord in the interwar years is difficult, since it is not clear whether any country was hegemonic in material terms during those two decades. The United States, though considerably ahead in productivity, did not replace Britain as the most important financial center and lagged behind in volume of trade. Although American domestic oil production was more than sufficient for domestic needs during these years, Britain still controlled the bulk of major Middle Eastern oil fields. Nevertheless, what prevented American leadership of a cooperative world political economy in these years was less lack of economic resources than an absence of political willingness to make and enforce rules for the system. Britain, despite its efforts, was too weak to do so effectively (Kindleberger, 1973). The crucial factor in producing discord lay in American politics, not in the material factors to which the theory points.

Unlike the crude basic force model, a refined version of hegemonic stability theory does not assert an automatic link between power and leadership. Hegemony is defined as a situation in which "one state is powerful enough to maintain the essential rules governing interstate

---

[2] See Krasner, 1976. Krasner's analysis focuses on liberalism, or openness, as the dependent variable rather than on order or cooperation. Cooperation and liberalism are conceptually distinct, and as we will see in chapter 9, in recent years they can also be distinguished empirically. In Krasner's highly aggregated analysis of the last 150 years, however, the distinction does not make a significant difference, since open systems have on the whole also been more predictable and less characterized by conflict—hence more orderly—than the protectionist ones.

relations, and willing to do so" (Keohane and Nye, 1977, p. 44). This interpretive framework retains an emphasis on power but looks more seriously than the crude power theory at the internal characteristics of the strong state. It does not assume that strength automatically creates incentives to project one's power abroad. Domestic attitudes, political structures, and decision making processes are also important.

This argument's reliance on state decisions as well as power capabilities puts it into the category of what March calls "force activation models." Decisions to exercise leadership are necessary to "activate" the posited relationship between power capabilities and outcomes. Force activation models are essentially *post hoc* rather than *a priori*, since one can always "save" such a theory after the fact by thinking of reasons why an actor would not have wanted to use all of its available potential power. In effect, this modification of the theory declares that states with preponderant resources will be hegemonic except when they decide not to commit the necessary effort to the tasks of leadership, yet it does not tell us what will determine the latter decision. As a causal theory this is not very helpful, since whether a given configuration of power will lead the potential hegemon to maintain a set of rules remains indeterminate unless we know a great deal about its domestic politics.[3]

Only the cruder theory generates predictions. When I refer without qualification to the theory of hegemonic stability, therefore, I will be referring to this basic force model. We have seen that the most striking contention of this theory—that hegemony is both a necessary and a sufficient condition for cooperation—is not strongly supported by the experience of this century. Taking a longer period of about 150 years, the record remains ambiguous.[4] International economic relations were relatively cooperative both in the era of British hegemony during the mid-to-late nineteenth century and in the two decades of American dominance after World War II. But only in the second of these periods was there a trend toward the predicted disruption of established rules and increased discord. And a closer examination of the British experience casts doubt on the causal role of British hegemony in producing cooperation in the nineteenth century.

Both Britain in the nineteenth century and the United States in the

---

[3] It should also be evident, in view of our discussion in chapter 2, that the refined version of hegemonic stability theory is not systemic, since it depends for its explanatory power on variations in the internal characteristics of actors.

[4] See footnote 2 above.

Table 3.1. Material Resources of Britain and the United States as Hegemons: Proportions of World Trade and Relative Labor Productivity

	Proportion of World Trade	Relative Labor Productivity*
Britain, 1870	24.0	1.63
Britain, 1890	18.5	1.45
Britain, 1913	14.1	1.15
Britain, 1938	14.0	.92
United States, 1950	18.4	2.77
United States, 1960	15.3	2.28
United States, 1970	14.4	1.72
United States, 1977	13.4	1.45

* As compared with the average rate of productivity in the other members of the world economy.

SOURCE: Lake, 1983, table 1 (p. 525) and table 3 (p. 541).

twentieth met the material prerequisites for hegemony better than any other states since the Industrial Revolution. In 1880 Britain was the financial center of the world, and it controlled extensive raw materials, both in its formal empire and through investments in areas not part of the Imperial domain. It had the highest per capita income in the world and approximately double the share of world trade and investment of its nearest competitor, France. Only in the aggregate size of its economy had it already fallen behind the United States (Krasner, 1976, p. 333). Britain's share of world trade gradually declined during the next sixty years, but in 1938 it was still the world's largest trader, with 14 percent of the world total. In the nineteenth century Britain's relative labor productivity was the highest in the world, although it declined rather precipitously thereafter. As table 3.1 shows, Britain in the late nineteenth century and the United States after World War II were roughly comparable in their proportions of world trade, although until 1970 or so the United States had maintained much higher levels of relative productivity than Britain had done three-quarters of a century earlier.

Yet, despite Britain's material strength, it did not always enforce its preferred rules. Britain certainly did maintain freedom of the seas. But it did not induce major continental powers, after the 1870s, to retain liberal trade policies. A recent investigation of the subject has concluded that British efforts to make and enforce rules were less extensive and less successful than hegemonic stability theory would lead us to believe they were (McKeown, 1983a, especially p. 88).[5]

Attempts by the United States after World War II to make and enforce rules for the world political economy were much more effective than Britain's had ever been. America after 1945 did not merely replicate earlier British experience; on the contrary, the differences between Britain's "hegemony" in the nineteenth century and America's after World War II were profound. As we have seen, Britain had never been as superior in productivity to the rest of the world as the United States was after 1945. Nor was the United States ever as dependent on foreign trade and investment as Britain. Equally important, America's economic partners—over whom its hegemony was exercised, since America's ability to make the rules hardly extended to the socialist camp—were also its military allies; but Britain's chief trading partners had been its major military and political rivals. In addition, one reason for Britain's relative ineffectiveness in maintaining a free trade regime is that it had never made extensive use of the principle of reciprocity in trade (McKeown, 1983a). It thus had sacrificed potential leverage over other countries that preferred to retain their own restrictions while Britain practiced free trade. The policies of these states might well have been altered had they been confronted with a choice between a closed British market for their exports on the one hand and mutual lowering of barriers on the other. Finally, Britain had an empire to which it could retreat, by selling less advanced goods to its colonies rather than competing in more open markets (De Cecco, 1975; Hobsbawm, 1968; Kindleberger, 1978b; Lewis, 1978). American hegemony, rather than being one more instance of a general phenomenon, was essentially unique in the scope and efficacy of the instruments at the disposal of a hegemonic state and in the degree of success attained.

That the theory of hegemonic stability is supported by only one or at most two cases casts doubt on its general validity. Even major proponents of the theory refrain from making such claims. In an article published in 1981, Kindleberger seemed to entertain the possibility that two or more countries might "take on the task of providing leadership together, thus adding to legitimacy, sharing the burdens,

---

[5] The question of whether Britain was always consistent in its espousal of liberalism is analytically a separate issue from that of its ability to make and enforce rules, since liberalism should not be equated with cooperation. For the nineteenth century, however, as footnote 2 indicates, the order that Britain sought was a liberal one. For discussions of cases outside of Europe in which the rise of British hegemony may have led to restrictions on trade, see Laitin, 1982, and Lawson, 1983.

and reducing the danger that leadership is regarded cynically as a cloak for domination and exploitation" (p. 252). In *War and Change in World Politics* (1981), Gilpin promulgated what appeared to be a highly deterministic conception of hegemonic cycles: "the conclusion of one hegemonic war is the beginning of another cycle of growth, expansion, and eventual decline" (p. 210). Yet he denied that his view was deterministic, and he asserted that "states can learn to be more enlightened in their definitions of their interests and can learn to be more cooperative in their behavior" (p. 227). Despite the erosion of hegemony, "there are reasons for believing that the present disequilibrium in the international system can be resolved without resort to hegemonic war" (p. 234).

The empirical evidence for the general validity of hegemonic stability theory is weak, and even its chief adherents have doubts about it. In addition, the logical underpinnings of the theory are suspect. Kindleberger's strong claim for the necessity of a single leader rested on the theory of collective goods. He argued that "the danger we face is not too much power in the international economy, but too little, not an excess of domination, but a superfluity of would-be free riders, unwilling to mind the store, and waiting for a storekeeper to appear" (1981, p. 253). As we will see in more detail in later chapters, some of the "goods" produced by hegemonic leadership are not genuinely collective in character, although the implications of this fact are not necessarily as damaging to the theory as might be imagined at first. More critical is the fact that in international economic systems a few actors typically control a preponderance of resources. This point is especially telling, since the theory of collective goods does not properly imply that cooperation among a few countries should be impossible. Indeed, one of the original purposes of Olson's use of the theory was to show that in systems with only a few participants these actors "can provide themselves with collective goods without relying on any positive inducements apart from the good itself" (Olson, 1965, p. 33; quoted in McKeown, 1983a, p. 79). Logically, hegemony should not be a necessary condition for the emergence of cooperation in an oligopolistic system.

The theory of hegemonic stability is thus suggestive but by no means definitive. Concentrated power alone is not sufficient to create a stable international economic order in which cooperation flourishes, and the argument that hegemony is necessary for cooperation is both theoretically and empirically weak. If hegemony is redefined as the ability and willingness of a single state to make and enforce rules, furthermore, the claim that hegemony is sufficient for cooperation becomes virtually tautological.

The crude theory of hegemonic stability establishes a useful, if somewhat simplistic, starting-point for an analysis of changes in international cooperation and discord. Its refined version raises a looser but suggestive set of interpretive questions for the analysis of some eras in the history of the international political economy. Such an interpretive framework does not constitute an explanatory systemic theory, but it can help us think of hegemony in another way—less as a concept that helps to explain outcomes in terms of power than as a way of describing an international system in which leadership is exercised by a single state. Rather than being a component of a scientific generalization—that power is a necessary or sufficient condition for cooperation—the concept of hegemony, defined in terms of willingness as well as ability to lead, helps us think about the incentives facing the potential hegemon. Under what conditions, domestic and international, will such a country decide to invest in the construction of rules and institutions?

Concern for the incentives facing the hegemon should also alert us to the frequently neglected incentives facing other countries in the system. What calculus do they confront in considering whether to challenge or defer to a would-be leader? Thinking about the calculations of secondary powers raises the question of deference. Theories of hegemony should seek not only to analyze dominant powers' decisions to engage in rule-making and rule-enforcement, but also to explore why secondary states defer to the leadership of the hegemon. That is, they need to account for the legitimacy of hegemonic regimes and for the coexistence of cooperation, as defined in the next chapter, with hegemony. We will see later in this chapter that Gramsci's notion of "ideological hegemony" provides some valuable clues helping us understand how cooperation and hegemony fit together.

MILITARY POWER AND HEGEMONY
IN THE WORLD POLITICAL ECONOMY

Before taking up these themes, we need to clarify the relationship between this analysis of hegemony in the world political economy and the question of military power. A hegemonic state must possess enough military power to be able to protect the international political economy that it dominates from incursions by hostile adversaries. This is essential because economic issues, if they are crucial enough to basic national values, may become military-security issues as well. For instance, Japan attacked the United States in 1941 partly in response to the freezing of Japanese assets in the United States, which denied Japan "access to all the vitally needed supplies outside her own control, in particular her most crucial need, oil" (Schroeder, 1958, p. 53). During and after World War II the United States used its military power to assure itself access to the petroleum of the Middle East; and at the end of 1974 Secretary of State Henry A. Kissinger warned that the United States might resort to military action if oil-exporting countries threatened "some actual strangulation of the industrialized world" (Brown, 1983, p. 428).

Yet the hegemonic power need not be militarily dominant world-wide. Neither British nor American power ever extended so far. Britain was challenged militarily during the nineteenth century by France, Germany, and especially Russia; even at the height of its power after World War II the United States confronted a recalcitrant Soviet adversary and fought a war against China. The military conditions for economic hegemony are met if the economically preponderant country has sufficient military capabilities to prevent incursions by others that would deny it access to major areas of its economic activity.

The sources of hegemony therefore include sufficient military power to deter or rebuff attempts to capture and close off important areas of the world political economy. But in the contemporary world, at any rate, it is difficult for a hegemon to use military power directly to attain its economic policy objectives with its military partners and allies. Allies cannot be threatened with force without beginning to question the alliance; nor are threats to cease defending them unless they conform to the hegemon's economic rules very credible except in extraordinary circumstances. Many of the relationships within the hegemonic international political economy dominated by the United States after World War II approximated more closely the ideal type of "complex interdependence"—with multiple issues, multiple channels of contact among societies, and inefficacy of military force for most policy objectives—than the converse ideal type of Realist theory (Keohane and Nye, 1977, ch. 2).

This does not mean that military force has become useless. It has certainly played an indirect role even in U.S. relations with its closest allies, since Germany and Japan could hardly ignore the fact that American military power shielded them from Soviet pressure. It has played a more overt role in the Middle East, where American military power has occasionally been directly employed and has always cast a shadow and where U.S. military aid has been conspicuous. Yet changes in relations of military power have not been the major factors affecting patterns of cooperation and discord among the advanced industrialized countries since the end of World War II. Only in the case of Middle Eastern oil have they been highly significant as forces contributing to changes in international economic regimes, and even in that case (I argue in chapter 9) shifts in economic interdependence, and therefore in economic power, were more important. Throughout the period between 1945 and 1983 the United States remained a far stronger military power than any of its allies and the only country capable of defending them from the Soviet Union or of intervening effectively against serious opposition in areas such as the Middle East. In exploring the relationship between hegemony and order in this chapter, as in examining hegemonic cooperation in chapter 8 and the decline of hegemonic regimes in chapter 9, I concentrate principally on economic sources of power, and on shifts in economic power as explanations for change. By abstracting from military issues, we can focus more clearly on the economic origins of change.

Some readers may wish to criticize this account by arguing that military power has been more important than claimed here. By considering military power only as a background condition for postwar American hegemony rather than as a variable, I invite such a debate. Any such critique, however, should keep in mind what I am trying to explain in this chapter and in Part III: not the sources of hegemony (in domestic institutions, basic resources, and technological advances any more than in military power), but rather the effects of changes in hegemony on cooperation among the advanced industrialized countries. I seek to account for the impact of American dominance on the creation of international economic regimes and the effects of an erosion of that preponderant position on those regimes. Only if *these* problems—not other questions that might be interesting—could be understood better by exploring more deeply the impact of changes in relations of military power would this hypothetical critique be damaging to my argument.

MARXIAN NOTIONS OF HEGEMONY

For Marxists, the fundamental forces affecting the world political economy are those of class struggle and uneven development. International history is dynamic and dialectical rather than cyclical. The maneuvers of states reflect the stages of capitalist development and the contradictions of that development. For a Marxist, it is futile to discuss hegemony, or the operation of international institutions, without understanding that they operate, in the contemporary world system, within a capitalist context shaped by the evolutionary patterns and functional requirements of capitalism. Determinists may call these requirements laws. Historicists may see the patterns as providing some clues into a rather open-ended process that is nevertheless affected profoundly by what has gone before: people making their own history, but not just as they please.

Any genuinely Marxian theory of world politics begins with an analysis of capitalism. According to Marxist doctrine, no smooth and progressive development of productive forces within the confines of capitalist relations of production can persist for long. Contradictions are bound to appear. It is likely that they will take the form of tendencies toward stagnation and decline in the rate of profit (Cohen, 1978; Fine and Harris, 1979; Mandel, 1974), but they may also be reflected in crises of legitimacy for the capitalist state, even in the absence of economic crisis (Habermas, 1973/1976). Any "crisis of hegemony" will necessarily be at the same time—and more fundamentally—a crisis of capitalism (Arrighi, 1982; Campen and MacEwan, 1982; Sweezy and Magdoff, 1972).

For Marxists, theories of hegemony are necessarily partial, since they do not explain changes in the contradictions facing capitalism. Nevertheless, Marxists have often used the concept of hegemony, implicitly defined simply as dominance, as a way of analyzing the surface manifestations of world politics under capitalism. For Marxists as well as mercantilists, wealth and power are complementary: each depends on the other. As David Sylvan (1981) has pointed out, the analyses of the Marxist Fred Block and the Realist Robert Gilpin are quite similar: both emphasize the role of U.S. hegemony in creating order after the Second World War and the disturbing effects of the erosion of American power.

Immanuel Wallerstein's work also illustrates this point. He is at pains to stress that modern world history should be seen as the history of capitalism as a world system. Apart from "relatively minor accidents" resulting from geography, peculiarities of history, or luck, "it is the operations of the world-market forces which accentuate the differences, institutionalize them, and make them impossible to surmount over the long run" (1979, p. 21). Nevertheless, when considering particular epochs, Wallerstein emphasizes hegemony and the role of military force. Dutch economic hegemony in the seventeenth century was destroyed not by the operation of the world-market system or contradictions of capitalism, but by the force of British and French arms (Wallerstein, 1980, pp. 38-39).

The Marxian adoption of mercantilist categories raises analytical ambiguities having to do with the relationship between capitalism and the state. Marxists who adopt this approach have difficulty maintaining a class focus, since their unit of analysis shifts to the country, rather than the class, for purposes of explaining international events. This is a problem for both Block and Wallerstein, as it often appears that their embrace of state-centered analysis has relegated the concept of class to the shadowy background of political economy (Brenner, 1977; Skocpol, 1977; Sylvan, 1981). The puzzle of the relationship between the state and capitalism is also reflected in the old debate between Lenin and Kautsky about "ultra-imperialism" (Lenin, 1917/ 1939, pp. 93-94). Lenin claimed that contradictions among the capitalist powers were fundamental and could not be resolved, against Kautsky's view that capitalism could go through a phase in which capitalist states could maintain unity for a considerable period of time.

The successful operation of American hegemony for over a quarter-century after the end of World War II supports Kautsky's forecast that ultra-imperialism could be stable and contradicts Lenin's thesis that capitalism made inter-imperialist war inevitable.[6] It does not, however, resolve the issue of whether ultra-imperialism could be maintained in the absence of hegemony. An analysis of the contemporary situation in Marxian terminology would hold that one form of ultra-imperialism—American hegemony—is now breaking down, leading to increased disorder, and that the issue at present is "whether all this will ultimately result in a new capitalist world order, in a revolutionary reconstitution of world society, or in the common ruin of the contending classes and nations" (Arrighi, 1982, p. 108). The issue from a Marxian standpoint is whether ultra-imperialism could be revived by new efforts at inter-capitalist collaboration or, on the contrary, whether fundamental contradictions in capitalism or in the coexistence of capitalism with the state system prevent any such recovery.

The key question of this book—how international cooperation can be maintained among the advanced capitalist states in the absence of American hegemony—poses essentially the same problem. The view taken here is similar to that of Kautsky and his followers, although the terminology is different. My contention is that the common interests of the leading capitalist states, bolstered by the effects of existing international regimes (mostly created during a period of American hegemony), are strong enough to make sustained cooperation possible, though not inevitable. One need not go so far as Murray (1971) and

---

[6] For a different interpretation of this debate, see Mandel (1974), pp. 332-42.

Hymer (1972) in projecting the "internationalization of capital" to understand the strong interests that capitalists have in maintaining some cooperation in the midst of rivalry. Uneven development in the context of a state system maintains rivalry and ensures that cooperation will be incomplete and fragile (Chase-Dunn, 1981), but it does not imply that the struggle must become violent or that compromises that benefit all sides are impossible.

Despite the similarities between my concerns and those of many Marxists, I do not adopt their categories in this study. Marxian explications of the "laws of capitalism" are not sufficiently well established that they can be relied upon for inferences about relations among states in the world political economy or for the analysis of future international cooperation. Insofar as there are fundamental contradictions in capitalism, they will surely have great impact on future international cooperation; but the existence and nature of these contradictions seem too murky to justify incorporating them into my analytical framework.[7]

As this discussion indicates, Marxian insights into international hegemony derive in part from combining Realist conceptions of hegemony as dominance with arguments about the contradictions of capitalism. But this is not the only Marxian contribution to the debate. In the thought of Antonio Gramsci and his followers, hegemony is distinguished from sheer dominance. As Robert W. Cox has expressed it:

> Antonio Gramsci used the concept of hegemony to express a unity between objective material forces and ethico-political ideas—in Marxian terms, a unity of structure and superstructure—in which power based on dominance over production is rationalized through an ideology incorporating compromise or consensus between dominant and subordinate groups (1977, p. 387). A hegemonial structure of world order is one in which power takes a primarily consensual form, as distinguished from a non-hegemonic order in which there are manifestly rival powers and no

---

[7] An example of the boldness of much of this Marxist literature, but also of its ambiguities and lack of empirical support, is provided by the theory of "long waves," or "Kondratieff waves," which has been adopted by Mandel (1974) and has also been taken up by non-Marxists such as Walt W. Rostow (1975). An excellent review essay on this literature, which comes to the conclusion that attempts to identify or explain long waves have "come to a dead end," can be found in Eklund (1980).

power has been able to establish the legitimacy of its dominance (1981, p. 153, n. 27).

The value of this conception of hegemony is that it helps us understand the willingness of the partners of a hegemon to defer to hegemonial leadership. Hegemons require deference to enable them to construct a structure of world capitalist order. It is too expensive, and perhaps self-defeating, to achieve this by force; after all, the key distinction between hegemony and imperialism is that a hegemon, unlike an empire, does not dominate societies through a cumbersome political superstructure, but rather supervises the relationships between politically independent societies through a combination of hierarchies of control and the operation of markets (Wallerstein, 1974, pp. 15-17). Hegemony rests on the subjective awareness by elites in secondary states that they are benefiting, as well as on the willingness of the hegemon itself to sacrifice tangible short-term benefits for intangible long-term gains.

Valuable as the conception of ideological hegemony is in helping us understand deference, it should be used with some caution. First, we should not assume that leaders of secondary states are necessarily the victims of "false consciousness" when they accept the hegemonic ideology, or that they constitute a small, parasitical elite that betrays the interests of the nation to its own selfish ends. It is useful to remind ourselves, as Robert Gilpin has, that during both the *Pax Britannica* and the *Pax Americana* countries other than the hegemon prospered, and that indeed many of them grew faster than the hegemon itself (1975, p. 85; 1981, pp. 175-85). Under some conditions—not necessarily all—it may be not only in the self-interest of peripheral elites, but conducive to the economic growth of their countries, for them to defer to the hegemon.[8]

We may also be permitted to doubt that ideological hegemony is as enduring internationally as it is domestically. The powerful ideology of nationalism is not available for the hegemon, outside of its own

---

[8] This is not to say that hegemony in general benefits small or weak countries. There certainly is no assurance that this will be the case. Hegemons may prevent middle-sized states from exploiting small ones and may construct a structure of order conducive to world economic growth; but they may also exploit smaller states economically or distort their patterns of autonomous development through economic, political, or military intervention. The issue of whether hegemony helps poor countries cannot be answered unconditionally, because too many other factors intervene. Until a more complex and sophisticated theory of the relationships among hegemony, other factors, and welfare is developed, it remains an empirically open question.

country, but rather for its enemies. Opponents of hegemony can often make nationalism the weapon of the weak and may also seek to invent cosmopolitan ideologies that delegitimize hegemony, such as the current ideology of a New International Economic Order, instead of going along with legitimating ones. Thus the potential for challenges to hegemonic ideology always exists.

CONCLUSIONS

Claims for the general validity of the theory of hegemonic stability are often exaggerated. The dominance of a single great power may contribute to order in world politics, in particular circumstances, but it is not a sufficient condition and there is little reason to believe that it is necessary. But Realist and Marxian arguments about hegemony both generate some important insights, which will be incorporated into the interpretation in Part III of the operation and decline of hegemonic cooperation.

Hegemony is related in complex ways to cooperation and to institutions such as international regimes. Successful hegemonic leadership itself depends on a certain form of asymmetrical cooperation. The hegemon plays a distinctive role, providing its partners with leadership in return for deference; but, unlike an imperial power, it cannot make and enforce rules without a certain degree of consent from other sovereign states. As the interwar experience illustrates, material predominance alone does not guarantee either stability or effective leadership. Indeed, the hegemon may have to invest resources in institutions in order to ensure that its preferred rules will guide the behavior of other countries.

Cooperation may be fostered by hegemony, and hegemons require cooperation to make and enforce rules. Hegemony and cooperation are not alternatives; on the contrary, they are often found in symbiotic relationships with one another. To analyze the relationships between hegemony and cooperation, we need a conception of cooperation that is somewhat tart rather than syrupy-sweet. It must take into account the facts that coercion is always possible in world politics and that conflicts of interest never vanish even when there are important shared interests. As we will see in more detail in the next chapter, cooperation should be defined not as the absence of conflict—which is always at least a potentially important element of international relations—but as a process that involves the use of discord to stimulate mutual adjustment.

PART II

Theories of Cooperation and International Regimes

Part II

Theory of Competition for
Resources and the
Implications for Community
Structure

· 4 ·

COOPERATION AND
INTERNATIONAL REGIMES

Hegemonic leadership can help to create a pattern of order. Cooperation is not antithetical to hegemony; on the contrary, hegemony depends on a certain kind of asymmetrical cooperation, which successful hegemons support and maintain. As we will see in more detail in chapter 8, contemporary international economic regimes were constructed under the aegis of the United States after World War II. In accounting for the creation of international regimes, hegemony often plays an important role, even a crucial one.

Yet the relevance of hegemonic cooperation for the future is questionable. Chapter 9 shows that the United States is less preponderant in material resources now than it was in the 1950s and early 1960s. Equally important, the United States is less willing than formerly to define its interests in terms complementary to those of Europe and Japan. The Europeans, in particular, are less inclined to defer to American initiatives, nor do they believe so strongly that they must do so in order to obtain essential military protection against the Soviet Union. Thus the subjective elements of American hegemony have been eroded as much as the tangible power resources upon which hegemonic systems rest. But neither the Europeans nor the Japanese are likely to have the capacity to become hegemonic powers themselves in the foreseeable future.[1]

This prospect raises the issue of cooperation "after hegemony," which is the central theme of this book and especially of the theories developed in Part II. It also leads back to a crucial tension between economics and politics: international coordination of policy seems highly beneficial in an interdependent world economy, but cooperation in world politics is particularly difficult. One way to relax this tension would be to deny the premise that international economic policy co-

---

[1] Historically, as noted in chapter 1, hegemonies have usually arisen only after major wars. The two principal modern powers that could be considered hegemonic leaders—Britain after 1815 and the United States after 1945—both emerged victorious from world conflicts. I am assuming, in regarding hegemony as unlikely in the foreseeable future, that any world war would have such disastrous consequences that no country would emerge as hegemonic over a world economy resembling that of the present. For a discussion of the cycle of hegemony, see Gilpin (1981) and Modelski (1978 and 1982).

ordination is valuable by assuming that international markets will automatically yield optimal results (Corden, 1981). The decisive objection to this argument is that, in the absence of cooperation, governments will interfere in markets unilaterally in pursuit of what they regard as their own interests, whatever liberal economists may say. They will intervene in foreign exchange markets, impose various restrictions on imports, subsidize favored domestic industries, and set prices for commodities such as petroleum (Strange, 1979). Even if one accepted cooperation to maintain free markets, but no other form of policy coordination, the further objection could be raised that economic market failure would be likely to occur (Cooper, 1983, pp. 45-46). Suboptimal outcomes of transactions could result, for a variety of reasons including problems of collective action. It would take an ideological leap of faith to believe that free markets lead necessarily to optimal results.

Rejecting the illusion that cooperation is never valuable in the world political economy, we have to cope with the fact that it is very difficult to organize. One recourse would be to lapse into fatalism—acceptance of destructive economic conflict as a result of political fragmentation. Although this is a logically tenable position for those who believe in the theory of hegemonic stability, even its most powerful theoretical advocate shies away from its bleak normative implications (Gilpin, 1981). A fatalistic view is not taken here. Without ignoring the difficulties that beset attempts to coordinate policy in the absence of hegemony, this book contends that nonhegemonic cooperation is possible, and that it can be facilitated by international regimes.

In making this argument, I will draw a distinction between the creation of international regimes and their maintenance. Chapter 5 seeks to show that when shared interests are sufficiently important and other key conditions are met, cooperation can emerge and regimes can be created without hegemony. Yet this does not imply that regimes can be created easily, much less that contemporary international economic regimes actually came about in this way. In chapter 6 I argue that international regimes are easier to maintain than to create, and that recognition of this fact is crucial to understanding why they are valued by governments. Regimes may be maintained, and may continue to foster cooperation, even under conditions that would not be sufficiently benign to bring about their creation. Cooperation is possible after hegemony not only because shared interests can lead to the creation of regimes, but also because the conditions for maintaining existing international regimes are less demanding than those required for creating them. Although hegemony helps to explain the creation of contemporary international regimes, the decline of hegemony does not necessarily lead symmetrically to their decay.

This chapter analyzes the meaning of two key terms: "cooperation" and "international regimes." It distinguishes cooperation from harmony as well as from discord, and it argues for the value of the concept of international regimes as a way of understanding both cooperation and discord. Together the concepts of cooperation and international regimes help us clarify what we want to explain: how do patterns of rule-guided policy coordination emerge, maintain themselves, and decay in world politics?

HARMONY, COOPERATION, AND DISCORD

Cooperation must be distinguished from harmony. Harmony refers to a situation in which actors' policies (pursued in their own self-interest without regard for others) *automatically* facilitate the attainment of others' goals. The classic example of harmony is the hypothetical competitive-market world of the classical economists, in which the Invisible Hand ensures that the pursuit of self-interest by each contributes to the interest of all. In this idealized, unreal world, no one's actions damage anyone else; there are no "negative externalities," in the economists' jargon. Where harmony reigns, cooperation is unnecessary. It may even be injurious, if it means that certain individuals conspire to exploit others. Adam Smith, for one, was very critical of guilds and other conspiracies against freedom of trade (1776/1976). Cooperation and harmony are by no means identical and ought not to be confused with one another.

Cooperation requires that the actions of separate individuals or organizations—which are not in pre-existent harmony—be brought into conformity with one another through a process of negotiation, which is often referred to as "policy coordination." Charles E. Lindblom has defined policy coordination as follows (1965, p. 227):

A set of decisions is coordinated if adjustments have been made in them, such that the adverse consequences of any one decision for other decisions are to a degree and in some frequency avoided, reduced, or counterbalanced or overweighed.

Cooperation occurs when actors adjust their behavior to the actual or anticipated preferences of others, through a process of policy coordination. To summarize more formally, *intergovernmental cooperation takes place when the policies actually followed by one gov-*

51

ernment are regarded by its partners as facilitating realization of their own objectives, as the result of a process of policy coordination.

With this definition in mind, we can differentiate among cooperation, harmony, and discord, as illustrated by figure 4.1. First, we ask whether actors' policies automatically facilitate the attainment of others' goals. If so, there is harmony: no adjustments need to take place. Yet harmony is rare in world politics. Rousseau sought to account for this rarity when he declared that even two countries guided by the General Will in their internal affairs would come into conflict if they had extensive contact with one another, since the General Will of each would not be general for both. Each would have a partial, self-interested perspective on their mutual interactions. Even for Adam Smith, efforts to ensure state security took precedence over measures to increase national prosperity. In defending the Navigation Acts, Smith declared: "As defence is of much more importance than opulence, the act of navigation is, perhaps, the wisest of all the commercial regulations of England" (1776/1976, p. 487). Waltz summarizes the point by saying that "in anarchy there is no automatic harmony" (1959, p. 182).

Yet this insight tells us nothing definitive about the prospects for cooperation. For this we need to ask a further question about situations in which harmony does not exist. Are attempts made by actors (governmental or nongovernmental) to adjust their policies to each others' objectives? If no such attempts are made, the result is discord: a situation in which governments regard each others' policies as hindering the attainment of their goals, and hold each other responsible for these constraints.

Discord often leads to efforts to induce others to change their policies; when these attempts meet resistance, policy conflict results. Insofar as these attempts at policy adjustment succeed in making policies more compatible, however, cooperation ensues. The policy coordination that leads to cooperation need not involve bargaining or negotiation at all. What Lindblom calls "adaptive" as opposed to "manipulative" adjustment can take place: one country may shift its policy in the direction of another's preferences without regard for the effect of its action on the other state, defer to the other country, or partially shift its policy in order to avoid adverse consequences for its partner. Or nonbargained manipulation—such as one actor confronting another with a *fait accompli*—may occur (Lindblom, 1965, pp. 33-34 and ch. 4). Frequently, of course, negotiation and bargaining indeed take place, often accompanied by other actions that are designed to induce others to adjust their policies to one's own. Each government

Figure 4.1. Harmony, Cooperation, and Discord

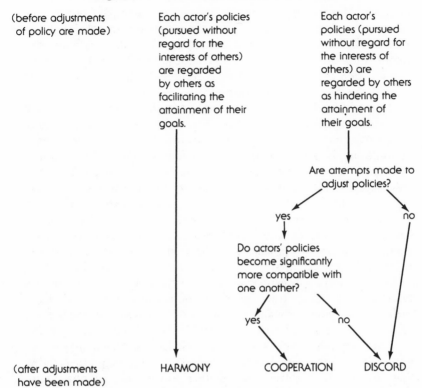

(before adjustments of policy are made)

Each actor's policies (pursued without regard for the interests of others) are regarded by others as facilitating the attainment of their goals.

Each actor's policies (pursued without regard for the interests of others) are regarded by others as hindering the attainment of their goals.

Are attempts made to adjust policies?

yes   no

Do actors' policies become significantly more compatible with one another?

yes   no

(after adjustments have been made)

HARMONY   COOPERATION   DISCORD

pursues what it perceives as its self-interest, but looks for bargains that can benefit all parties to the deal, though not necessarily equally.

Harmony and cooperation are not usually distinguished from one another so clearly. Yet, in the study of world politics, they should be. Harmony is apolitical. No communication is necessary, and no influence need be exercised. Cooperation, by contrast, is highly political: somehow, patterns of behavior must be altered. This change may be accomplished through negative as well as positive inducements. Indeed, studies of international crises, as well as game-theoretic experiments and simulations, have shown that under a variety of conditions strategies that involve threats and punishments as well as promises and rewards are more effective in attaining cooperative outcomes than those that rely entirely on persuasion and the force of good example (Axelrod, 1981, 1984; Lebow, 1981; Snyder and Diesing, 1977).

Cooperation therefore does not imply an absence of conflict. On

53

the contrary, it is typically mixed with conflict and reflects partially successful efforts to overcome conflict, real or potential. Cooperation takes place only in situations in which actors perceive that their policies are actually or potentially in conflict, not where there is harmony. Cooperation should not be viewed as the absence of conflict, but rather as a reaction to conflict or potential conflict. Without the specter of conflict, there is no need to cooperate.

The example of trade relations among friendly countries in a liberal international political economy may help to illustrate this crucial point. A naive observer, trained only to appreciate the overall welfare benefits of trade, might assume that trade relations would be harmonious: consumers in importing countries benefit from cheap foreign goods and increased competition, and producers can increasingly take advantage of the division of labor as their export markets expand. But harmony does not normally ensue. Discord on trade issues may prevail because governments do not even seek to reduce the adverse consequences of their own policies for others, but rather strive in certain respects to increase the severity of those effects. Mercantilist governments have sought in the twentieth century as well as the seventeenth to manipulate foreign trade, in conjunction with warfare, to damage each other economically and to gain productive resources themselves (Wilson, 1957; Hirschman, 1945/1980). Governments may desire "positional goods," such as high status (Hirsch, 1976), and may therefore resist even mutually beneficial cooperation if it helps others more than themselves. Yet even when neither power nor positional motivations are present, and when all participants would benefit in the aggregate from liberal trade, discord tends to predominate over harmony as the initial result of independent governmental action.

This occurs even under otherwise benign conditions because some groups or industries are forced to incur adjustment costs as changes in comparative advantage take place. Governments often respond to the ensuing demands for protection by attempting, more or less effectively, to cushion the burdens of adjustment for groups and industries that are politically influential at home. Yet unilateral measures to this effect almost always impose adjustment costs abroad, and discord continually threatens. Governments enter into international negotiations in order to reduce the conflict that would otherwise result. Even substantial potential common benefits do not create harmony when state power can be exercised on behalf of certain interests and against others. In world politics, harmony tends to vanish: attainment of the gains from pursuing complementary policies depends on cooperation.

Observers of world politics who take power and conflict seriously should be attracted to this way of defining cooperation, since my definition does not relegate cooperation to the mythological world of relations among equals in power. Hegemonic cooperation is not a contradiction in terms. Defining cooperation in contrast to harmony should, I hope, lead readers with a Realist orientation to take cooperation in world politics seriously rather than to dismiss it out of hand. To Marxists who also believe in hegemonic power theories, however, even this definition of cooperation may not seem to make it relevant to the contemporary world political economy. From this perspective, mutual policy adjustments cannot possibly resolve the contradictions besetting the system because they are attributable to capitalism rather than to problems of coordination among egoistic actors lacking common government. Attempts to resolve these contradictions through international cooperation will merely transfer issues to a deeper and even more intractable level. Thus it is not surprising that Marxian analyses of the international political economy have, with few exceptions, avoided sustained examinations of the conditions under which cooperation among major capitalist countries can take place. Marxists see it as more important to expose relationships of exploitation and conflict between major capitalist powers on the one hand and the masses of people in the periphery of world capitalism on the other. And, from a Leninist standpoint, to examine the conditions for international cooperation without first analyzing the contradictions of capitalism, and recognizing the irreconcilability of conflicts among capitalist countries, is a bourgeois error.

This is less an argument than a statement of faith. Since sustained international coordination of macroeconomic policies has never been tried, the statement that it would merely worsen the contradictions facing the system is speculative. In view of the lack of evidence for it, such a claim could even be considered rash. Indeed, one of the most perceptive Marxian writers of recent years, Stephen Hymer (1972), recognized explicitly that capitalists face problems of collective action and argued that they were seeking, with at least temporary prospects of success, to overcome them. As he recognized, any success in internationalizing capital could pose grave threats to socialist aspirations and, at the very least, would shift contradictions to new points of tension. Thus even were we to agree that the fundamental issue is posed by the contradictions of capitalism rather than the tensions inherent in a state system, it would be worthwhile to study the conditions under which cooperation is likely to occur.

55

INTERNATIONAL REGIMES AND COOPERATION

One way to study cooperation and discord would be to focus on particular actions as the units of analysis. This would require the systematic compilation of a data set composed of acts that could be regarded as comparable and coded according to the degree of cooperation that they reflect. Such a strategy has some attractive features. The problem with it, however, is that instances of cooperation and discord could all too easily be isolated from the context of beliefs and behavior within which they are embedded. This book does not view cooperation atomistically as a set of discrete, isolated acts, but rather seeks to understand patterns of cooperation in the world political economy. Accordingly, we need to examine actors' expectations about future patterns of interaction, their assumptions about the proper nature of economic arrangements, and the kinds of political activities they regard as legitimate. That is, we need to analyze cooperation within the context of international institutions, broadly defined, as in chapter 1, in terms of practices and expectations. Each act of cooperation or discord affects the beliefs, rules, and practices that form the context for future actions. Each act must therefore be interpreted as embedded within a chain of such acts and their successive cognitive and institutional residues.

This argument parallels Clifford Geertz's discussion of how anthropologists should use the concept of culture to interpret the societies they investigate. Geertz sees culture as the "webs of significance" that people have created for themselves. On their surface, they are enigmatical; the observer has to interpret them so that they make sense. Culture, for Geertz, "is a context, something within which [social events] can be intelligibly described" (1973, p. 14). It makes little sense to describe naturalistically what goes on at a Balinese cock-fight unless one understands the meaning of the event for Balinese culture. There is not a world culture in the fullest sense, but even in world politics, human beings spin webs of significance. They develop implicit standards for behavior, some of which emphasize the principle of sovereignty and legitimize the pursuit of self-interest, while others rely on quite different principles. Any act of cooperation or apparent cooperation needs to be interpreted within the context of related actions, and of prevailing expectations and shared beliefs, before its meaning can be properly understood. Fragments of political behavior become comprehensible when viewed as part of a larger mosaic.

The concept of international regime not only enables us to describe patterns of cooperation; it also helps to account for both cooperation and discord. Although regimes themselves depend on conditions that are conducive to interstate agreements, they may also facilitate further efforts to coordinate policies. The next two chapters develop an argument about the functions of international regimes that shows how they can affect the propensity even of egoistic governments to cooperate. To understand international cooperation, it is necessary to comprehend how institutions and rules not only reflect, but also affect, the facts of world politics.

Defining and Identifying Regimes

When John Ruggie introduced the concept of international regimes into the international politics literature in 1975, he defined a regime as "a set of mutual expectations, rules and regulations, plans, organizational energies and financial commitments, which have been accepted by a group of states" (p. 570). More recently, a collective definition, worked out at a conference on the subject, defined international regimes as "sets of implicit or explicit principles, norms, rules and decision-making procedures around which actors' expectations converge in a given area of international relations. Principles are beliefs of fact, causation, and rectitude. Norms are standards of behavior defined in terms of rights and obligations. Rules are specific prescriptions or proscriptions for action. Decision-making procedures are prevailing practices for making and implementing collective choice" (Krasner, 1983, p. 2).

This definition provides a useful starting-point for analysis, since it begins with the general conception of regimes as social institutions and explicates it further. The concept of norms, however, is ambiguous. It is important that we understand norms in this definition simply as standards of behavior defined in terms of rights and obligations. Another usage would distinguish norms from rules and principles by stipulating that participants in a social system regard norms, but not rules and principles, as morally binding regardless of considerations of narrowly defined self-interest. But to include norms, thus defined, in a definition of necessary regime characteristics would be to make the conception of regimes based strictly on self-interest a contradiction in terms. Since this book regards regimes as largely based on self-interest, I will maintain a definition of norms simply as standards of behavior, whether adopted on grounds of self-interest or otherwise. Only in chapter 7 will the possibility again be taken seriously that some regimes may contain norms and principles justified on the basis

57

of values extending beyond self-interest, and regarded as obligatory on moral grounds by governments.

The principles of regimes define, in general, the purposes that their members are expected to pursue. For instance, the principles of the postwar trade and monetary regimes have emphasized the value of open, nondiscriminatory patterns of international economic transactions; the fundamental principle of the nonproliferation regime is that the spread of nuclear weapons is dangerous. Norms contain somewhat clearer injunctions to members about legitimate and illegitimate behavior, still defining responsibilities and obligations in relatively general terms. For instance, the norms of the General Agreement on Tariffs and Trade (GATT) do not require that members resort to free trade immediately, but incorporate injunctions to members to practice nondiscrimination and reciprocity and to move toward increased liberalization. Fundamental to the nonproliferation regime is the norm that members of the regime should not act in ways that facilitate nuclear proliferation.

The rules of a regime are difficult to distinguish from its norms; at the margin, they merge into one another. Rules are, however, more specific: they indicate in more detail the specific rights and obligations of members. Rules can be altered more easily than principles or norms, since there may be more than one set of rules that can attain a given set of purposes. Finally, at the same level of specificity as rules, but referring to procedures rather than substances, the decisionmaking procedures of regimes provide ways of implementing their principles and altering their rules.

An example from the field of international monetary relations may be helpful. The most important principle of the international balance-of-payments regime since the end of World War II has been that of liberalization of trade and payments. A key norm of the regime has been the injunction to states not to manipulate their exchange rates unilaterally for national advantage. Between 1958 and 1971 this norm was realized through pegged exchange rates and procedures for consultation in the event of change, supplemented with a variety of devices to help governments avoid exchange-rate changes through a combination of borrowing and internal adjustment. After 1973 governments have subscribed to the same norm, although it has been implemented more informally and probably less effectively under a system of floating exchange rates. Ruggie (1983b) has argued that the abstract principle of liberalization, subject to constraints imposed by the acceptance of the welfare state, has been maintained throughout the postwar period: "embedded liberalism" continues, reflecting a fundamental element of

58

continuity in the international balance-of-payments regime. The norm of nonmanipulation has also been maintained, even though the specific rules of the 1958-71 system having to do with adjustment have been swept away.

The concept of international regime is complex because it is defined in terms of four distinct components: principles, norms, rules, and decisionmaking procedures. It is tempting to select one of these levels of specificity—particularly, principles and norms or rules and procedures—as *the* defining characteristic of regimes (Krasner, 1983; Ruggie, 1983b). Such an approach, however, creates a false dichotomy between principles on the one hand and rules and procedures on the other. As we have noted, at the margin norms and rules cannot be sharply distinguished from each other. It is difficult if not impossible to tell the difference between an "implicit rule" of broad significance and a well-understood, relatively specific operating principle. Both rules and principles may affect expectations and even values. In a strong international regime, the linkages between principles and rules are likely to be tight. Indeed, it is precisely the linkages among principles, norms, and rules that give regimes their legitimacy. Since rules, norms, and principles are so closely intertwined, judgments about whether changes in rules constitute changes *of* regime or merely changes *within* regimes necessarily contain arbitrary elements.

Principles, norms, rules, and procedures all contain injunctions about behavior: they prescribe certain actions and proscribe others. They imply obligations, even though these obligations are not enforceable through a hierarchical legal system. It clarifies the definition of regime, therefore, to think of it in terms of injunctions of greater or lesser specificity. Some are far-reaching and extremely important. They may change only rarely. At the other extreme, injunctions may be merely technical, matters of convenience that can be altered without great political or economic impact. In-between are injunctions that are both specific enough that violations of them are in principle identifiable and that changes in them can be observed, and sufficiently significant that changes in them make a difference for the behavior of actors and the nature of the international political economy. It is these intermediate injunctions—politically consequential but specific enough that violations and changes can be identified—that I take as the essence of international regimes.[2]

[2] Some authors have defined "regime" as equivalent to the conventional concept of international system. For instance, Puchala and Hopkins (1983) claim that "a regime

59

A brief examination of international oil regimes, and their injunctions, may help us clarify this point. The pre-1939 international oil regime was dominated by a small number of international firms and contained explicit injunctions about where and under what conditions companies could produce oil, and where and how they should market it. The rules of the Red Line and Achnacarry or "As-Is" agreements of 1928 reflected an "anti-competitive ethos": that is, the basic principle that competition was destructive to the system and the norm that firms should not engage in it (Turner, 1978, p. 30). This principle and this norm both persisted after World War II, although an intergovernmental regime with explicit rules was not established, owing to the failure of the Anglo-American Petroleum Agreement (discussed in chapter 8). Injunctions against price-cutting were reflected more in the practices of companies than in formal rules. Yet expectations and practices of major actors were strongly affected by these injunctions, and in this sense the criteria for a regime—albeit a weak one—were met. As governments of producing countries became more assertive, however, and as formerly domestic independent companies entered international markets, these arrangements collapsed; after the mid-to-late 1960s, there was no regime for the issue-area as a whole, since no injunctions could be said to be accepted as obligatory by all influential actors. Rather, there was a "tug of war" (Hirschman, 1981) in which all sides resorted to self-help. The Organization of Petroleum Exporting Countries (OPEC) sought to create a producers' regime based on rules for prorationing oil production, and consumers established an emergency oil-sharing system in the new International Energy Agency to counteract the threat of selective embargoes.

If we were to have paid attention only to the principle of avoiding competition, we would have seen continuity: whatever the dominant actors, they have always sought to cartelize the industry one way or another. But to do so would be to miss the main point, which is that momentous changes have occurred. At the other extreme, we could have fixed our attention on very specific particular arrangements, such

exists in every substantive issue-area in international relations where there is discernibly patterned behavior" (p. 63). To adopt this definition would be to make either "system" or "regime" a redundant term. At the opposite extreme, the concept of regime could be limited to situations with genuine normative content, in which governments followed regime rules *instead of* pursuing their own self-interests when the two conflicted. If this course were chosen, the concept of regime would be just another way of expressing ancient "idealist" sentiments in international relations. The category of regime would become virtually empty. This dichotomy poses a false choice between using "regime" as a new label for old patterns and defining regimes as utopias. Either strategy would make the term irrelevant.

as the various joint ventures of the 1950s and 1960s or the specific provisions for controlling output tried by OPEC after 1973, in which case we would have observed a pattern of continual flux. The significance of the most important events—the demise of old cartel arrangements, the undermining of the international majors' positions in the 1960s, and the rise of producing governments to a position of influence in the 1970s—could have been missed. Only by focusing on the intermediate level of relatively specific but politically consequential injunctions, whether we call them rules, norms, or principles, does the concept of regime help us identify major changes that require explanation.

As our examples of money and oil suggest, we regard the scope of international regimes as corresponding, in general, to the boundaries of issue-areas, since governments establish regimes to deal with problems that they regard as so closely linked that they should be dealt with together. Issue-areas are best defined as sets of issues that are in fact dealt with in common negotiations and by the same, or closely coordinated, bureaucracies, as opposed to issues that are dealt with separately and in uncoordinated fashion. Since issue-areas depend on actors' perceptions and behavior rather than on inherent qualities of the subject-matters, their boundaries change gradually over time. Fifty years ago, for instance, there was no oceans issue-area, since particular questions now grouped under that heading were dealt with separately; but there was an international monetary issue-area even then (Keohane and Nye, 1977, ch. 4). Twenty years ago trade in cotton textiles had an international regime of its own—the Long-Term Agreement on Cotton Textiles—and was treated separately from trade in synthetic fibers (Aggarwal, 1981). Issue-areas are defined and redefined by changing patterns of human intervention; so are international regimes.

Self-Help and International Regimes

The injunctions of international regimes rarely affect economic transactions directly: state institutions, rather than international organizations, impose tariffs and quotas, intervene in foreign exchange markets, and manipulate oil prices through taxes and subsidies. If we think about the impact of the principles, norms, rules, and decision-making procedures of regimes, it becomes clear that insofar as they have any effect at all, it must be exerted on national controls, and especially on the specific interstate agreements that affect the exercise of national controls (Aggarwal, 1981). International regimes must be distinguished from these specific agreements; as we will see in chapter

6, a major function of regimes is to facilitate the making of specific cooperative agreements among governments.

Superficially, it could seem that since international regimes affect national controls, the regimes are of superior importance—just as federal laws in the United States frequently override state and local legislation. Yet this would be a fundamentally misleading conclusion. In a well-ordered society, the units of action—individuals in classic liberal thought—live together within a framework of constitutional principles that define property rights, establish who may control the state, and specify the conditions under which subjects must obey governmental regulations. In the United States, these principles establish the supremacy of the federal government in a number of policy areas, though not in all. But world politics is decentralized rather than hierarchic: the prevailing principle of sovereignty means that states are subject to no superior government (Ruggie, 1983a). The resulting system is sometimes referred to as one of "self-help" (Waltz, 1979).

Sovereignty and self-help mean that the principles and rules of international regimes will necessarily be weaker than in domestic society. In a civil society, these rules "specify terms of exchange" within the framework of constitutional principles (North, 1981, p. 203). In world politics, the principles, norms, and rules of regimes are necessarily fragile because they risk coming into conflict with the principle of sovereignty and the associated norm of self-help. They may promote cooperation, but the fundamental basis of order on which they would rest in a well-ordered society does not exist. They drift around without being tied to the solid anchor of the state.

Yet even if the principles of sovereignty and self-help limit the degree of confidence to be placed in international agreements, they do not render cooperation impossible. Orthodox theory itself relies on mutual interests to explain forms of cooperation that are used by states as instruments of competition. According to balance-of-power theory, cooperative endeavors such as political-military alliances necessarily form in self-help systems (Waltz, 1979). Acts of cooperation are accounted for on the grounds that mutual interests are sufficient to enable states to overcome their suspicions of one another. But since even orthodox theory relies on mutual interests, its advocates are on weak ground in objecting to interpretations of system-wide cooperation along these lines. There is no logical or empirical reason why mutual interests in world politics should be limited to interests in combining forces against adversaries. As economists emphasize, there can also be mutual interests in securing efficiency gains from voluntary exchange or oligopolistic rewards from the creation and division of rents resulting from the control and manipulation of markets.

International regimes should not be interpreted as elements of a new international order "beyond the nation-state." They should be comprehended chiefly as arrangements motivated by self-interest: as components of systems in which sovereignty remains a constitutive principle. This means that, as Realists emphasize, they will be shaped largely by their most powerful members, pursuing their own interests. But regimes can also affect state interests, for the notion of self-interest is itself elastic and largely subjective. Perceptions of self-interest depend both on actors' expectations of the likely consequences that will follow from particular actions and on their fundamental values. Regimes can certainly affect expectations and may affect values as well. Far from being contradicted by the view that international behavior is shaped largely by power and interests, the concept of international regime is consistent both with the importance of differential power and with a sophisticated view of self-interest. Theories of regimes can incorporate Realist insights about the role of power and interest, while also indicating the inadequacy of theories that define interests so narrowly that they fail to take the role of institutions into account.

Regimes not only are consistent with self-interest but may under some conditions even be necessary to its effective pursuit. They facilitate the smooth operation of decentralized international political systems and therefore perform an important function for states. In a world political economy characterized by growing interdependence, they may become increasingly useful for governments that wish to solve common problems and pursue complementary purposes without subordinating themselves to hierarchical systems of control.

Conclusions

In this chapter international cooperation has been defined as a process through which policies actually followed by governments come to be regarded by their partners as facilitating realization of their own objectives, as the result of policy coordination. Cooperation involves mutual adjustment and can only arise from conflict or potential conflict. It must therefore be distinguished from harmony. Discord, which is the opposite of harmony, stimulates demands for policy adjustments, which can either lead to cooperation or to continued, perhaps intensified, discord.

Since international regimes reflect patterns of cooperation and discord over time, focusing on them leads us to examine long-term patterns of behavior, rather than treating acts of cooperation as isolated events. Regimes consist of injunctions at various levels of generality, ranging from principles to norms to highly specific rules and decisionmaking procedures. By investigating the evolution of the norms and rules of a regime over time, we can use the concept of international regime both to explore continuity and to investigate change in the world political economy.

From a theoretical standpoint, regimes can be viewed as intermediate factors, or "intervening variables," between fundamental characteristics of world politics such as the international distribution of power on the one hand and the behavior of states and nonstate actors such as multinational corporations on the other. The concept of international regime helps us account for cooperation and discord. To understand the impact of regimes, it is not necessary to posit idealism on the part of actors in world politics. On the contrary, the norms and rules of regimes can exert an effect on behavior even if they do not embody common ideals but are used by self-interested states and corporations engaging in a process of mutual adjustment.

· 5 ·

RATIONAL-CHOICE AND
FUNCTIONAL EXPLANATIONS

A simple explanation for the failure of a given attempt at cooperation in world politics is always available: that the interests of the states involved were incompatible with one another. This would imply that discord was a natural, if not inevitable, result of the characteristics of the actors and their positions relative to one another. Indeed, on this account, low levels of cooperation might still be Pareto-optimal; that is, given the interests of the actors, there might be no more cooperative solution that would make all of them better off.

This is one possible account of discord. But it reminds one uncomfortably of Voltaire's *Candide*, whose hero keeps proclaiming, in the wake of terrible disasters, that all is for the best in this, the "best of all possible worlds." It is difficult to prove that the frequent disasters of international politics are not inherent in the interests of the actors; but if we believed they were, we would be forced into the fatalistic and ultimately absurd position that such events as World War I were in the interests of the Austrian, German, and Russian empires, all of which disappeared as a result of the conflict. More generally, this view would have us believe, implausibly, that objective interests determine world events regardless of the information available to governments and transnational actors, their perceptions of likely consequences of action, or the sequence of interactions in which they engage.

The implausibility of this view is reinforced by recent deductive theories based on assumptions of rationality. Game theory and discussions of collective action emphasize that rational individuals who would all benefit from cooperating may nevertheless be unable to do so. For one reason or another, they may fail to coordinate their actions to reach the desired position. Even if they are rational as individuals, the group of which they are part will not necessarily behave as a rational actor. To infer conflicting interests from discord, without obtaining direct evidence on those alleged conflicts of interest, is therefore to run the risk of serious error (Hardin, 1982, p. 1). Actors may fail to cooperate even when their interests are entirely identical. In Shakespeare's *Romeo and Juliet*, for instance, Romeo and Juliet have the same interest—to marry one another—but the inability of Friar

John to deliver a message from Friar Laurence to Romeo leads to the failure of Friar Laurence's plan and the death of both lovers.

The fact that attempts at cooperation may fail despite mutual interests recalls our discussion of Institutionalist thought in chapter 1. Institutionalist writers have always stressed that cooperation can be fostered by institutions. This implies that actual cooperation, in the absence of institutions, is often less than potential cooperation. It does not, however, mean that cooperation is inevitable, or that it must continue to increase.

Institutionalists have sometimes been inclined to proclaim the growth of cooperation or even supranational authority, only to find their theory apparently falsified as their hopes are dashed. Even when they avoid excessive optimism, they have been bedeviled by ambiguity about actors' motivations. Realists are at least clear about their assumptions: states, the principal actors in world politics, are rational egoists. As we saw in chapter 2, the assumption of egoism implies that the preferences of actors in world politics are based on their assessments of their own welfare, not that of others. The rationality assumption states that they "seek to maximize value across a set of consistently ordered objectives" (Snyder and Diesing, 1977, p. 81). These assumptions permit Realist analysts to generate predictions about state behavior on the basis of relatively sparse information about their environments. Knowledge of the structure of the situation facing decisionmakers provides the analyst with clues to state action, since leaders, being rational egoists, will respond to the incentives and constraints provided by the environment in ways calculated to increase the wealth, security, and power of their states. Instead of having to do research on what leaders are actually thinking, we can obtain the necessary information merely by conducting thought-experiments in our own offices. As Hans J. Morgenthau expressed it some years ago (1948/1966, p. 5):

> [To understand foreign policy] we put ourselves in the position of a statesman who must meet a certain problem of foreign policy under certain circumstances, and we ask ourselves what the rational alternatives are from which a statesman may choose . . . and which of these rational alternatives this particular statesman, acting under these circumstances, is likely to choose. It is the testing of this rational hypothesis against the actual facts and their consequences that gives meaning to the facts of international politics and makes a theory of politics possible.

Institutionalists are less explicit about their models of actor behavior, since they have more complex ideas about "self-interest" and how it can change. This ambiguity has led, unfortunately, to the common belief that because they believe in the possibility of cooperation, they must "smuggle in" idealistic assumptions about motivations. Critics can point to idealistic premises or to ambiguity in the works of some writers who emphasize the role of institutions in promoting cooperation, and dismiss their theory as based on illusions about people and states.

My argument anticipates this objection by adopting the Realist model of rational egoism. In this chapter and the next one I assume, with the Realists, that actors are rational egoists. I propose to show, on the basis of their own assumptions, that the characteristic pessimism of Realism does not necessarily follow. I seek to demonstrate that Realist assumptions about world politics are consistent with the formation of institutionalized arrangements, containing rules and principles, which promote cooperation. Once the argument has been established in this way, it can be modified (as in chapter 7) by relaxing the key assumptions of rationality and egoism to allow for the impacts of bounded rationality, changes in preferences, and empathy on state behavior.

SINGLE-PLAY PRISONERS' DILEMMA AND THE PROBLEM OF COLLECTIVE ACTION

The difficulties of cooperating are illustrated best not by either purely conflictual games (in which discord appears to be determined by the structure of interests) or fundamentally cooperative ones (in which only melodramatic bad luck or its equivalent can prevent cooperation), but by what Thomas Schelling has called "mixed-motive games": games characterized by a combination of "mutual dependence and conflict, of partnership and competition" (1960/1980, p. 89). In these games, both players can benefit from mutual cooperation, but each can gain more from double-crossing the other one—that is, from "defection."[1]

Several mixed-motive games have been identified as relevant to world politics (Snyder and Diesing, 1977; Snidal, 1981; Oye, 1983b; Stein,

---

[1] For purposes of exposition, this discussion uses game-theoretic terminology and matrices to discuss the problem of collective action. It is important, however, to recognize that what Oran Young calls "manipulative" models of bargaining are equally important for an exploration of this issue from the actors' standpoint. Manipulative models emphasize "the presence of both strategic interaction and imperfect information." As we will see later in this chapter, both of these conditions are highly relevant to the problem of the functions performed by international regimes. On manipulative models of bargaining, see Young, 1975, especially pp. 303-18, and Schelling, 1960/ 1980 and 1978.

1983). Of particular interest is the well-known game of "Prisoners' Dilemma," since it demonstrates that under certain conditions rational actors find themselves unable to reach a Pareto-optimal solution, despite a certain degree of convergence of interests between them. Not all situations in world politics or the international political economy take the form of Prisoners' Dilemma, but many do, and the issues posed by Prisoners' Dilemma are central to the problems of discord and cooperation discussed in this book (Taylor, 1976).

Prisoners' Dilemma is based on the fable of two guilty partners in crime who are being questioned separately by the District Attorney. Each prisoner knows that if neither confesses, the DA will only have sufficient evidence to convict them for misdemeanors, leading to thirty-day prison terms for each. If both confess, however, they will each be sentenced to a year in the penitentiary. This prospect might seem to give both an incentive not to confess, except that the clever DA has promised that if either confesses while the other refuses, the confessor will not be prosecuted at all, while his recalcitrant partner is punished severely with a five-year sentence.

Under these conditions, each prisoner recognizes that on grounds of narrow self-interest he should confess *whatever his partner does.* If his partner also confesses, his own confession at least saves him from the punitive five-year sentence, and if his partner refuses to confess, his own confession lets him go free (at his partner's expense) rather than being convicted of a misdemeanor. As a result of these calculations, we are urged to conclude that two rational, self-interested individuals in such a situation will both confess and will receive prison sentences that they could have avoided by cooperating with each other and "stonewalling" the District Attorney. That is, to "defect" from cooperating with one's partner (to confess to the DA) seems to be the dominant strategy for both players.

A familiar game-theory matrix for Prisoners' Dilemma, with a numerical example included, is provided below. If both players cooperate with each other (not confessing to the DA), they receive the reward, R. If they defect (both confess), they are punished, P. If one defects while the other cooperates, the defector receives the benefit, T, of succumbing to temptation and tricking his partner, while the cooperator receives the sucker payoff, S. To insure that an even chance of exploiting or being exploited is worse than mutual cooperation, the standard definition of Prisoners' Dilemma includes the provision that the reward for cooperation is greater than twice the sum of the payoffs for tricking the other actor and being the sucker.

The logic of collective action, as explained by Mancur Olson, Jr. (1965), is similar in its essentials to this logic of Prisoners' Dilemma

Prisoners' Dilemma

		Column's Choice	
		COOPERATE	DEFECT
Row's choice:	COOPERATE	R, R (3, 3)	S, T (1, 4)
	DEFECT	T, S (4, 1)	P, P (2, 2)
Payoff ordering:	T > R > P > S	Condition: R > (S + T)/2	

(Hardin, 1982, ch. 2). In situations calling for collective action, co-operation is necessary to obtain a good that (insofar as it is produced at all) will be enjoyed by all members of a set of actors, whether they have contributed to its provision or not. When each member's contribution to the cost of the good is small as a proportion of its total cost, self-interested individuals are likely to calculate that they are better off by not contributing, since their contribution is costly to them but has an imperceptible effect on whether the good is produced. Thus, as in Prisoners' Dilemma, the dominant strategy for an egoistic individualist is to defect, by not contributing to the production of the good. Generalizing this calculation yields the conclusion that the collective good will not be produced, or will be underproduced, despite the fact that its value to the group is greater than its cost.

Both Prisoners' Dilemma and the problem of collective action have great heuristic value. They warn us against the fallacy of composition, which in world politics would lead us to believe that the sources of discord must lie in the nature of the actors rather than in their patterns of interaction. Prisoners' Dilemma and the logic of collective action both suggest, on the contrary, the power of "third image" explanations, which attribute causality to the nature of the international system rather than the nature of states (Waltz, 1959). Both Prisoners' Dilemma and collective action arguments focus attention on issues of enforcement, commitment, and strategic interaction, all of which are significant for world politics. Perhaps even more important, these models, especially Prisoners' Dilemma, draw our attention to ways in which barriers to information and communication in world politics can impede cooperation and create discord even when common interests exist.

LIMITATIONS OF RATIONAL-CHOICE MODELS: CHOICE, ANOMIE, AND ETHICS

Single-play Prisoners' Dilemma is often taken as a paradigm for international politics, showing why discord is prevalent and cooperation rare. It is sometimes used also to support arguments that international institutions are doomed to futility. Such is not my argument. I seek to show, in this chapter and the next, that if we use rational-choice theory properly, we should expect a substantial amount of cooperation in the international relations of the advanced market-economy countries, and that rational-choice theory and the theory of collective goods help to show why institutions are significant in world politics, and even crucial to successful cooperation. Before developing this argument, however, it is important to examine some objections to the use of rational-choice theory in the first place.

The assumption of rational egoism creates an abstract, unreal world for analysis. It can mislead us if we take premises for reality and seek to apply our conclusion in a simple-minded way to the world that we observe. Yet it is valuable as a simplifying assumption with which to build theory, since it provides a baseline premised on a relatively uncomplicated situation characterized by purely self-interested and rational behavior. That is, rational-choice theory provides us with a set of hypothetical expectations that we can then test against experience. Max Weber (1905/1949, pp. 166, 185-86) discussed such an approach to "the logical analysis of history" when he argued that, "in order to penetrate to the real causal interrelationships, *we construct unreal ones.*" We build what he called "ideal types." The construction of unreal expectations based on assumptions of rational egoism contributes to a causal analysis without committing us to the view that the assumptions of the theory are necessarily true.

Thus rational-choice models have great value, but they cannot be applied mechanically to world politics. Their assumptions can easily be distorted in such a way as to do violence to reality. Insofar as this is the case, their conclusions will not be compelling and may even be profoundly misleading. Three important potential distortions of these models are worth mentioning. First, we may assume too easily that actors' decisions are in some meaningful sense voluntary, thus running the risk of ignoring inequalities of power among actors. A second pitfall is to equate the premise of egoism with an atomistic assumption about the role of the individual in society. Finally, rationality may be confused with egoism. All three of these potential distortions suggest the need to be very careful in applying rational-choice theory to world politics.

Choice and Constraint

Using rational-choice theory for the study of international cooperation implies that the relevant decisions of governments, and other actors, about whether to cooperate can be treated as if they were voluntary. But the notion of "voluntary" action in a world in which both military and economic instruments of coercion are available seems problematical at best. Anyone who has thought about Hobbes's tendentious discussion of "voluntary" agreements in *Leviathan* realizes the dangers of casuistry entailed in applying voluntaristic analysis to politics. Hobbes holds that, in the state of nature, covenants entered into out of fear are obligatory; indeed, "even in commonwealths, if I be forced to redeem myself from a thief by promising him money, I am bound to pay it till the civil law discharge me" (1651/1958, ch. 14, p. 117). Thus in a state of nature (which Hobbes asserts is the condition of sovereigns relative to one another) I am bound by promises made under duress—with a gun at my head—since I have rationally chosen to make these pledges rather than to be shot.

This odd notion that such severely constrained choices create moral and political obligations is not inherent in rational-choice theory used for positive analysis. But the focus of this theory on choice rather than on prior constraints can be highly misleading if we are not careful; we could assume that since our mode of analysis is voluntaristic, the process is genuinely voluntaristic as well. My response to this problem in analyzing international cooperation is to distinguish two aspects of the process by which international regimes come into being: imposition of constraints, and decisionmaking. Constraints are dictated both by environmental factors such as geography and by powerful actors. Regimes can be more or less "imposed"; that is, decisions to join them can be more or less constrained by powerful actors (Young, 1983).

In formal terms, we could regard any regime as having been created or maintained voluntarily in the Hobbesian sense: independent actors with the ability to refuse consented to join it. But if these actors were weak, acting under fear of invasion or economic collapse, most people would not regard their accession as purely voluntary. In such a situation, we should focus first on the constraints unequally imposed on actors before examining their choices. More generally, we need to be aware that any agreement resulting from bargaining will be affected by the different opportunity costs of alternatives faced by the various actors—that is, by which party has the greater need for agreement with the other (Harsanyi, 1962/1971; Hirschman, 1945/1980). Relationships of power and dependence in world politics will therefore be important determinants of the characteristics of international regimes. Actors' choices will be constrained in such a way that the preferences of the most powerful actors will be accorded the greatest weight. Thus, in applying rational-choice theory to the formation and maintenance of international regimes, we have to be continually sensitive to the structural context within which agreements are made. Voluntary choice does not imply equality of situation; in explaining outcomes, prior constraints may be more important than the process of choice itself.

If we keep these prior restrictions on choice in mind, we can employ rational-choice analysis in a sophisticated way without implying either that actors are equal in power or that their actions are necessarily voluntary in the sense of being unconstrained. We can use rational-choice analysis to understand decisions to construct international regimes while keeping in mind that a crucial part of the whole process—the establishment of a context of power relations involving different opportunity costs for different actors—has to be considered separately. Indeed, used in a sophisticated way, rational-choice analysis should draw our attention to constraints, since choices must be made within a context of power as well as values. A constraint-choice approach draws attention to the question of why disadvantaged actors join international regimes even though they may receive fewer benefits than other members—an issue ignored by arguments that regard certain regimes as simply imposed. Weak actors as well as powerful actors make choices that we need to understand, even if they make them within more severe constraints.

In a voluntaristic rational-choice analysis, each actor is assumed to have calculated that it will be at least as well off as a member of an international regime as outside of it—given the prior structure of constraints. Otherwise, it would not have joined. Yet the importance of prior constraints, and of the inequalities of power that lie behind them, reminds us that the results of voluntary bargaining will not necessarily be entirely benign. There is no guarantee that the formation of international regimes will yield overall welfare benefits. To strengthen their bargaining positions, powerful actors may impose constraints on weaker ones prior to formation of a new regime, or may threaten adverse results if the weaker countries refuse to go along with a hegemonic scheme. For instance, we will see in chapter 8 that during World War II and in the immediate postwar years the United States controlled the level of British financial reserves and tightened its grip on Middle Eastern oil. Both of these measures made Britain more dependent on American good will than otherwise, thus increasing the opportunity costs of British resistance to American plans. From a liberal economic standpoint, construction of a stable international monetary regime, centered on the dollar, and of a nondiscriminatory trade regime provided welfare benefits for everyone; but elements of British society that sought maintenance of the Imperial Preference system (whether for reasons of Empire or a desire to construct socialism) did not share that view. Even some of those who agreed to the American terms regarded adherence to these regimes as a lamentable and costly necessity rather than a beneficial opportunity (Block, 1977; Gardner, 1956/1980).

Even if the members of an international regime are content with its arrangements, outsiders may suffer from its creation. Indeed, some regimes (such as alliances or cartel-type regimes) are specifically designed to impose costs on nonmembers. Although it would be difficult or perhaps impossible to compare these costs with the benefits to members, there is no reason necessarily to assume that the benefits would be greater than the costs. Since the point is often missed, it should be underlined: although international regimes may be valuable to their creators, *they do not necessarily improve world welfare.* They are not *ipso facto* "good."

Egoism and Anomie

The second major pitfall in using rational-choice analysis to study cooperation and discord in the contemporary world economy lies in the danger that the assumption of rational egoism will be equated with the assumption that actors are anomic individuals, outside of human society. This premise, which as we will see is not intrinsically necessary for rational-choice theory, is also Hobbesian. The players exist in a state of nature with respect to one another. An obvious aspect of this situation is that they are unable to enforce commitments. But in a larger sense they are profoundly separate from one another, not linked by shared experiences, ethical precepts, or expectations of future interactions with identifiable individuals.

The apparently compelling conclusion of single-play Prisoners' Dilemma—that defecting is a dominant strategy—depends on this atomistic assumption. Players are assumed to be "possessive individualists" (Macpherson, 1962; Ruggie, 1983a, p. 277). They are rational in the calculating sense: they seek to maximize their expected utility, uninfluenced by ethical principles or standards of fairness. Yet egoistic players linked by a common society, with expectations of interaction, may act as if they shared ethical standards. Suppose, for instance, that the two prisoners in our example were members of a society of criminals such as the Mafia. Under these conditions, we would expect them *not* to confess. This behavior would not necessarily reflect any irrationality on their part, or any ethical principles, but rather result from the effects of their common membership in an ongoing organization on their payoff matrices. To confess would be equivalent to signing one's own death warrant: a confessor could expect to be murdered on leaving prison, if not before. Thus the subjective game matrix for these prisoners would be as follows:

		Column	
		COOPERATE	DEFECT
Row	COOPERATE	R, R (4, 4)	S, T (3, 2)
	DEFECT	T, S (2, 3)	P, P (1, 1)

This game is, of course, not Prisoners' Dilemma, despite the District Attorney's attempt to make it such. Mutual cooperation—not confessing—is the dominant strategy for both players, and the equilibrium is therefore found in the upper-left cell at R, R.

Rationality and Ethics

Even when social ties are less cohesive and coercive than those of the Mafia, apparent Prisoners' Dilemma games may have quite different payoff matrices if at least one player holds ethical views that value cooperation and censure actions harmful to others. If Row is a strongly ethical person who would be tormented by guilt for defecting in response to an experimenter's temptation, while Column is the anomic self-interested individual of game theory, the subjective matrix of a supposedly Prisoners' Dilemma game would look like this:

		Column	
		COOPERATE	DEFECT
Row	COOPERATE	R, R (4, 3)	S, T (3, 4)
	DEFECT	T, S (2, 1)	P, P (1, 2)

In this game, Row's dominant strategy is to cooperate, Column's is to defect, and the outcome S, T is a stable equilibrium that neither player has an incentive to alter. Row prefers being the "sucker" to doing wrong.

By itself, this difference between players' ethics does not pose a difficulty for rational-choice theory. We can understand Row's behavior as rational, since she tries to maximize her expected utility, although she is not egotistical, since she incorporates others' preferences into her own utility function. Altruists and saints can be as rational as the crassest materialist or most resolute bully. It is the assumption of egoism, not that of rationality, that their behavior violates. Theorists of rational choice sometimes fail to recognize this fact, assuming on the contrary that such behavior must be the result of irrationality rather than of a nonegoistic preference function. Hardin (1982, pp. 117-24), for instance, labels as "extrarational" such activities as contributing, on Kantian moral grounds, to organizations promoting one's view of the common good.

Rational-choice analysis does not necessarily imply that people are egoists. But to use rational-choice logic one needs to make *some* assumptions about the values and interests of the actors, precisely because the logic alone is empirically empty. Any rational-choice analysis has to assume a prior context of power, expectations, values, and conventions, which affect how interests are determined as well as what calculations, given interests, are made (Field, 1981). We can just as well assume that the actors are imbued with values transmitted by society, or that they follow principles of fairness, as that they are pure possessive individualists.

ITERATED PRISONERS' DILEMMA AND COLLECTIVE ACTION IN SMALL GROUPS

With these limitations of rational-choice theory in mind, we can consider once again the game of Prisoners' Dilemma. The apparently compelling conclusion referred to above—that defecting is a dominant strategy—depends on the assumption that the game is only played once, or at most a small number of times. If the game is played repeatedly by the same players—that is, in "iterated" Prisoners' Dilemma—"it is generally agreed that players may rationally cooperate" (Hardin, 1982, p. 145; see also Taylor, 1976, ch. 5).[2] The essential reason for this difference is that, in multiple-play Prisoners' Dilemma, defection is in the long run unrewarding, since the short-run gains thereby obtained will normally be outweighed by the mutual punishment that will ensue over the long run. For cooperation to take place, of course, future rewards must be valued; if, on the contrary, the

---

[2] It is often held that any Prisoners' Dilemma game with a very large but finite number of plays, known in advance, will lead to the same noncooperative solution as the single-play game. But Russell Hardin (1982, pp. 145-50) has given strong reasons to believe that rational players would not go through the contorted calculations necessary for this perverse and self-defeating result to obtain; and it is certainly difficult to believe that ordinary players, outside of the theorist's office, would do so.

players emphasize with Keynes that "in the long run we're all dead," they may prefer to defect to obtain better results in the present. Incentives to cooperate also depend on the willingness of one's opponent to retaliate against defection. When playing against a saint or a patsy, it may pay to be a bully. Robert Axelrod (1981, 1984) has shown that when future rewards are sufficiently valued, a strategy of "tit for tat" does well in a variety of situations—in technical terms, it is robust and collectively stable. A player following this strategy begins by cooperating, then does whatever her opponent did on the last move, retaliating for defection and reciprocating for acts of cooperation. When both players use this strategy, complete mutual cooperation results. Axelrod shows that, even among pure egoists, cooperation can "emerge" if a large enough initial cluster of potential cooperators exists.

As we noted in chapter 4, such cooperation need not involve any negotiation at all, since mutual adjustment can take place without direct communication between the participants. In this book, however, we focus on coordination achieved through bargaining. Such bargaining typically occurs not only in one bargaining episode but in several, over a period of time. Negotiations on international monetary arrangements, trade, and energy take place continuously and are expected to continue indefinitely into the future. Furthermore, the fact that many closely related negotiations take place simultaneously increases the "multiple-play" rather than "single-play" character of the game. Usually, unlike the actors in Prisoners' Dilemma, governments can reverse decisions to cooperate if they discover that their partners are reneging on their own agreements. This possibility has an effect similar to that of iteration of the game, since it reduces the incentives to defect. Thus even insofar as international negotiations can be modeled in the simple form of Prisoners' Dilemma—and we will see later that to do so requires a number of questionable simplifying assumptions—the pessimistic standard conclusion of single-play Prisoners' Dilemma does not follow (Wagner, 1983).

The theory of collective action can also help to account for cooperation. Olson concluded from his analysis that large groups seeking to provide collective (public) goods should be extremely difficult to form, since each member would have an incentive not to contribute to provision of the good. He argued, however, that small groups might be "privileged"; that is, they might be able to provide such goods, either because it was in the interests of a single actor to do so unilaterally or because a small number of individuals, who were able to monitor each other's behavior and react strategically to one another, could do so. The latter situation is similar to that of iterated Prisoners' Dilemma: when decisions to contribute are not made only once, but are taken frequently over time, it may pay to cooperate because otherwise one's partners may defect, leaving oneself worse off. Strategic interaction, in a situation involving collective goods as well as in Prisoners' Dilemma, can foster cooperation.

Contemporary international relations are beset by dilemmas of collective action, but these dilemmas are rendered less intractable by the small number of states involved. Even in global negotiations, the number of states does not exceed about one hundred and fifty, many of which do not play significant roles. Among the advanced industrialized countries, negotiations rarely depend on more than a few crucial participants. For example, the institutionalized economic summits involve only seven leaders, and the entire Organization of Economic Cooperation and Development (the umbrella organization for the advanced industrialized countries) has only twenty-four members, of very unequal size and influence. Rather than having so many actors that the contributions of each exert no effects on the propensity of others to contribute, international political-economic bargaining among the advanced industrialized countries involves a small number of governments intensely interacting with one another and carefully monitoring each other's behavior. Even if no hegemon exists, a small number of strong actors may be able to accomplish this task together. As we saw in chapter 3, there is nothing in Olson's theory that precludes effective oligopolistic collaboration among a few actors, each of which monitors and reacts to the behavior of each of the others.

Olson also argued that the success of certain large groups relying on a diffuse membership to provide public goods was explained by their provision of private goods as a by-product of membership. Farmers joining the Farm Bureau, for instance, might not only contribute to the collective good of lobbying for governmental benefits, but they might also thereby gain access to cheap insurance or a farmers' cooperative. Thus the logic of collective action would lead organizations to seek to privatize some of what they provide.

International regimes frequently do the same thing (Oye, 1983b). Duncan Snidal (1979) has pointed out that the benefits provided by international regimes rarely meet the classic criteria for a public good: impossibility of excluding noncontributors and jointness of supply (additional consumption of the good by new consumers does not affect others' consumption of it). For instance, only members of the International Energy Agency are entitled to receive oil under the emergency sharing arrangements, although other consumers may benefit if the

77

IEA succeeds in deterring another producer embargo coupled with a rapid rise in world petroleum prices. Only members of the International Monetary Fund (IMF) can borrow from the Fund, although nonmembers may also be the beneficiaries of IMF action to stabilize exchange rates or avoid a debt collapse. And the trade regime centered on the General Agreement on Tariffs and Trade (GATT) is set up in such a way that countries that refuse to accept the rules can be excluded from benefits, in this case the benefits of most-favored-nation treatment. Thus the theory of collective goods is as valuable in explaining the forms that cooperation must take, to avoid problems of collective action, as it is in accounting for discord.

Rational-choice analysis is used in this book not to reinforce the conventional wisdom that cooperation must be rare in world politics, but to show that it can be pursued even by purely rational, narrowly self-interested governments, unmoved by idealistic concern for the common good or by ideological commitment to a certain pattern of international relations. That is, rational egoists can have incentives to form international regimes. Prisoners' Dilemma and models of collective action help to demonstrate this point. So do less familiar but quite suggestive approaches based on theories of market failure in economics, which will be discussed below. Together these theories based on assumptions of rationality emphasize the significance of actors' reputations and the importance of international institutions within which repeated interactions among the same actors take place over a substantial period of time.

EGOISTIC COOPERATION AND THE CREATION OF INTERNATIONAL REGIMES

We saw in chapter 3 that hegemonic powers may help to create international regimes, although some reasons were given there to doubt that hegemony was necessary for regime formation. The finding in this chapter that cooperation can develop among egoists without a hegemon reinforces those doubts by providing a stronger theoretical basis for them. Whether a hegemon exists or not, international regimes depend on the existence of patterns of common or complementary interests that are perceived or capable of being perceived by political actors. This makes common action to produce joint gains rational. A hegemon may help to create shared interests by providing rewards for cooperation and punishments for defection, but where no hegemon exists, similar rewards and punishments can be provided if conditions are favorable. Outcomes must be determined by a relatively small number of actors that can monitor each other's compliance with rules and practices and that follow strategies making other governments' welfare dependent on their continued compliance with agreements and understandings.

Thus intensive interaction among a few players helps to substitute for, or to supplement, the actions of a hegemon. As a hegemon's power erodes, a gradual shift may take place from hegemonic to post-hegemonic cooperation. Increasingly, incentives to cooperate will depend not only on the hegemon's responses but on those of other sizable states. Such a transition may be difficult in practice, since expectations may lag behind reality; but nothing in rational-choice analysis renders it impossible.

The ability to create cooperation when it is desired by governments will also depend on existing patterns of regimes. The creation of new international regimes may be facilitated by the mutual confidence created by old ones. Regimes rarely emerge from chaos; on the contrary, they are built on one another. We should therefore think as much about the evolution of regimes as about their creation *ex nihilo*. This intricate connection between the operation of old regimes and the creation of new ones means that a functional analysis of regimes, such as is developed in the rest of this chapter and in chapter 6, is crucial for understanding not only why regimes are created and maintained, but also how they evolve over time.

As we have seen, incentives to form international regimes depend most fundamentally on the existence of shared interests. These interests may reflect the gains to be obtained from exploiting others more effectively—creating and sharing "rents"—as in raw material cartels. But they may also be based on a mutual desire to increase the efficiency of the exchanges in which they engage. In the latter case, it will matter how dense is the "policy space": that is, how closely linked different issues are to one another. The incentives to form international regimes will be greater in dense policy spaces than in areas with lower issue density, owing to the fact that *ad hoc* agreements in a dense policy space will tend to interfere with one another, unless they are based on a common set of principles and rules. Where issue density is low, *ad hoc* agreements may well be sufficient; but where it is high, regimes will reduce the costs of continually taking into account the effect of one set of agreements on others. Each new agreement can be compared more efficiently with a given set of rules and procedures than with each other agreement; the existence of the regime establishes standards for consistency. For this reason there is likely to be increasing demand for international regimes as interdependence grows and policy spaces become more dense.

FUNCTIONAL EXPLANATIONS AND THEORIES OF MARKET FAILURE

Taking a rational-choice approach to studying behavior directs our attention in the first instance to the incentives facing actors. If we assume rationality, asking why an actor behaved in a certain way is equivalent to asking what its incentives were: that is, what were the opportunity costs of its various alternative courses of action?[3]

Opportunity costs are determined by the nature of the environment as well as by the characteristics of the actor. Institutions, interpreted within a rational-choice framework, affect the context of choice and therefore the opportunity costs of alternatives. In using rational-choice analysis to study institutions, therefore, we are immediately led toward a functional argument. According to this line of analysis, "institutions are functional if reasonable men might create and maintain them in order to meet social needs or achieve social goals" (Simon, 1978, p. 3). Economic reasoning, as Simon argues, can readily be "translated" into the language of functional analysis and vice versa.

In general, functional explanations account for causes in terms of their effects. That is, "the character of what is explained is determined by its effect on what explains it" (Cohen, 1978, p. 278). So, for example, investment is explained by profit, as in the statement "The increased profitability of oil drilling has increased investment in the oil industry." Of course, in a temporal sense investment is the cause of profit, since profits follow successful investment. But in this functional formulation the causal path is reversed: effect explains cause. In our example, this inverse link between effect and cause is provided by the rationality assumption; *anticipated* profits lead to investment.

Functional explanations in social theory, like the functional explanations of international regimes developed in this chapter, are generally *post hoc* in nature. We observe such institutions and then rationalize their existence. Rational-choice theory, as applied to social institutions, assumes that institutions can be accounted for by examining the incentives facing the actors who created and maintain them. Institutions exist because they could have reasonably been expected to increase the welfare of their creators.

---

[3] I follow the definition of opportunity costs provided in the *International Encyclopedia of the Social Sciences* (1968) by Alchian: the value of "the highest-valued opportunity necessarily forsaken" (p. 404).

Nevertheless, functional arguments such as these must be used with caution. Even if the institutions in question perform the functions ascribed to them, they may have emerged for different reasons. For instance, the fact that private property rights help individuals coordinate their behavior under capitalism does not refute the arguments of Marx or Rousseau that they were invented by people who sought to exploit others rather than to cooperate with them (Heymann, 1973, p. 872). Furthermore, functional arguments do not demonstrate either that existing institutions had to emerge or that institutions that failed to emerge would have been inferior. The crucial reason for inconclusiveness on this point is that these arguments do not consider whether hypothetical alternative institutions could have performed just as well or better. We have seen from the theory of collective action that valuable institutions that would benefit a set of individuals will not necessarily be created. Thus it is logically possible that institutions superior to those that exist might have evolved under different conditions. Functional arguments do not, therefore, establish that existing institutions are *uniquely* well adapted to the interests of the actors who maintain them. As Simon indicates, "this kind of argument may demonstrate the sufficiency of a particular pattern for performing an essential function, but cannot demonstrate its necessity—cannot show that there may not be alternative, functionally equivalent, behavior patterns that would satisfy the same need" (1978, p. 4).

Fortunately, functional analysis does not have to show that a given set of institutions was uniquely well adapted to the environment in order to make a causal argument. To demonstrate, for example, that the limited liability corporation was invented to facilitate large-scale economic projects would not require showing that it was the *only* institution that could have done so. But a sound functional argument does have to provide good reasons to believe in a causal connection between the functions that an institution performs on the one hand and its existence on the other. From this standpoint, the most important danger lurking behind functional explanations is the *post hoc ergo propter hoc* fallacy: institutions may be interpreted as having arisen because of the functions they must have served, when they in fact appeared for purely adventitious reasons.

One way of avoiding this fallacy is to show that the actors being investigated are rational, and that the institutions and the social practices to be explained were designed to fulfill anticipated functions. In this way, effects can explain causes. For instance, we could say that the formation of the International Energy Agency is explained by its anticipated effects on the security of consumer governments' oil supplies and the solidity of U.S.-centered alliances. The only other plausible way of guarding against the *post hoc ergo propter hoc* fallacy is to demonstrate that those institutions and practices that fail to fulfill specified functional requirements will disappear as a result. Darwinian theories of natural selection, and economic theories of marginal-cost pricing in a competitive economy, rest on the latter logic. Dysfunctional mutations, and firms that fail to follow marginal-cost pricing, will vanish. In world politics, however, states rarely disappear. Thus the functional argument as applied to our subject-matter must rest on the premise of rational anticipation. Unless actors can be assumed to anticipate the effects of their behavior, effects cannot possibly explain causes, and understanding the functions of international regimes will not help to explain their occurrence.[4]

In developing a functional theory of international regimes, I will rely in part on the logic of Prisoners' Dilemma and theories of collective action, as discussed above. But I will also make use of theories of "market failure" as developed by contemporary economists. As we will see, the concept of market failure will be helpful in building our theory. Yet since this literature is unfamiliar to most students of world politics, it is necessary at this point to explicate a few of its basic ideas.

Market failure refers to situations in which the outcomes of market-mediated interactions are suboptimal, given the utility functions of actors and the resources at their disposal. That is, agreements that would be beneficial to all parties are not made. George Akerlof (1970) has provided a telling example of this phenomenon in discussing the "market for lemons." As Akerlof explains it, owners of defective used cars ("lemons") have a greater incentive to sell their vehicles than do owners of "creampuffs." Since prospective buyers know that they are unable reliably to determine when a used car is a "lemon," they will insist on paying less than the real value of a good-quality used car, in order to adjust for the risk they run of being stuck with a sour one. As a result, owners of good used cars will be unable to sell them for their real value and may therefore be unwilling to sell them at the discounted price that the market will bear. Some mutually profitable

---

[4] G. A. Cohen makes it clear that the validity of functional explanations does not depend on the validity of the doctrine of functionalism, as developed in anthropology particularly by Malinowski and Radcliffe-Brown (1978, pp. 283-85). Cohen makes the point that purposive (rational-choice) and Darwinian theory constitute the two major forms of functional explanation, although he also argues, unconvincingly to me, that "Lamarckian" and "self-deception" variants of functional theory can be identified (pp. 287-89). For a useful set of distinctions on functionalism, see Nagel, 1961, especially "Functionalism and social science," pp. 520-35; for an argument justifying rules in society in terms of their functions for coordinating human actions, see Heymann, 1973.

trades will thus not take place: buyers who would purchase a good used car at a given price, and sellers who would sell it at that price, will be unable to consummate the deal because of what Akerlof calls "quality uncertainty."

In situations of market failure, the difficulties are attributed not to inadequacies of the actors themselves (who are presumed to be rational utility-maximizers), but rather to the structure of the system and the institutions, or lack thereof, that characterize it (Arrow, 1974)[5]. Specific attributes of the system impose transaction costs (including information costs) that create barriers to effective cooperation among the actors. Thus institutional defects are responsible for failures of coordination. To correct these defects, conscious institutional innovation may be necessary. For instance, a useful innovation in the used-car market is the institution of automobile dealers who have reputations in the community. Dealers with good reputations will be able to sell cars at prices higher than those obtained by individuals who put advertisements in the newspaper. The effect of dealers' reputations on buyers' confidence may enable exchanges to take place between buyers and sellers, intermediated by the dealers, that could not otherwise have occurred.

The literatures on collective action, Prisoners' Dilemma, and market failure all suggest the plausibility of a functional explanation for the development of institutions. Institutions, according to this argument, are formed as ways to overcome the deficiencies that make it impossible to consummate even mutually beneficial agreements. Their anticipated effects—whether these are welfare gains resulting from the sale of used cars by a reliable dealer or benefits accruing to governments from being able to concert their actions in the world political economy—explain their causes.

Conclusions

In this chapter we have shown that rational-egoist models do not necessarily predict that discord will prevail in relations among independent actors in a situation of anarchy. On the contrary, it matters a great deal not only whether anyone may be excluded from collectively

---

[5] Collective goods theory, as discussed earlier in this chapter, identifies one class of market-failure problems, which arise in part because the nature of the goods being produced and the number of actors involved give rise to problems of transaction costs and information such as those discussed below. As in the "market for lemons" example, however, market failures can also occur without the goods involved being collective at all.

provided benefits, but whether interactions among the same players can be expected to continue over time. If the egoists monitor each other's behavior and if enough of them are willing to cooperate on condition that others cooperate as well, they may be able to adjust their behavior to reduce discord. They may even create and maintain principles, norms, rules, and procedures—institutions referred to in this book as regimes. These regimes facilitate nonnegotiated adjustment by providing guidelines for actors' behavior: in particular, as we will see in chapter 7, regimes may provide "rules of thumb" for actors laboring under the constraints of bounded rationality. But even for classically rational actors engaged in bargaining, regimes can be useful in helping them to achieve mutually beneficial agreements, as chapter 6 shows. Properly designed institutions can help egoists to cooperate even in the absence of a hegemonic power.

Rational-choice analysis therefore helps us criticize, in its own terms, Realism's bleak picture of the inevitability of either hegemony or conflict. By reexamining Realism in the light of rational-choice theory and with sensitivity to the significance of international institutions, we can become aware of its weaknesses as well as its strengths. We can strip away some of the aura of verisimilitude that surrounds Realism and reconsider the logical and empirical foundations of its claims to our intellectual allegiance.

· 6 ·

A FUNCTIONAL THEORY OF
INTERNATIONAL REGIMES

Chapter 5 discussed how international regimes could be created and emphasized their value for overcoming what could be called "political market failure." Now we turn to a more detailed examination of this argument by exploring why political market failure occurs and how international regimes can help to overcome it. This investigation will help us understand both why states often comply with regime rules and why international regimes can be maintained even after the conditions that facilitated their creation have disappeared. The functional theory developed in this chapter will therefore suggest some reasons to believe that even if U.S. hegemonic leadership may have been a crucial factor in the creation of some contemporary international economic regimes, the continuation of hegemony is not necessarily essential for their continued viability.

POLITICAL MARKET FAILURE
AND THE COASE THEOREM

Like imperfect markets, world politics is characterized by institutional deficiencies that inhibit mutually advantageous cooperation. We have noted the prevalence, in this self-help system, of conflicts of interest between actors. In economic terms, these conflicts can be regarded as arising in part from the existence of externalities: actors do not bear the full costs, or receive the full benefits, of their own actions.[1] Yet in a famous article Ronald Coase (1960) argued that the presence of externalities alone does not necessarily prevent effective coordination among independent actors. Under certain conditions, declared Coase, bargaining among these actors could lead to solutions that are Pareto-optimal regardless of the rules of legal liability.

To illustrate the Coase theorem and its counter-intuitive result, suppose that soot emitted by a paint factory is deposited by the wind onto clothing hanging outdoors in the yard of an old-fashioned laundry. Assume that the damage to the laundry is greater than the $20,000 it would cost the laundry to enclose its yard and install indoor drying

---

[1] For an elaborated version of this definition, see Davis and North, 1971, p. 16.

equipment; so if no other alternative were available, it would be worthwhile for the laundry to take these actions. Assume also, however, that it would cost the paint factory only $10,000 to eliminate its emissions of air pollutants. Social welfare would clearly be enhanced by eliminating the pollution rather than by installing indoor drying equipment, but in the absence of either governmental enforcement or bargaining, the egoistic owner of the paint factory would have no incentive to spend anything to achieve this result.

It has frequently been argued that this sort of situation requires centralized governmental authority to provide the public good of clean air. Thus if the laundry had an enforceable legal right to demand compensation, the factory owner would have an incentive to invest $10,000 in pollution control devices to avoid a $20,000 court judgment. Coase argued, however, that the pollution would be cleaned up equally efficiently even if the laundry had no such recourse. If the law, or the existence of a decentralized self-help system, gave the factory a right to pollute, the laundry owner could simply pay the factory owner a sum greater than $10,000, but less than $20,000, to install anti-soot equipment. Both parties would agree to some such bargain, since both would benefit.

In either case, the externality of pollution would be eliminated. The key difference would not be one of economic efficiency, but of distribution of benefits between the factory and the laundry. In a self-help system, the laundry would have to pay between $10,000 and $20,000 and the factory would reap a profit from its capacity to pollute. But if legal liability rules were based on "the polluter pays principle," the laundry would pay nothing and the factory would have to invest $10,000 without reaping a financial return. Coase did not dispute that rules of liability could be evaluated on grounds of fairness, but insisted that, given his assumptions, efficient arrangements could be consummated even where the rules of liability favored producers of externalities rather than their victims.

The Coase theorem has frequently been used to show the efficacy of bargaining without central authority, and it has occasionally been applied specifically to international relations (Conybeare, 1980). The principle of sovereignty in effect establishes rules of liability that put the burden of externalities on those who suffer from them. The Coase theorem could be interpreted, therefore, as predicting that problems of collective action could easily be overcome in international politics through bargaining and mutual adjustment—that is, through cooperation as we have defined it. The further inference could be drawn that the discord observed must be the result of fundamental conflicts of interest rather than problems of coordination. The Coase theorem, in other words, could be taken as minimizing the importance of Olson's perverse logic of collective action or of the problems of coordination emphasized by game theory. However, such a conclusion would be incorrect for two compelling sets of reasons.

In the first place, Coase specified three crucial conditions for his conclusion to hold. These were: a legal framework establishing liability for actions, presumably supported by governmental authority; perfect information; and zero transaction costs (including organization costs and the costs of making side-payments). It is absolutely clear that none of these conditions is met in world politics. World government does not exist, making property rights and rules of legal liability fragile; information is extremely costly and often held unequally by different actors; transaction costs, including costs of organization and side-payments, are often very high. Thus an *inversion* of the Coase theorem would seem more appropriate to our subject. In the absence of the conditions that Coase specified, coordination will often be thwarted by dilemmas of collective action.

Second, recent critiques of Coase's argument reinforce the conclusion that it cannot simply be applied to world politics, and suggest further interesting implications about the functions of international regimes. It has been shown on the basis of game theory that, with more than two participants, the Coase theorem cannot necessarily be demonstrated. Under certain conditions, there will be no stable solution: any coalition that forms will be inferior, for at least one of its members, to another possible coalition. The result is an infinite regress. In game-theoretic terminology, the "core" of the game is empty. When the core is empty, the assumption of zero transaction costs means that agreement is hindered rather than facilitated: "in a world of zero transaction costs, the inherent instability of all coalitions could result in endless recontracting among the firms" (Aivazian and Callen, 1981, p. 179; Veljanovski, 1982).

What do Coase and his critics together suggest about the conditions for international cooperation through bargaining? First, it appears that approximating Coase's first two conditions—that is, having a clear legal framework establishing property rights and low-cost information available in a roughly equal way to all parties—will tend to facilitate cooperative solutions. But the implications of reducing transaction costs are more complex. If transaction costs are too high, no bargains will take place; but if they are too low, under certain conditions an infinite series of unstable coalitions may form.

Inverting the Coase theorem allows us to analyze international institutions largely as responses to problems of property rights, uncertainty, and transaction costs. Without consciously designed institutions, these problems will thwart attempts to cooperate in world politics even when actors' interests are complementary. From the deficiency of the "self-help system" (even from the perspective of purely self-interested national actors) we derive a need for international regimes. Insofar as they fill this need, international regimes perform the functions of establishing patterns of legal liability, providing relatively symmetrical information, and arranging the costs of bargaining so that specific agreements can more easily be made. Regimes are developed in part because actors in world politics believe that with such arrangements they will be able to make mutually beneficial agreements that would otherwise be difficult or impossible to attain.

This is to say that the architects of regimes anticipate that the regimes will facilitate cooperation. Within the functional argument being constructed here, these expectations explain the formation of the regimes: the *anticipated effects* of the regimes account for the actions of governments that establish them. Governments believe that *ad hoc* attempts to construct particular agreements, without a regime framework, will yield inferior results compared to negotiations within the framework of regimes. Following our inversion of the Coase theorem, we can classify the reasons for this belief under the categories of legal liability (property rights), transaction costs, and problems of uncertainty. We will consider these issues in turn.

Legal Liability

Since governments put a high value on the maintenance of their own autonomy, it is usually impossible to establish international institutions that exercise authority over states. This fact is widely recognized by officials of international organizations and their advocates in national governments as well as by scholars. It would therefore be mistaken to regard international regimes, or the organizations that constitute elements of them, as characteristically unsuccessful attempts to institutionalize centralized authority in world politics. They cannot establish patterns of legal liability that are as solid as those developed within well-ordered societies, and their architects are well aware of this limitation.

Of course, the lack of a hierarchical structure of world politics does not prevent regimes from developing bits and pieces of law (Henkin, 1979, pp. 13-22). But the principal significance of international regimes does not lie in their formal legal status, since any patterns of legal liability and property rights established in world politics are subject to being overturned by the actions of sovereign states. International regimes are more like the "quasi-agreements" that William Fellner (1949) discusses when analyzing the behavior of oligopolistic firms than they are like governments. These quasi-agreements are legally unenforceable but, like contracts, help to organize relationships in mutually beneficial ways (Lowry, 1979, p. 276). Regimes also resemble conventions: practices, regarded as common knowledge in a community, that actors conform to not because they are uniquely best, but because others conform to them as well (Hardin, 1982; Lewis, 1969; Young, 1983). What these arrangements have in common is that they are designed not to implement centralized enforcement of agreements, but rather to establish stable mutual expectations about others' patterns of behavior and to develop working relationships that will allow the parties to adapt their practices to new situations. Contracts, conventions, and quasi-agreements provide information and generate patterns of transaction costs: costs of reneging on commitments are increased, and the costs of operating within these frameworks are reduced.

Both these arrangements and international regimes are often weak and fragile. Like contracts and quasi-agreements, international regimes are frequently altered: their rules are changed, bent, or broken to meet the exigencies of the moment. They are rarely enforced automatically, and they are not self-executing. Indeed, they are often matters for negotiation and renegotiation. As Puchala has argued, "attempts to enforce EEC regulations open political cleavages up and down the supranational-to-local continuum and spark intense politicking along the cleavage lines" (1975, p. 509).

Transaction Costs

Like oligopolistic quasi-agreements, international regimes alter the relative costs of transactions. Certain agreements are forbidden. Under the provisions of the General Agreement on Tariffs and Trade (GATT), for instance, it is not permitted to make discriminatory trade arrangements except under specific conditions. Since there is no centralized government, states can nevertheless implement such actions, but their lack of legitimacy means that such measures are likely to be costly. Under GATT rules, for instance, retaliation against such behavior is justified. By elevating injunctions to the level of principles and rules, furthermore, regimes construct linkages between issues. No longer does a specific discriminatory agreement constitute merely a particular act without general significance; on the contrary, it becomes a "violation of GATT" with serious implications for a large number of other issues. In the terms of Prisoners' Dilemma, the situation has been transformed from a single-play to an iterated game. In market-failure terms, the transaction costs of certain possible bargains have been increased, while the costs of others have been reduced. In either case, the result is the same: incentives to violate regime principles are reduced. International regimes reduce transaction costs of legitimate bargains and increase them for illegitimate ones.

International regimes also affect transaction costs in the more mundane sense of making it cheaper for governments to get together to negotiate agreements. It is more convenient to make agreements within a regime than outside of one. International economic regimes usually incorporate international organizations that provide forums for meetings and secretariats that can act as catalysts for agreement. Insofar as their principles and rules can be applied to a wide variety of particular issues, they are efficient: establishing the rules and principles at the outset makes it unnecessary to renegotiate them each time a specific question arises.

International regimes thus allow governments to take advantage of potential economies of scale. Once a regime has been established, the marginal cost of dealing with each additional issue will be lower than it would be without a regime. As we saw in chapter 5, if a policy area is sufficiently dense, establishing a regime will be worthwhile. Up to a point there may even be what economists call "increasing returns to scale." In such a situation, each additional issue could be included under the regime at lower cost than the previous one. As Samuelson notes, in modern economies, "increasing returns is the prime case of deviations from perfect competition" (1967, p. 117). In world politics, we should expect increasing returns to scale to lead to more extensive international regimes.

In view of the benefits of economies of scale, it is not surprising that specific agreements tend to be "nested" within regimes. For instance, an agreement by the United States, Japan, and the European Community in the Multilateral Trade Negotiations to reduce a particular tariff will be affected by the rules and principles of GATT—that is, by the trade regime. The trade regime, in turn, is nested within a set of other arrangements, including those for monetary relations, energy, foreign investment, aid to developing countries, and other issues, which together constitute a complex and interlinked pattern of relations among the advance market-economy countries. These, in turn, are related to military-security relations among the major states.[2]

The nesting patterns of international regimes affect transaction costs by making it easier or more difficult to link particular issues and to arrange side-payments, giving someone something on one issue in return for her help on another.[3] Clustering of issues under a regime facilitates side-payments among these issues: more potential *quids* are available for the *quo*. Without international regimes linking clusters of issues to one another, side-payments and linkages would be difficult to arrange in world politics; in the absence of a price system for the exchange of favors, institutional barriers would hinder the construction of mutually beneficial bargains.

Suppose, for instance, that each issue were handled separately from all others, by a different governmental bureau in each country. Since a side-payment or linkage always means that a government must give up something on one dimension to get something on another, there would always be a bureaucratic loser within each government. Bureaus that would lose from proposed side-payments, on issues that matter to them, would be unlikely to bear the costs of these linkages willingly on the basis of other agencies' claims that the national interest required it.

Of course, each issue is not considered separately by a different governmental department or bureau. On the contrary, issues are grouped together, in functionally organized departments such as Treasury, Commerce, and Energy (in the United States). Furthermore, how governments organize themselves to deal with foreign policy is affected by how issues are organized internationally; issues considered by different regimes are often dealt with by different bureaucracies at home. Linkages and side-payments among issues grouped in the same regime thus become easier, since the necessary internal tradeoffs will tend to take place within rather than across bureaus; but linkages among issues falling into different regimes will remain difficult, or even become more so (since the natural linkages on those issues will be with issues within the same regime).

Insofar as issues are dealt with separately from one another on the international level, it is often hard, in simply bureaucratic terms, to arrange for them to be considered together. There are bound to be

---

[2] For the idea of "nesting," I am indebted to Aggarwal (1981). Snidal (1981) also relies on this concept, which was used in a similar context some years ago by Barkun (1968), p. 17.

[3] On linkage, see especially the work of Kenneth A. Oye (1979, 1983b). See also Stein, 1980, and Tollison and Willett, 1979.

difficulties in coordinating policies of different international organizations—GATT, the IMF, and the IEA all have different memberships and different operating styles—in addition to the resistance that will appear to such a move within member governments. Within regimes, by contrast, side-payments are facilitated by the fact that regimes bring together negotiators to consider sets of issues that may well lie within the negotiators' bureaucratic bailiwicks at home. GATT negotiations, as well as deliberations on the international monetary system, have been characterized by extensive bargaining over side-payments and the politics of issue-linkage (Hutton, 1975). The well-known literature on "spillover" in bargaining, relating to the European Community and other integration schemes, can also be interpreted as concerned with side-payments. According to these writings, expectations that an integration arrangement can be expanded to new issue-areas permit the broadening of potential side-payments, thus facilitating agreement (Haas, 1958).

We conclude that international regimes affect the costs of transactions. The value of a potential agreement to its prospective participants will depend, in part, on how consistent it is with principles of legitimacy embodied in international regimes. Transactions that violate these principles will be costly. Regimes also affect bureaucratic costs of transactions: successful regimes organize issue-areas so that productive linkages (those that facilitate agreements consistent with the principles of the regime) are facilitated, while destructive linkages and bargains that are inconsistent with regime principles are discouraged.

Uncertainty and Information

From the perspective of market-failure theories, the informational functions of regimes are the most important of all. Recall that what Akerlof called "quality uncertainty" was the crucial problem in the "market for lemons" example. Even in games of pure coordination with stable equilibria, this may be a problem. Conventions—commuters meeting under the clock at Grand Central Station, suburban families on a shopping trip "meeting at the car"—become important. But in simple games of coordination, severe information problems are not embedded in the structure of relationships, since actors have incentives to reveal information and their own preferences fully to one another. In these games the problem is to reach some point of agreement; but it may not matter much which of several possible points is chosen (Schelling, 1960/1978). Conventions are important and ingenuity may be required, but serious systemic impediments to the acquisition and exchange of information are lacking (Lewis, 1969; Young, 1983).

Yet as we have seen in our discussions of collective action and Prisoners' Dilemma, many situations—both in game theory and in world politics—are characterized by conflicts of interest as well as common interests. In such situations, actors have to worry about being deceived and double-crossed, just as the buyer of a used car has to guard against purchasing a "lemon." The literature on market failure elaborates on its most fundamental contention—that, in the absence of appropriate institutions, some mutually advantageous bargains will not be made because of uncertainty—by pointing to three particularly important sources of difficulty: *asymmetrical information*; *moral hazard*; and *irresponsibility*.

ASYMMETRICAL INFORMATION

Some actors may know more about a situation than others. Expecting that the resulting bargains would be unfair, "outsiders" will be reluctant to make agreements with "insiders" (Williamson, 1975, pp. 31-33). This is essentially the problem of "quality uncertainty" as discussed by Akerlof. Recall that this is a problem not merely of insufficient information, but rather of *systematically biased* patterns of information, which are recognized in advance of any agreement both by the holder of more information (the seller of the used car) and by its less well-informed prospective partner (the potential buyer of the "lemon" or "creampuff," as the case may be). Awareness that others have greater knowledge than oneself, and are therefore capable of manipulating a relationship or even engaging successful deception and double-cross, is a barrier to making agreements. When this suspicion is unfounded—that is, the agreement would be mutually benefical—it is an obstacle to improving welfare through cooperation.

This problem of asymmetrical information only appears when dishonest behavior is possible. In a society of saints, communication would be open and no one would take advantage of superior information. In our imperfect world, however, asymmetries of information are not rectified simply by communication. Not all communication reduces uncertainty, since communication may lead to asymmetrical or unfair bargaining outcomes as a result of deception. Effective communication is not measured well by the amount of talking that used-car salespersons do to customers or that governmental officials do to one another in negotiating international regimes! The information that is required in entering into an international regime is not merely information about other governments' resources and formal negotiating positions, but also accurate knowledge of their future positions. In part, this is a matter of estimating whether they will keep their commitments. As the "market for lemons" example suggests, and as we will see in more detail below, a government's reputation therefore becomes an important asset in persuading others to enter into agreements with it. International regimes help governments to assess others' reputations by providing standards of behavior against which performance can be measured, by linking these standards to specific issues, and by providing forums, often through international organizations, in which these evaluations can be made.[4] Regimes may also include international organizations whose secretariats act not only as mediators but as providers of unbiased information that is made available, more or less equally to all members. By reducing asymmetries of information through a process of upgrading the general level of available information, international regimes reduce uncertainty. Agreements based on misapprehension and deception may be avoided; mutually beneficial agreements are more likely to be made.

Regimes provide information to members, thereby reducing risks of making agreements. But the information provided by a regime may be insufficiently detailed. A government may require precise information about its prospective partners' internal evaluations of a particular situation, their intentions, the intensity of their preferences, and their willingness to adhere to an agreement even in adverse future circumstances. Governments also need to know whether other participants will follow the spirit as well as the letter of agreements, whether they will share the burden of adjustment to unexpected adverse change, and whether they are likely to seek to strengthen the regime in the future.

The significance of asymmetrical information and quality uncertainty in theories of market failure therefore calls attention to the importance not only of international regimes but also of variations in the degree of closure of different states' decisionmaking processes. Some governments maintain secrecy much more zealously than others. American officials, for example, often lament that the U.S. government

---

[4] This point was suggested to me by reading Elizabeth Colson's account of how stateless societies reach consensus on the character of individuals: through discussions and gossip that allow people to "apply the standards of performance in particular roles in making an overall judgement about the total person; this in turn allows them to predict future behavior" (1974, p. 53).

leaks information "like a sieve" and claim that this openness puts the United States at a disadvantage vis-à-vis its rivals.

Surely there are disadvantages in openness. The real or apparent incoherence in policy that often accompanies it may lead the open government's partners to view it as unreliable because its top leaders, whatever their intentions, are incapable of carrying out their agreements. A cacophony of messages may render all of them uninterpretable. But some reflection on the problem of making agreements in world politics suggests that there are advantages for the open government that cannot be duplicated by countries with more tightly closed bureaucracies. Governments that cannot provide detailed and reliable information about their intentions—for instance, because their decisionmaking processes are closed to the outside world and their officials are prevented from developing frank informal relationships with their foreign counterparts—may be unable convincingly to persuade their potential partners of their commitment to the contemplated arrangements. Observers from other countries will be uncertain about the genuineness of officials' enthusiasm or the depth of their support for the cooperative scheme under consideration. These potential partners will therefore insist on discounting the value of prospective agreements to take account of their uncertainty. As in the "market for lemons," some potential agreements, which would be beneficial to all parties, will not be made because of "quality uncertainty"—about the quality of the closed government's commitment to the accord.[5]

MORAL HAZARD

Agreements may alter incentives in such a way as to encourage less cooperative behavior. Insurance companies face this problem of "moral hazard." Property insurance, for instance, may make people less careful with their property and therefore increase the risk of loss (Arrow, 1974). The problem of moral hazard arises quite sharply in international banking. The solvency of a major country's largest banks may be essential to its financial system, or even to the stability of the entire international banking network. As a result, the country's central bank

---

[5] In 1960 Thomas Schelling made a similar argument about the problem of surprise attack. Asking how we would prove that we were not planning a surprise attack if the Russians suspected we were, he observed that "evidently it is not going to be enough just to tell the truth. . . . There has to be some way of authenticating certain facts, the facts presumably involving the disposition of forces" (p. 247). To authenticate facts requires becoming more open to external monitoring as a way of alleviating what Akerlof later called "quality uncertainty."

may have to intervene if one of these banks is threatened. The U.S. Federal Reserve, for instance, could hardly stand idly by while the Bank of America or Citibank became unable to meet its liabilities. Yet this responsibility creates a problem of moral hazard, since the largest banks, in effect, have automatic insurance against disastrous consequences of risky but (in the short-run at least) profitable loans. They have incentives to follow risk-seeking rather than risk-averse behavior at the expense of the central bank (Hirsch, 1977).

IRRESPONSIBILITY

Some actors may be irresponsible, making commitments that they may not be able to carry out. Governments or firms may enter into agreements that they intend to keep, assuming that the environment will continue to be benign; if adversity sets in, they may be unable to keep their commitments. Banks regularly face this problem, leading them to devise standards of creditworthiness. Large governments trying to gain adherents to international agreements may face similar difficulties: countries that are enthusiastic about cooperation are likely to be those that expect to gain more, proportionately, than they contribute. This is a problem of self-selection, as discussed in the market-failure literature. For instance, if rates are not properly adjusted, people with high risks of heart attack will seek life insurance more avidly that those with longer life expectancies; people who purchased "lemons" will tend to sell them earlier on the used-car market than people with "creampuffs" (Akerlof, 1970; Arrow, 1974). In international politics, self-selection means that for certain types of activities—such as sharing research and development information—weak states (with much to gain but little to give) may have more incentive to participate than strong ones, but less incentive actually to spend funds on research and development.[6] Without the strong states, the enterprise as a whole will fail.

From the perspective of the outside observer, irresponsibility is an aspect of the problem of public goods and free-riding; but from the standpoint of the actor trying to determine whether to rely on a potentially irresponsible partner, it is a problem of uncertainty. Either way, informational costs and asymmetries may prevent mutually beneficial agreement.

---

[6] Bobrow and Kudrle found evidence of severe problems of collective goods in the IEA's energy research and development program, suggesting that "commercial interests and other national rivalries appear to have blocked extensive international cooperation" (1979, p. 170).

Regimes and Market Failure

International regimes help states to deal with all of these problems. As the principles and rules of a regime reduce the range of expected behavior, uncertainty declines, and as information becomes more widely available, the asymmetry of its distribution is likely to lessen. Arrangements within regimes to monitor actors' behavior—discussed more fully below under the heading of "compliance"—mitigate problems of moral hazard. Linkages among particular issues within the context of regimes raise the costs of deception and irresponsibility, since the consequences of such behavior are likely to extend beyond the issue on which they are manifested. Close ties among officials involved in managing international regimes increase the ability of governments to make mutually beneficial agreements, because intergovernmental relationships characterized by ongoing communication among working-level officials, informal as well as formal, are inherently more conducive to exchange of information than are traditional relationships between closed bureaucracies. In general, regimes make it more sensible to cooperate by lowering the likelihood of being double-crossed. Whether we view this problem through the lens of game theory or that of market failure, the central conclusion is the same: international regimes can facilitate cooperation by reducing uncertainty. Like international law, broadly defined, their function is "to make human actions conform to predictable patterns so that contemplated actions can go forward with some hope of achieving a rational relationship between means and ends" (Barkun, 1968, p. 154).

Thus international regimes are useful to governments. Far from being threats to governments (in which case it would be hard to understand why they exist at all), they permit governments to attain objectives that would otherwise be unattainable. They do so in part by facilitating intergovernmental agreements. Regimes facilitate agreements by raising the anticipated costs of violating others' property rights, by altering transaction costs through the clustering of issues, and by providing reliable information to members. Regimes are relatively efficient institutions, compared with the alternative of having a myriad of unrelated agreements, since their principles, rules, and institutions create linkages among issues that give actors incentives to reach mutually beneficial agreements. They thrive in situations where states have common as well as conflicting interests on multiple, overlapping issues and where externalities are difficult but not impossible to deal with through bargaining. Where these conditions exist, international regimes can be of value to states.

We have seen that it does not follow from this argument that regimes necessarily increase global welfare. They can be used to pursue particularistic and parochial interests as well as more widely shared objectives. Nor should we conclude that all potentially valuable regimes will necessarily be instituted. As we have seen, even regimes that promise substantial overall benefits may be difficult to invent.

COMPLIANCE WITH INTERNATIONAL REGIMES

International regimes are decentralized institutions. Decentralization does not imply an absence of mechanisms for compliance, but it does mean that any sanctions for violation of regime principles or rules have to be enacted by the individual members (Young, 1979, p. 35). The regime provides procedures and rules through which such sanctions can be coordinated. Decentralized enforcement of regime rules and principles is neither swift nor certain. Yet, in many instances, rules are obeyed. Indeed, Louis Henkin goes so far as to say that "almost all nations observe almost all principles of international law and almost all of their obligations almost all of the time" (1979, p. 47). In the world political economy, we observe a good deal of compliance even when governments have incentives, on the basis of myopic self-interest, to violate the rules. Although the United States eventually broke the Bretton Woods arrangements unilaterally on August 15, 1971, for some years before that the U. S. government followed rules that constricted American freedom of action. Japanese fishermen have apparently complied, in general, with prescriptions of the International North Pacific Fisheries Convention (Young, 1979, pp. 79-88). Examples of regime compliance could also be drawn from such issue-areas as commodity trade and air transport (Cahn, 1980; Jonsson, 1981).

The extent of international compliance should not be overstated. As we will see, the trade and monetary regimes both became weaker during the 1970s. American and European policies became more protectionist in textiles, steel, and other threatened sectors (Aggarwal, 1983; Verreydt and Waelbroeck, 1982; Woolcock, 1982). Nevertheless, despite the economic disruptions of the 1970s and 1980s, there has been no headlong rush to reduce trade drastically. Indeed, only in the severe recessions of 1975 and 1982-83 did the volume of industrialized countries' exports fall; in every other year they rose by more than the real gross national product of those countries (IMF, 1983, tables B-1 and B-8, pp. 170, 176). The form that protectionism takes, furthermore, is, like hypocrisy, "the tribute that vice pays to virtue": much contemporary protectionism is designed to avoid running directly afoul of international agreements. For instance, American protectionism in manufactured goods consists largely of "voluntary export restraints" rather than unilaterally imposed import quotas, despite the fact that import quotas do not require laborious international negotiations and capture more rents for the government or private firms in the importing country (Bergsten, 1975b). Voluntary export restraints are often chosen because they bypass GATT restrictions without directly violating explicit GATT prohibitions; yet this advantage is gained at the expense of frequently building in loopholes permitting imports to continue to increase rapidly (Yoffie, 1983). Certainly liberalism in world trade has been under pressure, but the pattern as a whole does not suggest disregard on the part of governments for compliance with international agreements. Although governments sometimes break international rules, they often comply with them.

The puzzle of compliance is why governments, seeking to promote their own interests, ever comply with the rules of international regimes when they view these rules as in conflict with what I will call their "myopic self-interest." Myopic self-interest refers to governments' perception of the relative costs and benefits to them of alternative courses of action with regard to a particular issue, *when that issue is considered in isolation from others.* An action is in a government's myopic self-interest if it has the highest expected value of any alternative, apart from the indirect effects that actions on the specific issue in question would have on other issues. That governments often comply with rules that conflict with their myopic self-interest poses a potential anomaly for theories, such as Realism or the functional theory developed in this chapter, that assume rational, egoistic action in world politics. Why should an egoistic actor behave, on a given issue, in a way that is inconsistent with its self-interest on that issue? If we observe compliance with the rules of international regimes, is this not inconsistent with the assumption of egoism?

The murky language of national interests allows some Realists, such as Hans J. Morgenthau, to avoid this issue. Morgenthau notes the existence of functional organizations such as the specialized agencies of the United Nations system, but contents himself with the observation that when there is a conflict between the national interest and the operation of such agencies, "the national interest wins out over the international objective" (1948/1966, p. 509). This begs the question of whether the national interest is defined myopically, without regard to the effects of one's actions on other issues or other values, or in a more farsighted way, taking into account the impact of violating international rules and norms on other state objectives. Yet the crucial issues are precisely those of how interests are defined, and how institutions affect states' definitions of their own interests. An understanding of the puzzle of compliance requires an examination of how international regimes affect the calculations of self-interest in which rational, egoistic governments engage.

Such an exploration is pursued below through two distinct but related lines of argument. The first looks at a given regime in isolation, examining its value to governments as opposed to the feasible alternatives. This explanation of the puzzle of compliance emphasizes the difficulty of establishing international regimes in the first place. Because regimes are difficult to construct, it may be rational to obey their rules if the alternative is their breakdown, since even an imperfect regime may be superior to any politically feasible replacement. The second line of argument sets regimes in the context of other regimes in world politics. We view each issue and each regime as part of a larger network of issues and regimes. Much as iterated Prisoners' Dilemma leads to very different results from the single-play version of the game, so does an analysis of a given regime in the context of others produce a different structure of incentives than considering each regime in isolation.

The Value of Existing Regimes

We have seen that it is difficult even for perfectly rational individuals to make agreements with one another in the absence of provisions for central enforcement of contracts. In world politics, international regimes help to facilitate the making of agreements by reducing barriers created by high transaction costs and uncertainty. But these very difficulties make it hard to create the regimes themselves in the first place.

The importance of transaction costs and uncertainty means that regimes are easier to maintain than they are to create. Complementary interests are necessary but not sufficient conditions for their emergence. The construction of international regimes may require active efforts by a hegemonic state, as the IMF and GATT did after World War II; or regime-creation in the absence of hegemony may be spurred on by the pressures of a sudden and severe crisis, such that which led to the IEA. Even with complementary interests, it is difficult to overcome problems of transaction costs and uncertainty.

Once an international regime has been established, however, it begins to benefit from the relatively high and symmetrical level of information that it generates, and from the ways in which it makes regime-supporting bargains easier to consummate. We will see in chapter 9 that the international organizations at the center of the international monetary and trade regimes have outlived the period of U.S. hegemony that brought them into being. Viewing international regimes as information-providing and transaction cost-reducing entities rather than as quasi-governmental rule-makers helps us to understand such persistence. Effective international regimes facilitate informal contact and communication among officials. Indeed, they may lead to "transgovernmental" networks of acquaintance and friendship: supposedly confidential documents of one government may be seen by officials of another; informal coalitions of like-minded officials develop to achieve common purposes; and critical discussions by professionals probe the assumptions and assertions of state policies (Neustadt, 1970; Keohane and Nye, 1974; Keohane, 1978). These transgovernmental relationships may increase opportunities for cooperation in world politics by providing policymakers with high-quality information about what their counterparts are likely to do.[7]

Appreciating the significance of these information-producing patterns of action that become embedded in international regimes helps us to understand further why the erosion of American hegemony during the 1970s was not accompanied by an immediate collapse of cooperation, as the crude theory of hegemonic stability would have predicted. Since the level of institutionalization of postwar regimes was extremely high by historical standards, with intricate and extensive networks of communication among working-level officials, we should expect the lag between the decline of American hegemony and the disruption of international regimes to be quite long and the "inertia" of the existing regimes relatively great.

This argument about the role of information in maintaining regimes can be reinforced by examining some work on oligopolistic cooperation and competition that has similar analytic concerns. Oliver Williamson (1965, p. 584) argues on the basis of organization theory that communication among members of a group tends to increase cooperation, or what he calls "adherence to group goals." Cooperation among oligopolists will also be fostered by a record of past cooperation. Using these assumptions, Williamson constructs a model that has two points of equilibrium, one at high levels and one at low levels of cooperation. Once a given equilibrium has been reached, substantial changes in the environment are necessary to alter it:

---

[7] At the very highest levels of government, however, these transgovernmental interactions are often quite limited (Russell, 1973; Putnam and Bayne, 1984)

If the system is operating at a low level of adherence and communication (i.e., the competitive solution), a substantial improvement in the environment will be necessary before the system will shift to a high level of adherence and communication. *Indeed, the condition of the environment required to drive the system to the collusive solution is much higher than the level required to maintain it once it has achieved this position. Similarly, a much more unfavorable condition of the environment is required to move the system from a high to a low level equilibrium than is required to maintain it there* (p. 592).[8]

Like Williamson's oligopolies, international regimes are easier to maintain than to construct. The principles, rules, institutions, and procedures of international regimes, and the informal patterns of interaction that develop in conjunction with them, become useful to governments as arrangements permitting communication and therefore reducing transaction costs and facilitating the exchange of information. As they prove themselves in this way, the value of the functions they perform increases. Thus even if power becomes more diffused among members, making problems of collective action more severe, this disadvantage may be outweighed by the agreement-facilitating effects of the information provided by the regime.

Arthur Stinchcombe (1968) has made a similar point in discussing "sunk costs."[9] He writes that "when an action in the past has given rise to a permanently useful resource, we speak of this resource as a 'sunk cost.'" Sunk costs, such as those invested in reputation and good will (or, we might add, in institutions such as international regimes), cannot be recovered and therefore "ought not enter into current calculations of rational policy." But "if these sunk costs make a traditional pattern of action cheaper, and if new patterns are not enough more profitable to justify throwing away the resource, the sunk costs tend to preserve a pattern of action from one year to the next" (pp. 120-21). In these terms, international regimes embody sunk costs, and we can understand why they persist even when all members would prefer somewhat different mixtures of principles, rules, and institutions.

Ironically, if regimes were costless to build, there would be little point in constructing them. In this case, agreements would also be

---

[8] I am indebted to Timothy McKeown for introducing me to Williamson's argument and its implications for the study of international relations.

[9] I am indebted to Stephen D. Krasner for this reference.

costless. Under these circumstances, governments could wait until specific problems arose, then make agreements to deal with them; they would have no need to construct international regimes to facilitate agreements. It is precisely the costliness of agreements, and of regimes themselves, that make them important. The high costs of regime-building help existing regimes to persist.

Networks of Issues and Regimes

In thinking about compliance, we should recall the previous discussion of how regimes facilitate the making of agreements. To some extent, it is governments' anticipation that international regimes will increase compliance that accounts for their willingness to enter into these arrangements in the first place. Insofar as regimes create incentives for compliance, they also make it more attractive for conscientious potential members to join them. We saw that, by linking issues to one another, regimes create situations that are more like iterated, open-ended Prisoners' Dilemma, in which cooperation may be rational, than like single-play Prisoners' Dilemma, in which it is not. Violation of one's commitments on a given issue, in pursuit of myopic self-interest, will affect others' actions on other questions. Pursuit of its farsighted self-interest may therefore lead a government to eschew its myopic self-interest.

As the Prisoners' Dilemma example suggests, social pressure, exercised through linkages among issues, provides the most compelling set of reasons for governments to comply with their commitments. That is, egoistic governments may comply with rules because if they fail to do so, other governments will observe their behavior, evaluate it negatively, and perhaps take retaliatory action. Sometimes retaliation will be specific and authorized under the rules of a regime; sometimes it will be more general and diffuse.

Suppose, for example, that a member of GATT is under pressure from domestic manufacturers of nuts and bolts to enact import quotas on these products. Even if the government perceives that it has a myopic self-interest in doing so, it knows that such an action in violation of the rules would have negative implications for it on other trade questions—let us say, in opening markets for its semiconductors abroad. The principles and rules of the regime, since they facilitate linkage among issues, will in such circumstances render pursuit of myopic self-interest less attractive. Indeed, the prospect of discord as a result of its rule-violation may lead the government to continue to engage in cooperation, whereas if it could have gotten away with the violation without risking discord, it would have gone ahead.

This hypothetical example helps us understand why governments, having entered into regimes that they find beneficial, comply with the rules even in particular cases where the costs of so doing outweigh the benefits. Yet sometimes governments may find that the regimes to which they belong are no longer beneficial to them. What happens to incentives for compliance when the regime as a whole seems malign?

If there were only one regime in world politics, or each regime existed in isolation, the egoistic government would rationally cease to comply with its rules. Regimes would be abandoned when governments calculated that the opportunity costs of belonging to a regime were higher than those of some feasible alternative course of action. In the contemporary world political economy, however, there are multiple issues and multiple contacts among governments; thus governments belong to many regimes.[10] Disturbing one regime does not merely affect behavior in the issue-area regulated by it, but is likely to affect other regimes in the network as well. For a government rationally to break the rules of a regime, the net benefits of doing so must outweigh the net costs of the effects of this action on other international regimes. Insofar as its partners retaliate in those domains for its actions against the first regime, it may find that it is inhibited from pursuing its myopic self-interest.

All of these incentives for compliance rest on the prospects of retaliatory linkage: as in Axelrod's (1981) simulation of Prisoners' Dilemma, "tit for tat" is a more effective strategy to induce cooperation than submissiveness. We have seen that GATT contains provisions for retaliation; and the Bretton Woods Agreement of 1944 furnishes another relevant example. Under Article VII (the "scarce currency clause"), a surplus country that declined to replenish the IMF's depleted holdings of its currency could find its exports discriminated against with the sanction of the IMF itself (Hirsch, 1967, p. 433). Yet retaliation for specific violations is not a reliable way to maintain international regimes; indeed, the GATT provisions for retaliation have been in-

---

[10] Multiple issues and multiple contacts among societies are two aspects of "complex interdependence" (Keohane and Nye, 1977). Both facilitate agreements by multiplying points of interaction among governments and therefore increasing incentives to comply with commitments in a situation characterized by practices of "tit for tat" reciprocity. The third characteristic of complex interdependence—lack of efficacy of resorts to force—has similar effects, since it helps to guarantee that the game will not be truncated by sudden violent acts.

voked only once, and then ineffectively (Jackson, 1983). Individual governments find it costly to retaliate. Familiar problems of collective action arise: if a given state's violation of a particular rule does not have a large effect on any one country, retaliation is unlikely to be severe, even if the aggregate effect of the violation is large. If international regimes depended entirely for compliance on specific retaliations against transgressors, they would be weak indeed.

In the absence of specific retaliation, governments may still have incentives to comply with regime rules and principles if they are concerned about precedent or believe that their reputations are at stake. Governments worry about establishing bad precedents because they fear that their own rule-violations will promote rule-violations by others, even if no specific penalty is imposed on themselves. That is, breaking rules may create an individual benefit, but it produces a "collective bad." The effect of the collective bad on the utility of the individual government may under certain circumstances outweigh the benefit.

Putting the point this way makes it evident that precedent is a weak reed to lean on. No matter how much international lawyers may preach about the adverse consequences of rule-violation, even the most dim-witted egoist can see that, from her standpoint, the proper comparison is not between the benefits from her rule-breaking and its total costs to everyone, but between its benefits and its costs *to her*. The problem of collective action raises its ugly head again.

The dilemmas of collective action are partially solved through the device of reputation. Unlike the costs of establishing bad precedents, the costs of acquiring a bad reputation as a result of rule-violations are imposed specifically on the transgressor. As long as a continuing series of issues is expected to arise in the future, and as long as actors monitor each other's behavior and discount the value of agreements on the basis of past compliance, having a good reputation is valuable even to the egoist whose role in collective activity is so small that she would bear few of the costs of her own malefactions.

Our analysis of uncertainty earlier in this chapter suggests how important reputation can be even to governments not concerned with personal honor and self-respect. Under conditions of uncertainty and decentralization, governments will decide whom to make agreements with, and on what terms, largely on the basis of their expectations about their partners' willingness and ability to keep their commitments. A good reputation makes it easier for a government to enter into advantageous international agreements; tarnishing that reputation imposes costs by making agreements more difficult to reach.[11]

The importance òf reputation as an incentive to conform to standards of behavior in world politics has an interesting parallel in the practices of stateless societies. "Primitive" societies without centralized patterns of authority develop what one anthropologist has called "rule(s) and standards which define appropriate action" (Colson, 1974, p. 52). Like international regimes, these rules help to limit conflicts of interest by reducing ambiguity—in this case, by providing information about which types of behavior are legitimate. A principal sanction for violating social norms and rules in these societies is the cost to the offending individual's reputation: "The one public crime in such societies was often that of being a bad character" (Colson, 1974, p. 53). As in world politics, the focus of public concern is less on what an actor has done in the past (as in a formal legal system) than on what she is likely to do in the future. That is, systems of social control in primitive societies, as in international relations, are "forward-looking." They depend on intense, continuing interaction among a small number of actors, who deal frequently with each other without formal laws enforced by a common government.

For reasons of reputation, as well as fear of retaliation and concern about the effects of precedents, egoistic governments may follow the rules and principles of international regimes even when myopic self-interest counsels them not to. As we have seen in this section, they could do so strictly on the basis of calculations of costs and benefits. Each time that they seem to have incentives to violate the provisions of regimes, they could calculate whether the benefits of doing so outweigh the costs, taking into account the effects on their reputations as well as the probability of retaliation and the effects of rule-violation on the system as a whole. They might often decide, in light of this cost-benefit calculation, to conform to the rules. Rational egoism can lead governments not only to make agreements, but to keep them even when they turn out poorly.

---

[11] Heymann makes this point succinctly for the general case: "Since coordinated actions to obtain outcomes of benefit to all parties often depend upon trust, each actor who wants to be a participant in, and thus beneficiary of, such cooperative schemes in the long run and on a number of separable occasions has an important stake in creating and preserving a reputation as a trustworthy party" (1973, p. 822). He also points out that the incentive to obey agreed-upon rules for the sake of one's reputation only operates when one's actions are not secret and others retain the capability to retaliate effectively against one's infractions.

CONCLUSIONS

This chapter has used theories of rational choice and of the functions performed by institutions to help us understand the creation, maintenance, and evolution of international regimes. My analysis has assumed that governments calculate their interests minutely on every issue facing them. It has not relied at all on assumptions about the "public interest" or the General Will; no idealism whatsoever is posited. I have tried to show that, even on the restrictive assumptions of Realism and game theory, gloomy conclusions about the inevitability of discord and the impossibility of cooperation do not logically follow. Egoistic governments can rationally seek to form international regimes on the basis of shared interests. Governments may comply with regime rules even if it is not in their myopic self-interest to do so. In a world of many issues, such apparent self-abnegation may actually reflect rational egoism.

In view of the difficulties of constructing international regimes, it is also rational to seek to modify existing ones, where possible, rather than to abandon unsatisfactory ones and attempt to start over. Thus regimes tend to evolve rather than to die. Governments that are in general sympathy with the principles and rules of regimes have incentives to try to maintain them, even when doing so requires sacrifices of myopic self-interest.

International regimes perform the valuable functions of reducing the costs of legitimate transactions, while increasing the costs of illegitimate ones, and of reducing uncertainty. International regimes by no means substitute for bargaining; on the contrary, they authorize certain types of bargaining for certain purposes. Their most important function is to facilitate negotiations leading to mutually beneficial agreements among governments. Regimes also affect incentives for compliance by linking issues together and by being linked together themselves. Behavior on one set of questions necessarily affects others' actions with regard to other matters.

Decisions by governments to join international regimes are made partially behind a "veil of ignorance," to use an analogy from John Rawls's discussion of the social contract (Rawls, 1971; Sandel, 1982). Of course, governments know better than Rawls's shadowy individuals which provisions are likely to benefit them; but they nevertheless cannot predict the future with perfect accuracy. Regimes can be affected in the future by many factors, including alterations in world power relations, changes in interests, perhaps as a result of new patterns of interdependence, and changes in membership, as newly independent countries join the regimes. Governments adopting the rules and principles of international regimes take on future obligations whose costs they cannot accurately calculate.

These commitments reduce the flexibility of governments and in particular limit their ability to act on the basis of myopic self-interest. To do so is likely to be costly not only to the regime itself but to the state's reputation. Governments of wealthy countries that join international lending networks recognize that once they become active participants in these regimes, they cannot predict how much they may be called upon to lend to their partners. Countries belonging to the IEA agree to provide oil in an emergency to members suffering the most serious shortfalls, according to a pre-arranged formula. Although it may be possible to predict which countries are likely to be creditors and which debtors, or which members of the IEA are likely to have oil to share, the magnitudes involved are unclear in advance. Governments recognize that it will be difficult to renege on their commitments without suffering costly damage to their reputations. Regimes rely not only on decentralized enforcement through retaliation but on governments' desires to maintain their reputations.

A decent respect for the realities of human life and the findings of social science requires us to acknowledge that the assumption of pure maximizing rationality is not fully realistic. Although, as we have seen, the assumption of rationality can be very useful for the construction of theory at the level of the international system, no serious recent study of decisionmaking concludes that modern governments actually behave according to the canons of pure rationality (Snyder and Diesing, 1977). Governments do not act as classical maximizers any more than other large organizations (March and Simon, 1958). In the next chapter, therefore, we will modify the assumption of rationality by introducing concepts such as "bounded rationality" and "satisficing," which have been widely used in the last quarter-century to describe how individuals, and particularly organizations, behave. These concepts do not deny or disparage the intelligence of human beings, nor do they challenge the assumption of egoism. But they do lead to some different ways of thinking about how governments make decisions and about international cooperation.

Up to this point we have assumed, with Realists, that governments are egoistic. This assumption, like that of perfect rationality, is a theoretically useful simplification of reality rather than a true reflection of it. Governments are composed of individuals, some of whom have values that extend beyond their own narrowly conceived self-interest. In view of the hypocrisy that typically characterizes governments' pronouncements on international relations—proclaiming dedication to principle while pursuing self-interested ends—we will be cautious about relaxing the assumption of egoism. But in chapter 7 we will explore the possibility that empathy could have profound effects on the prospects for international cooperation. Having shown that cooperation is explicable even on narrowly self-interested, egoistic assumptions about the actors in world politics, we can entertain the notion that more generous values may make a difference in the world political economy.

· 7 ·

BOUNDED RATIONALITY AND
REDEFINITIONS OF SELF-INTEREST

Chapters 5 and 6 developed an abstract argument about the functions of international regimes, on the assumption that governments behave as rational egoists. This chapter will relax both components of this assumption. In the first two sections I will view governments as incapable of meeting the stringent requirements of the classical theory of rationality and will inquire about the implications of this argument for a functional theory of international regimes. I will then broaden my conception of self-interest toward a less egoistical formulation, in order to see how cooperation in world politics may be affected if actors take into account others' welfare as part of their own sense of well-being. In the final section I will compare the value of such explanations, based on the assumption of empathy, with egoistic ones such as those used in chapters 5 and 6.

I first focus on problems of "bounded rationality." As mentioned at the close of chapter 6, classical rationality is an idealization. It makes more sense to view individuals—and especially governments—as constrained in their abilities to make calculations. It is costly for them to gather information and to make decisions. Under such conditions, the rules and principles of international regimes become even more useful than they would be to a decisionmaker who could make calculations costlessly; decisionmaking costs can be saved by automatically obeying regime rules rather than calculating the costs and benefits of complying in each individual case.

Up to this point I will have assumed that the preferences of a given decisionmaker remain constant: each actor worries about changes in others' preferences but not about changes in its own. But rules and institutions can be used to control one's future behavior as well as that of others. This fact is particularly relevant for collective actors such as governments whose leadership changes from time to time. In the second section, therefore, I relax the assumption that each actor has stable preferences and assess how leaders and bureaucrats could seek to use international regimes to guard against changes in *their own* governments' future preferences.

The third part of this chapter goes one step further by reassessing what I mean by egoism. I do not switch to an assumption of pure altruism, but I do entertain the possibility that governments will define their self-interest in such a way as to make their own well-being dependent on the welfare of others. Under these conditions, international regimes will be easier to construct.[1] To explore the strengths and limitations of empathy as an explanatory factor in world politics, I then consider whether two phenomena that appear relatively self-less—moralistic pronouncements and apparently unbalanced exchanges—can be better explained on egoistic or empathetic premises.

BOUNDED RATIONALITY AND REGIMES

The perfectly rational decisionmaker of chapters 5 and 6 may face uncertainty as a result of the behavior of others, or the forces of nature, but she is assumed to make her own calculations costlessly. Yet this individual, familiar in textbooks, is not made of human flesh and blood. Even the shrewdest speculator or the most brilliant scientist faces limitations on her capacity for calculation. To imagine that all available information will be used by a decisionmaker is to exaggerate the intelligence of the human species.

Decisionmakers are in practice subject to limitations on their own cognitive abilities, quite apart from the uncertainties inherent in their environments. Herbert Simon has made this point with his usual lucidity (1982, p. 162):

> Particularly important is the distinction between those theories that locate all the conditions and constraints in the environment, outside the skin of the rational actor, and those theories that postulate important constraints arising from the limitations of the actor himself as an information processor. Theories that incorporate constraints on the information-processing capacities of the actor may be called *theories of bounded rationality*.

Actors subject to bounded rationality cannot maximize in the classical sense, because they are not capable of using all the information

---

[1] This chapter does not discuss the implications of relaxing the assumption that the major entities in world politics are governments (Keohane and Nye, 1972), but there is no apparent reason to believe that such a shift in premises would make the creation or maintenance of international regimes less likely. Transnational organizations can cooperate in pursuit of shared interests and must take international institutions into account; if anything, their inability to rely either on nationalism to inspire loyalty or on force to attain their objectives may make them more likely to be responsive to regime injunctions.

that is potentially available. They cannot compile exhaustive lists of alternative courses of action, ascertaining the value of each alternative and accurately judging the probability of each possible outcome (Simon, 1955/1979a, p. 10). It is crucial to emphasize that the source of their difficulties in calculation lies not merely in the complexity of the external world, but in their own cognitive limitations. In this respect, behavioral theories of bounded rationality are quite different from recent neoclassical theories, such as the theories of market failure discussed in chapters 5 and 6, which retain the assumption of perfect maximization:

> [In new neoclassical theories] limits and costs of information are introduced, not as psychological characteristics of the decision maker, but as part of his technological environment. Hence, the new theories do nothing to alleviate the computational complexities facing the decision maker—do not see him coping with them by heroic approximation, simplifying and satisficing, but simply magnify and multiply them. Now he needs to compute not merely the shapes of his supply and demand curves, but in addition, the costs and benefits of computing those shapes to greater accuracy as well. Hence, to some extent, the impression that these new theories deal with the hitherto ignored phenomena of uncertainty and information transmission is illusory (Simon, 1979b, p. 504).

In Simon's own theory, people "satisfice" rather than maximize. That is, they economize on information by searching only until they find a course of action that falls above a satisfactory level—their "aspiration level." Aspiration levels are adjusted from time to time in response to new information about the environment (Simon, 1972, p. 168). In view of people's knowledge of their own cognitive limitations, this is often a sensible strategy; it is by no means irrational and may well be the best way to make most decisions.

In ordinary life, we satisfice all the time. We economize on information by developing habits, by devising operating rules to simplify calculation in situations that repeat themselves, and by adopting general principles that we expect, in the long run, to yield satisfactory results. I do not normally calculate whether to brush my teeth in the morning, whether to hit a tennis ball directed at me with my backhand or my forehand, or whether to tell the truth when asked on the telephone whether Robert Keohane is home. On the contrary, even apart from any moral scruples I might have (for instance, about lying), I assume that my interests will be furthered better by habitually brushing my teeth, applying the rule "when in doubt, hit it with your forehand because you have a lousy backhand," and adopting the general principle of telling the truth than by calculating the costs and benefits of every alternative in each case. I do not mean to deny that I might occasionally be advantaged by pursuing a new idea at my desk rather than brushing my teeth, hitting a particular shot with my backhand, or lying to an obnoxious salesman on the telephone. If I could costlessly compute the value of each alternative, it might indeed be preferable to make the necessary calculations each time I faced a choice. But since this is not feasible, given the costs of processing information, it is in my long-run interest to eschew calculation in these situations.

Simon's analysis of bounded rationality bears some resemblance to the argument made for rule-utilitarianism in philosophy, which emphasizes the value of rules in contributing to the general happiness.[2] Rule-utilitarianism was defined by John Austin in a dictum: "Our rules would be fashioned on utility; our conduct, on our rules" (Mackie, 1977, p. 136). The rule-utilitarian adopts these rules, or "secondary principles," in John Stuart Mill's terms, in the belief that they will lead, in general, to better results than a series of *ad hoc* decisions based each time on first principles.[3] A major reason for formulating and following such rules is the limited calculating ability of human beings. In explicating his doctrine of utilitarianism, Mill therefore anticipated much of Simon's argument about bounded rationality (1861/1951, p. 30):

> Nobody argues that the art of navigation is not founded on astronomy, because sailors cannot wait to calculate the Nautical Almanack. Being rational creatures, they go to sea with it ready

[2] In philosophy, utilitarianism refers to an ethical theory that purports to provide generalizable principles for moral human action. Since my argument here is a positive one, seeking to explain the behavior of egoistic actors rather than to develop or criticize an ethical theory, its relationship to rule-utilitarianism in philosophy, as my colleague Susan Okin has pointed out to me, is only tangential.

[3] John Mackie argues that even act-utilitarians "regularly admit the use of rules of thumb," and that whether one follows rules therefore does not distinguish act- from rule-utilitarianism (1977, p. 137). Conversely, Joseph Nye has pointed out to me that even rule-utilitarians must depart at some point from their rules for consequentialist reasons. The point here is not to draw a hard-and-fast dichotomy between the two forms of utilitarianism, but rather to point out the similarities between Mill's notion of relying on rules and Simon's conception of bounded rationality. If all utilitarians have to resort to rules of thumb to some extent, this only strengthens the point I am making about the importance of rules in affecting, but not determining, the behavior of governments. For a succinct discussion of utilitarianism in philosophy, see Urmson (1968).

calculated; and all rational creatures go out upon the sea of life with their minds made up on the common questions of right and wrong, as well as on many of the far more difficult questions of wise and foolish. And this, as long as foresight is a human quality, it is to be presumed they will continue to do.

If individuals typically satisfice rather than maximize, all the more so do governments and other large organizations (Allison, 1971; Steinbruner, 1974; Snyder and Diesing, 1977). Organizational decision-making processes hardly meet the requirements of classical rationality. Organizations have multiple goals, defined in terms of aspiration levels; they search until satisfactory courses of action are found; they resort to feedback rather than systematically forecasting future conditions; and they use "standard operating procedures and rules of thumb" to make and implement decisions (Cyert and March, 1963, p. 113; March and Simon, 1958).

The behavioral theory of the firm has made it clear that satisficing does not constitute aberrant behavior that should be rectified where possible; on the contrary, it is intelligent. The leader of a large organization who demanded that the organization meet the criteria of classical rationality would herself be foolish, perhaps irrationally so. An organization whose leaders behaved in this way would become paralyzed unless their subordinates found ways to fool them into believing that impossible standards were being met. This assertion holds even more for governments than for business firms, since governments' constituencies are more varied, their goals more diverse (and frequently contradictory), and success or failure more difficult to measure. Assumptions of unbounded rationality, however dear they may be to the hearts of classical Realist theorists (Morgenthau, 1948/ 1966) and writers on foreign policy, are idealizations. A large, complex government would tie itself in knots by "keeping its options open," since middle-level bureaucrats would not know how to behave and the top policymakers would be overwhelmed by minor problems. The search for complete flexibility is as quixotic as looking for the Holy Grail or the fountain of youth.

If governments are viewed as constrained by bounded rationality, what are the implications for the functional argument, presented in chapter 6, about the value of international regimes? Recall that, under rational-choice assumptions, international regimes are valuable to governments because they reduce transaction costs and particularly because they reduce uncertainty in the external environment. Each government is better able, with regimes in place, to predict that its

114

counterparts will follow predictably cooperative policies. According to this theory, governments sacrifice the ability to maximize their myopic self-interest by making calculations on each issue as it arises, in return for acquiring greater certainty about others' behavior.

Under bounded rationality, the inclination of governments to join or support international regimes will be reinforced by the fact that the alternatives to regimes are less attractive than they would be if the assumptions of classical rationality were valid. Actors laboring under bounded rationality cannot calculate the costs and benefits of each alternative course of action on each issue. On the contrary, they need to simplify their own decisionmaking processes in order to function effectively at all. The rules of thumb they devise will not yield better, and will generally yield worse, results (apart from decisionmaking costs) than classically rational action—whether these rules of thumb are adopted unilaterally or as part of an international regime. Thus a comparison between the value of a unilateral rule of thumb and that of a regime rule will normally be more favorable to the regime rule than a comparison between the value of costless, perfectly rational calculation and the regime rule.

When we abandon the assumption of classical rationality, we see that it is not international regimes that deny governments the ability to make classically rational calculations. The obstacle is rather the nature of governments as large, complex organizations composed of human beings with limited problem-solving capabilities. The choice that governments actually face with respect to international regimes is not whether to adhere to regimes at the expense of maximizing utility through continuous calculation, but rather on what rules of thumb to rely. Normally, unilateral rules will fit the individual country's situation better than rules devised multilaterally. Regime rules, however, have the advantage of constraining the actions of others. The question is whether the value of the constraints imposed on others justifies the costs of accepting regime rules in place of the rules of thumb that the country would have adopted on its own.

Thus if we accept that governments must adopt rules of thumb, the costs of adhering to international regimes appear less severe than they would be if classical rationality were a realistic possibility. Regimes merely substitute multilateral rules (presumably somewhat less congenial per se) for unilateral ones, with the advantage that other actors' behavior thereby becomes more predictably cooperative. International regimes neither enforce hierarchical rules on governments nor substitute their own rules for autonomous calculation; instead, they provide rules of thumb in place of those that governments would otherwise adopt.

Combining this argument with that of chapter 6, we can see how different our conception of international regimes is from the self-help system that is often taken as revealing the essence of international politics. In a pure self-help system, each actor calculates its interests on each particular issue, preserving its options until that decision has been made. The rational response to another actor's distress in such a system is to take advantage of it by driving a hard bargain, demanding as much as "the traffic will bear" in return for one's money, one's oil, or one's military support. Many such bargains are in fact struck in world politics, especially among adversaries; but one of the key features of international regimes is that they limit the ability of countries in a particularly strong bargaining position (however transitory) to take advantage of that situation. This limitation, as we have stressed, is not the result of altruism but of the fact that joining a regime changes calculations of long-run self-interest. To a government that values its ability to make future agreements, reputation is a crucial resource; and the most important aspect of an actor's reputation in world politics is the belief of others that it will keep its future commitments even when a particular situation, myopically viewed, makes it appear disadvantageous to do so. Thus even classically rational governments will sometimes join regimes and comply with their rules. To a government seeking to economize on decisionmaking costs, the regime is also valuable for providing rules of thumb; discarding it would require establishing a new set of rules to guide one's bureaucracy. The convenience of rules of thumb combines with the superiority of long-run calculations of self-interest over myopic ones to reinforce adherence to rules by egoistic governments, particularly when they labor under the constraints of bounded rationality.

PROTECTING AGAINST CHANGES IN PREFERENCES

In economics, preferences or "tastes" are usually taken as given: *de gustibus non est disputandum* (Stigler and Becker, 1977). Yet as James March (1978) has pointed out, rational choice involves making guesses about one's own future preferences as well as about future consequences of present actions. Individuals seek to affect their own future preferences—whether by Freudian repression, by sublimation, or otherwise.

Thinking about individuals seeking to affect their own future preferences leads the reflective observer to the philosophical problem of

116

"weakness of will" and to some difficult paradoxes for a theory based on human volition. But for collective entities such as governments, which change leadership more or less frequently, it is not at all paradoxical that present decisions would deliberately be made, in part, to limit future choices. The autonomy of a future administration, particularly one of a different persuasion, is not necessarily part of a present government's utility function. Indeed, constitutions are difficult to amend partly because the founders of republics fear that virtuous leaders will not always be in power and therefore believe that safeguards against the misguided actions of their successors are necessary.[4] Asked by a younger American what sort of government the ex-colonies had established, Benjamin Franklin reportedly replied, "A republic—if you can keep it."

In the ordinary course of government, people in power are not concerned with writing a constitution. But in pluralistic, competitive systems, any party or group in office can expect to be out of office fairly soon. A major strategic problem that any programmatically committed democratic government faces, therefore, is how to ensure that its policies are perpetuated even after it has left office. A common technique for doing this in domestic politics is to begin large-scale spending programs extending for years into the future. By expanding social programs, a social democratic government may create public expectations and patterns of savings that cannot be reversed by its more conservative successors; by beginning long-term programs of weapons acquisition, a government intent on building up national military power can make it difficult for its less bellicose or more complacent successors to reduce the defense budget.

Since these examples all involve domestic policies not requiring any international agreements, they can be legally reversed by a later government with different preferences, although it may be difficult or impossible in practice to do so. But policies that are incorporated in international agreements are much more difficult for future governments to alter. Governments are obliged to continue to abide by the terms of international agreements concluded by their predecessors unless they choose to run the risk of international retaliation.

This problem arises in its most acute form for revolutionary governments, such as the Sandinista government in Nicaragua, which found itself obliged to accept responsibility for the large debts incurred

[4] This point depends on a long-remembered remark made by Harvey Mansfield, Jr., in a course on American political thought at Harvard University in 1962 or 1963.

by the Somoza regime in order to keep its lines of credit open. But it is relevant for our subject—international regimes involving advanced market-economy countries—as well. During the early postwar years in the United States, for instance, isolationist sentiment remained strong, and the internationalists in power had reason to fear that they might be succeeded in office by an administration seeking to reduce U.S. involvements abroad. The international regimes created by American internationalists were in part a way of tying the hands of such a future isolationist government—of forcing it to be involved in America's new entanglements overseas. The proposed "Bricker Amendment" to the Constitution, which would have required the Senate's consent to a wide range of international agreements in addition to treaties, constituted an effort by conservatives in the 1950s to prevent the United States from becoming so entangled in international regimes that even a conservative leader would not be able to avoid supporting them.[5]

Examples of attempts to bind future governments will also be found in our account of postwar international economic regimes in Part III. The efforts by State Department officials to ensure the importation of foreign oil after the war through an Anglo-American Petroleum Agreement (discussed in chapter 8) also constituted an endeavor—in this instance, unsuccessful—to limit the ability of a future government to impose import quotas on petroleum. GATT provides another case in point. One effect of reaching multilateral trade agreements is to bind mutual concessions, thus making these tariff-cutting exercises difficult for future governments to reverse. GATT was not merely a device by which governments could influence each other's behavior, but one permitting them to restrict their successors' freedom of action. Likewise, the par-value system of the Bretton Woods monetary regime, before 1971, restricted the inflationary propensities of future governments, at least insofar as they would have to borrow internationally to finance the resulting current account deficits.[6]

---

[5] The Bricker Amendment failed to be adopted, and some of the results feared by its sponsors eventually came to pass, as President Reagan's strong support for the International Monetary Fund, if not for the United Nations, indicates.

[6] The validity of this point is apparently not limited to issues of political economy. Jeremy Stone has recently argued that "history shows that arms control agreements are needed, in cases like [the MX missile], to put weapons systems to rest permanently. From a dove's perspective, it is only because the campaign against ABM was closed out in favor of an ABM agreement with the Russians that we do not have ABM today. By contrast, the B-1 bomber, beaten down unilaterally, has risen from the ashes like a Phoenix precisely because we had not nailed down its oblivion with an arms control agreement precluding new manned bombers" (1983, p. 3).

More generally, decisions taken during one period of time to maintain an open economy have profoundly restraining effects on the ability of future governments to control economic transactions with the outside world. The OECD secretariat has pointed out that, in the typical member country, imports constitute about 20 percent of gross national product. As a result, a country that changes its monetary and fiscal policies to stimulate demand, seeking Keynesian growth, will quickly develop a current account deficit as imports are drawn into the country (OECD, 1983, p. 19). If fiscal policy is loose and monetary policy tight, and if international holders of capital have confidence in the country and its government (for ideological reasons or otherwise), such a policy may lead to a capital inflow, causing an appreciation of the exchange rate, as happened to the United States between 1981 and 1983. But at some point the growing current account deficit is likely to drive down the exchange rate, inducing the government eventually to tighten policy to avoid a currency crisis.

The restraints imposed by an open world economy are likely to be particularly severe for socialist governments seeking to pursue stimulative policies, although they may also affect conservative governments whose restrictive policies lead to unwanted capital inflows and appreciation of the exchange rate. When expansionary policies are pursued by a new socialist government, succeeding a conservative one that was formerly in office for some time, the adverse effects on the value of its currency are likely to be accentuated by capital flight and low levels of private investment.[7] The French socialist government of François Mitterand experienced such difficulties during 1981-82. International openness therefore makes it difficult to undertake changes in policy that are at odds with the policies of the major states in the world political economy. As the OECD puts it, "international linkages, real and financial, work powerfully to limit the degree of divergence that is possible for individual countries" (1983, p. 19).

Marxists argue that these international constraints of liberalism are profoundly biased in favor of capital and against labor. One of the strengths of Marxian literature on the international political economy is its emphasis on the political bias of international economic liberalism. Marxists have seen that policies of openness pursued by internationalist governments help to tie the hands of their socialist or

[7] This sentence is carefully qualified so as not to say that *any* government calling itself socialist faces these difficulties. Austria and Sweden have both combined social democracy with high rates of investment and relatively high rates of growth during substantial parts of the postwar era.

nationalist successors, by creating international economic and political patterns of interdependence whose disruption would entail high costs.[8] When international liberalism prevails, citizens may be reluctant to vote socialist governments into office, even if they regard socialism as superior to capitalism as a system, for fear of these economic disruptions. Furthermore, socialist governments in power and socialist or communist movements seeking power may be constrained by fear of capital flight, as the experiences of the British Labour Party (Panitch, 1976), the Italian communists (Putnam, 1978), and most recently the French socialists illustrate. The road to socialism may be blocked by liberal international regimes, constructed by conservative predecessors in conjunction with their capitalist allies.

The problem socialist governments face underlines the main point of this section: international regimes can be used to affect preferences of future governments by creating constraints on their freedom of action. Obviously, there is no assurance that this is "good," since that depends on one's own preferences about the future. But it is, from the standpoint of any existing administration, one of the functions served by international regimes. Current governments seek to tie the state, as it were, to the mast: to lash the tiller so that it cannot be untied, and the boat taken onto the rocks, by a different skipper.

EMPATHY AND INTERNATIONAL REGIMES

Idealists writing on international affairs have called for international cooperation in the interests of humanity as a whole, that is, on the basis of "cosmopolitan" values as discussed by Charles Beitz (1979a, 1979b). Idealism has a long history in Anglo-American thinking on foreign affairs and has been particularly prominent in American foreign policy (Osgood, 1953; Wolfers and Martin, 1956), although since World War II it has clearly been subordinate to the Realist emphasis

---

[8] The consequences of such biases for coalitional politics within advanced industrialized countries are, in my view, less clear than Marxists often admit. Fred Block, for instance, declares that "the openness of an economy provides a means to combat the demands of the working class for higher wages and for economic and social reforms" (1977, p. 3). One difficulty with this argument is that "the working class" and "capital" are theoretical constructs that do not necessarily have clear empirical counterparts in contemporary political economies. The antithesis between the two is harder to find in complex modern societies than in Marxian theory. People constitute themselves politically in a variety of ways, on the basis of diverse interests: economic position is important, but so are sectoral, cultural, religious, and other bases for the formation of interests.

on self-interest. This book has deliberately adopted Realist assumptions of egoism, as well as rationality, in order to demonstrate the possibilities for cooperation on Realist premises. Our critique has argued from the premises of Realist theory that cooperation is possible even under conditions often deemed to preclude it.

Yet even writers who by and large accept the Realist tradition sometimes admit that not all international behavior can be explained egoistically. Hans J. Morgenthau, for instance, declares that the ultimate goals of foreign policy may derive from legal and ethical principles. His distinctive argument is not that ideals are unimportant in determining goals, but that foreign policy analysis can ignore ideals because power is a necessary means: "the immediate aim is power" (1948/ 1966, p. 25; see also pp. 84-85). The flaw in this contention, which has often been pointed out, is that power is by no means homogeneous, so that the "search for power" takes many different forms, whose characteristics depend in part on the ultimate goals of the actor (Wolfers, 1962, pp. 81-102), as well as on the particular contexts within which attempts at exerting influence take place (Baldwin, 1979). In discussing these goals, Arnold Wolfers argued that states sometimes pursue policies of "self-abnegation." For Wolfers, self-abnegation "is the goal of those who place a higher value on such ends as international solidarity, lawfulness, rectitude, or peace than they place even on national security and self-preservation" (1962, p. 93). Wolfers regards pursuit of self-abnegation as rare but not impossible (p. 94):

Cases in which self-abnegation goals have precedence over national self-preservation may be rare in an era in which nationalism and the ethics of patriotism continue unabated. This does not preclude the possibility, however, that where influential groups of participants in the decision-making process place high value on a universal cause such as peace, pressures exerted by these groups may affect the cause of foreign policy. It may lead to a more modest interpretation of the national interest, to more concern for the interests of other nations, to more concessions for the sake of peace, or to more restraint in the use of power and violence. Whether the nation will profit or suffer in the end from the success of such "internationalist," "humanitarian," or "pacifist" pressures depends on the circumstances of the case; whichever it does, the abnegation goals will have proved themselves a reality.

Wolfers is particularly concerned with military and security issues, in which the price of self-abnegation may be national independence.

121

It is not surprising that policies of self-abnegation are rarely followed when threats to independence are severe. But if tendencies toward self-abnegation occasionally appear even when the costs of failure are so high, such policies may be more plausible when the stakes are lower, as in the world political economy. Wolfers's argument suggests, at a minimum, that we should not assume the universal validity of egoistic models. To reveal the inadequacy of the logic that derives the necessity of discord from fragmentation of power, it was useful to adopt the egoistic assumption of rationality. Having done this, however, we can now afford to relax it.

To relax the assumption of egoism by drawing a sharp distinction between egoism and altruism, however, would confuse the issue. Egoism can be farsighted as well as myopic. Altruism is difficult to identify clearly, since apparently altruistic behavior can always be reinterpreted as egoistic: the "altruist" may be seen as *preferring* to sacrifice herself rather than to violate a principle or see someone else suffer. Thus it is often impossible to determine whether to classify a given action as one of farsighted egoism or altruism. This difficulty is instructive, for it reflects the fact that the very idea of self-interest is so elastic. Rather than argue about egoism versus altruism, we need to ask how people and organizations define self-interest. What beliefs and values do they take into account?

The crucial issue here is how actors see their own interests relative to those of others. To what extent are their interests independent of those of others, and to what extent are they interdependent with others' welfare? Four different situations can be imagined:

1) Actors may be *indifferent* to the welfare of others. This would be the situation in a purely Hobbesian world in which exchanges took place between entities that would never have anything to do with each other again. But for the same reasons that single-play Prisoners' Dilemma is not a good representation of world politics, this is a deficient image of reality. Relationships among states are ongoing and persistent.

2) Actors may be interested in the welfare of others only insofar as the others can take action that affects them. In such a situation, we will refer to interests as being *instrumentally interdependent*. Egoists in iterated Prisoners' Dilemma have instrumentally interdependent interests: each takes into account the effect of her actions on those of the other players, not because she cares about their welfare per se but because they may retaliate against her own defection.

3) Actors may be interested in the welfare of others not only for instrumental reasons, but because improvements in others' welfare improve their own, and vice versa, whatever the other actor does. In this case, interests are *situationally interdependent*. As the world economy has become more tightly knit together since the end of World War II, situational interdependence has increased. It is bad for the U.S. economy for Europe or Japan to undergo a severe recession, reducing demand for American goods. Brazil's prosperity is important to the United States, even apart from what might happen politically as a result of economic collapse, because a bankrupt Brazil could not pay its debts to American banks. Close-knit trade and financial networks in the contemporary world, reflecting the growth of economic interdependence, can directly transmit welfare effects, good or bad, from one society to another. They therefore make the interests of even egoistically inclined actors situationally interdependent, *regardless* of any actions that any of them may take.

4) Finally, actors may be interested in the welfare of others for their own sake, even if this has no effect on their own material well-being or security. Public and private agencies in wealthy countries send relief to victims of disaster and provide considerable amounts of foreign aid. Much governmental aid can be explained on narrowly self-interested grounds, but this explanation may not be convincing in accounting for programs of small countries such as Holland or Sweden, and it seems largely irrelevant to activities of voluntary agencies such as Oxfam or CARE. We will label this *empathetic interdependence.*[9]

The distinction in chapter 5 between myopic and farsighted self-interest presupposed instrumental or situational interdependence. The farsightedness of an egoistic actor depends on the number and range

[9] In considering empathetic interdependence, I only take account of situations in which actors positively value benefits received by others. Under conditions of severe competition, which is characteristic of power conflicts and particularly of arms races, the reverse may be true: gains for one side are seen as losses for the other. Crowding effects and other negative externalities can lead people to value gains by others negatively, both within domestic society (Hirsch, 1976) and in the world political economy. By the argument I make here, negative evaluations of others' welfare gains should make international regimes harder to institute. It should also be noted that in discussing empathetic interdependence I assume that the parties involved have similar values: "benefits" in the eyes of one are also regarded as beneficial by the others. Otherwise, supposed empathy could become a rationale for domination, as in the ideology of "the white man's burden," which justified much nineteenth-century imperialism.

123

of issues that she treats as potentially related to her behavior on a given question. The myopic actor takes into account only the immediate issue, whereas the farsighted one also assesses the effects of the decision facing her on other interests she may have. Both, however, only consider their own welfare in making these calculations.[10] Raising the question of empathy takes us beyond this distinction to a deeper question of values.

To speak of empathy in world politics may seem to put one beyond the Realist pale. Yet, in a world of high mobility, instantaneous communication, and extensive transnational relations of various kinds (Keohane and Nye, 1972), it is not obvious that solidaristic relationships coincide with national boundaries. Paul Taylor has pointed out that feelings of community in Europe may on occasion prevail over utilitarian considerations: "the calculation of advantage from cooperation in relation to particular interests may be secondary to a preference for cooperation with a particular partner or partners" (1980, p. 373). Furthermore, public opinion research in Europe has shown that, when asked about intra-European relations, a large proportion of people display policy preferences that deviate from what one would expect on the basis of narrow self-interest. In response to a poll taken in 1977, for instance, over 70 percent of respondents in each of the nine European Community countries declared that if another member of the Community were in serious economic trouble, its partners should help it; and a plurality of respondents even said that their own representatives to the European Parliament should put European interests ahead of national ones (Inglehart and Rubier, 1978, pp. 78, 82-84). These responses may reflect a mixture of instrumental, situational, and empathetic interdependence. But, along with recent work questioning the moral significance of boundaries in world politics (Beitz, 1979a, 1979b), they suggest the possibility that, in limited ways, interests could be interpreted empathetically. In such situations, self-interests would by no means have disappeared. Rather, they would have been redefined so as to depend on the welfare of others being realized as well.

What we have called "egoism" so far in this book refers to conceptions of interests as independent or only instrumentally or situationally interdependent. Relaxing the assumption of egoism means

[10] Bounded rationality may help to account for myopic rather than farsighted decisionmaking, since the costliness of calculation is likely to reduce the range of relevant issues and interests considered.

entertaining the possibility that governments and other actors in world politics may redefine their interests so that they are empathetically dependent on those of others. The consequences for cooperation could be far-reaching. Governments that regard themselves as empathetically interdependent will be more inclined than egoists to reach for greater joint gains—solutions to international problems that lead to larger overall value—even at the expense of direct gains to themselves. They will be so inclined because they will also benefit vicariously from the gains achieved by others. Shared interests will therefore be greater. The set of possible agreements regarded as mutually beneficial will be at least as large as it is for egoists, and probably larger.

Egoism and Empathy as Competing Explanations

Empathetic explanations of behavior in world politics are limited to relatively small spheres of activity: situations in which actions do not have obvious explanations in terms of more narrowly defined self-interest. The presumption in a self-help system is that empathy will play a subordinate role. Even when behavior appears to be motivated by empathy, it may be possible to construct an alternative, and plausible, explanation for it on the premise of egoism. Examining these competing accounts may suggest some of the strengths and limitations of egoistic and empathetic interpretations of behavior associated with international regimes.

In this section we consider two patterns of behavior that seem difficult to explain on egoistic grounds: the moralistic overlay of rules in world politics, and the existence of exchange relationships that, at least for a substantial period of time, are unbalanced. I seek first to account for these phenomena through the use of rational-egoist models. In both cases, a line of argument can be constructed using such models to account for the behavior in question. This suggests the power of the premise of egoism, since even where action seems at first glance to be motivated by empathy, it can be reinterpreted as egoistic. Yet in neither case is the egoistic account entirely satisfactory. It should be clear that I have no intention of debunking explanations resting on the assumption of self-interest; rather, I wish to see how far they can legitimately run, and whether there are some phenomena, even at the margins of political economy, that are accounted for more adequately on the basis of empathetic interdependence.

125

Treating Rules as Moral Obligations

From a Realist perspective, it is remarkable how moralistic governments often are in discussing their obligations and those of others. The rules of international regimes are often discussed not merely as convenient devices for altering transaction costs and reducing uncertainty, as we have regarded them in this book, but as principles and rules that create obligations. Leaders of governments proclaim their adherence to these principles and rules; furthermore, they argue that other governments are morally obligated to keep their agreements as well. We have seen that international regimes can be valuable for purely egoistic states. But why do normative connotations, involving an intertwining of moral codes with international law, develop? As H.L.A. Hart (1961, p. 226) emphasizes, law need not be based on a system of morality, but can be maintained by calculations of long-term self-interest or for other reasons. If rational egoism were a sufficient explanation for international regimes, how could one explain the moralistic overlay of world politics?

A fairly straightforward argument on egoist grounds can be constructed in response. As we saw in chapter 6, even rules regarded as having no moral validity may be obeyed by egoists, since to violate them would damage not only a mutually beneficial set of arrangements but also the violator's reputation, and thus her ability to make future agreements. Now notice how much more effective these rules and principles can be if they do have moral content! Members of the group will suffer from less uncertainty about others' behavior, because defecting from agreements will be morally proscribed and therefore more damaging to a rule-violator's reputation than if the regime were regarded merely as a convenient device to facilitate the coordination of behavior. Since there will be less uncertainty, members of the group will be better able to make mutually beneficial agreements than they would have been if no moral code existed. In a discussion of cooperation that begins, as mine has, with the example of Prisoners' Dilemma, a philosopher has concluded that "prudence is not enough, that the rational calculation of long-term self-interest is not sufficient in itself (necessarily) to lead men to make mutually beneficial agreements or, once made, to keep them" (Mackie, 1977, pp. 119-20). He concludes that "the main moral is the practical value of the notion of obligation, or an invisible and indeed fictitious tie or bond, whether this takes the form of a general requirement to keep whatever agreements one makes or of various specific duties like those of military honour or of loyalty to comrades or to an organization" (p. 119).

Morality may therefore "pay" for the group as a whole. It may also pay for the individual government. Adhering to a moral code may identify an actor as a political cooperator, part of a cluster of players with whom mutually beneficial agreements can be made, as in Robert Axelrod's model (1981, 1984). That is, publicly accepting a set of principles as morally binding may perform a labelling function. If the code were too passive—turn the other cheek—the moralist could be exploited by the egoist, but if the code prescribes reciprocity in a "tit-for-tat" manner, it may be a valuable label for its adherents. Each egoistic government could privately dismiss moral scruples, but if a moral code based on reciprocity were widely professed, it would be advantageous for even those governments to behave as if they believed it. Vice would pay homage to virtue.

Thus we could account for the existence of professed moral principles in world politics on purely self-interested grounds. Perhaps rules would not really be regarded as moral obligations, but they would be treated publicly as if they were. However neat this explanation, though, it is probably too cynical. For representative governments such as those that rule the major market-economy countries, it is difficult to separate "real" from "public" motivations. Moralists such as Woodrow Wilson and Jimmy Carter sometimes gain high office; indeed, their moralism may appeal to the electorate. Furthermore, even officials without strong moral principles have to defend their policies, and it is often convenient to do so in moral terms. This requirement may lead them, in order to avoid cognitive dissonance, to take on some of the beliefs that they profess. The act of piety may engender piety itself, as in Pascal's famous wager.[11]

Unbalanced Exchange

International regimes sometimes seem to facilitate unbalanced material exchanges in which, at a given time, one side provides much more in the way of tangible resources than the other. These apparently

---

[11] Not being able to prove the existence of God in rational terms, Pascal argued that it is nevertheless rational to believe in God, since if there were no such being, we would have lost relatively little by being pious in life, compared to the eternity lost if we disbelieved, only to discover after death that a God of heaven and hell existed. This argument can, of course, be put in game-theoretic terms, with piety as the minimax solution. But Pascal's further twist on the argument was that if one behaved in a pious way, with all the necessary outward shows of faith, genuine faith might well follow. See Nannerl O. Keohane, 1980, p. 278.

onesided exchanges may involve resources provided in the present—such as aid or access to markets—as did the Marshall Plan, many of the trade arrangements characteristic of the 1950s, and some contemporary foreign aid. They may also involve promises to provide such resources in the future.

Unbalanced exchanges seem *prima facie* to contradict rational-egoist premises. Yet the theorist of egoism has a powerful response, which is to reinterpret them as, by definition, balanced exchanges. Each observable material flow is assumed to have an intangible counterpart. Often such an interpretation is justified, as in our discussion in chapter 8 of European and Japanese deference after World War II in exchange for American aid, reflecting the "influence effect" of the latter (Hirschman, 1945/1980). The United States sent material goods to Europe that were of greater value than those received. In return, the U.S. gained influence—the basis for what Klaus Knorr (1975, p. 25) calls "patronal leadership," which we have referred to as hegemonic leadership. The reverse flow of influence, resulting from deference by the client, suggests that a patron-client relationship can often be reconceptualized as an exchange relationship in which intangible as well as tangible flows of benefits take place.

This response rests on the assumption that reciprocity is the underlying principle of a self-help system: when we observe a flow of resources in one direction, there must be a reciprocal flow in the other. Before accepting this premise, however, it may be worthwhile to probe more deeply into the concept of reciprocity and its implications for international relations.

Norms of reciprocity seem to be virtually universal as elements of culture, making "two interrelated minimal demands: 1) people should help those who have helped them, and 2) people should not injure those who have helped them" (Gouldner, 1960, p. 171). But reciprocity takes different forms in different societies, or for the same relationships in the same society. In his discussion of "stone-age economics," Marshall Sahlins makes a useful distinction among what he calls "negative," "balanced," and "generalized" reciprocity (1972, ch. 5, especially pp. 185-220).

Negative reciprocity refers to attempts to maximize utility at the expense of others, through fraud and violence if necessary. At the limit, it corresponds to aggressive war in world politics. Negative reciprocity reflects a strategy that is not well adapted to situations in which each actor's welfare depends, at least in part, on securing the voluntary cooperation of others over a protracted period of time. Indeed, Sahlins finds (consistent with our argument about international regimes) that elaborate institutional arrangements develop among primitive peoples with the function of achieving "a social suppression of negative reciprocity" (p. 201).

Balanced reciprocity is characterized by simultaneous direct exchange of equally valued goods (pp. 194-95). Balanced reciprocity is closer than negative reciprocity to exchange relationships in the world political economy, since it is based on realization of mutual gains from trade. But the characterization of balanced reciprocity as *simultaneous* distinguishes it rather sharply from patterns of exchange facilitated by international regimes. Indeed, this distinction helps us clarify further the role played by regimes. International regimes can be thought of in part as arrangements that facilitate *nonsimultaneous* exchange. In purely simultaneous exchange, neither party has to accept obligations, rules, or principles, since the exchange is balanced at every moment. There is never a "debt" or a "credit." An extreme example is provided by the settlement between Iran and the United States in 1981, in which American diplomats held hostage by Iran were liberated in return for the release of Iranian financial assets in the United States. Elaborate arrangements were made, involving Algeria and Britain, to ensure that neither side could double-cross the other by withholding its part of the bargain after receiving what it wanted. In the complete absence of an international regime linking the United States with the revolutionary government of Iran, laborious negotiations were necessary to set up an *ad hoc* arrangement to permit balanced reciprocity that benefited both sides.

This sort of perfectly balanced reciprocity provides an unsatisfactory basis for long-term relationships. Sahlins comments that among primitive tribes "a measure of imbalance sustains the trade partnership, compelling as it does another meeting" (p. 201). In the world political economy, international regimes make temporary imbalances feasible, since they create incentives (in the form partly of obligations) to repay debts. Thus regimes perform functions similar to those of credit markets, and it is not surprising that much of their activity is devoted to providing information that facilitates agreement. This is true of contemporary investigations of "country risk" undertaken by banks that want to know their borrowers; and it was true of the medieval European Bourses, which provided information in the form of merchants' newsletters and exchanges of information at fairs.[12] Like international

---

[12] Helen Milner made this observation to me, suggesting that the history of the development of credit markets could be informative. The analogy seems to hold. Richard

regimes, furthermore, credit markets depend on institutional reputation, which cannot be created in a short period of time, or through promises or argument alone, but is based on past performance. As Walter Bagehot said, "every banker knows that if he has to *prove* that he is worthy of credit, however good may be his arguments, in fact his credit is gone. . . . Credit is a power which may grow, but cannot be constructed" (1873/1962, p. 33). The reputations of international organizations and governments grow over a substantial period of time; they can be quickly destroyed, but not so rapidly rebuilt.

Credit arrangements, like insurance contracts, provide for exchanges that are expected to benefit both parties in the long run, but not to be balanced at any given time. The principle of ultimate symmetry of benefits, however, is maintained. In Sahlins's third type of reciprocity, "generalized reciprocity," this constraint is lifted. Generalized reciprocity characterizes certain sustained one-way flows of transactions, which Sahlins terms "putatively altruistic." No obligations are specified in return for the transfer of resources; the expectation of reciprocity is indefinite. Receipt of a gift only creates "a diffuse obligation to reciprocate when necessary to the donor and/or possible for the recipient. . . . Failure to reciprocate does not cause the giver of stuff to stop giving: the goods move one way, in favor of the have-not, for a very long period" (pp. 193-94).

Within primitive societies, generalized or near-generalized reciprocity is limited to relatively close kinship and residential groups. We should therefore be cautious about assuming that whenever we see an apparently onesided flow of benefits in world politics, it should be considered a true example of generalized reciprocity, especially since the egoistic explanation for this phenomenon is so powerful. What Sahlins's categories do, however, is to broaden our conception of reciprocity and therefore call attention to the fact that apparently unbalanced exchanges can be interpreted in a variety of different ways. They may be regarded as balanced by the exchange of intangible for tangible benefits; they may involve credit or insurance, in which current benefits are exchanged for future ones; or they may be cases of "generalized reciprocity," without specified reciprocal obligations.

Insofar as apparently unbalanced exchanges can be reinterpreted as

---

Ehrenberg reports that the development of credit arrangements in the Bourses reduced transaction costs (since money did not need to be transported in the form of specie) and that "during the Middle Ages the best information as to the course of events in the world was regularly to be obtained in the fairs and the Bourses" (1928, p. 317). The Bourses also supplied credit ratings, which provided information but also served as a crude substitute for effective systems of legal liability.

balanced, they can be accounted for by instrumental self-interest. Regimes play an important role, as we have seen, in exchanges such as these: institutionalizing deference, as in America's period of hegemony, or providing information that facilitates credit or insurance agreements. Generalized reciprocity, by contrast, reflects either situational or empathetic interdependence of interests. One gives unrequited gifts either because doing so will help oneself, regardless of reciprocity, or because one cares about the recipient's welfare.

The notion of generalized reciprocity does not substitute for an egoistic interpretation of unbalanced exchanges, but it may supplement such an interpretation by helping us to broaden our notions both of self-interest and of reciprocity. For instance, an interpretation of the Marshall Plan and other U.S. measures toward Europe after 1947 as generalized reciprocity would clearly not be adequate alone, since in times of crisis, such as Suez, the United States did require deference. Nevertheless, ascribing some weight to situational or empathetic interdependence is plausible in view of the widespread perception in America that U.S. welfare depended on a prosperous and democratic Europe, and in view of the close personal ties that many American statesmen had with Europeans. Furthermore, a difficulty with the pure egoistic-exchange view is that it would be hard now, much less in 1947 or 1956, to determine whether the United States extracted "enough" deference to compensate for its aid. It seems best to view the Marshall Plan as a combination of an exchange relationship—material benefits in return for present and future deference—and generalized reciprocity based on situational and empathetic interdependence.

CONCLUSIONS: SELF-INTERESTS AND LEARNING

This chapter has experimented with relaxing the assumption of rational egoism on which the arguments of chapters 5 and 6 relied. I have attempted to show that the value of international regimes is likely to be higher for organizations with bounded rationality, leaders who wish to bind their successors, or governments that have empathy for one another than for classically rational egoists. Actors laboring under bounded rationality will value rules of thumb provided by regimes. If governments fear changes in preferences by their successors, they may seek to join regimes to bind those future administrations. And finally, if governments' definitions of self-interest incorporate empathy, they will be more able than otherwise to construct international regimes, since shared interests will be greater. Empathy, however, is more fragile

131

and elusive than bounded rationality: actions that may lend themselves to explanations based on empathy can also be interpreted in ways consistent with egoistic theories.

This chapter has questioned the solidity of the assumption of self-interest on which rational-egoist models rely. Since the notion of self-interest is so elastic, we have to examine what this premise means, rather than simply taking it for granted. A complete analysis of regimes would have to show how international regimes could change as a result not of shifts in the allegedly objective interests of states, or in the power distributions and institutional conditions facing govern-ments, but of changes in how people think about their interests—that is, as a result of actors' learning. Learning, as Ernst Haas has empha-sized, involves increasing appreciation of complexity and recognition of more elaborate cause-and-effect linkages among events that should be taken into account by policy (Haas, Williams, and Babai, 1977, p. 324). It is crucial for Haas precisely because self-interests are largely subjective: "Changing perceptions of values and interests among actors are associated with changed behavior, though not in obedience to any pattern of rationality imputed or imposed by the observer. There is no fixed 'national interest' and no 'optimal regime' " (1983, p. 57).

Although I agree with Haas about the importance of learning, I believe that a structural analysis of constraints and a functional un-derstanding of international regimes are both necessary to put the phenomenon of actor cognition into its proper political context. Thus it has seemed necessary to focus in this book on arguments about power and institutions. A comprehensive treatment of international regimes would indeed go beyond the acknowledgment that self-inter-ests can be redefined; but this book does not undertake such a task. My defense, or excuse, is simply that to do so would require another research effort comparable in magnitude to the one reflected in this volume. Nevertheless, it should be emphasized that insofar as the argument of this book is taken seriously, it points to the importance of pursuing further the line of research that Haas has pioneered. Taking into account the constraints of power distribution, the potential ben-efits of cooperation, and the value of regimes for facilitating cooper-ation, we should ask: under what conditions do actors learn, and what are the effects of learning?

PART III

Hegemony and Cooperation
in Practice

· 8 ·

HEGEMONIC COOPERATION
IN THE POSTWAR ERA

Chapter 1 observed that Realist and Institutionalist theories were both able to account for the order that characterized the world political economy during the twenty years after World War II, but that they did so in very different ways. Institutionalism emphasized the role of shared interests created by economic interdependence and the effects of institutions; Realism stressed the impact of American hegemony. Both perspectives are valuable but incomplete. A synthesis of Realism and Institutionalism is necessary.

Part II sought such a synthesis at the theoretical level. Chapters 5 and 6 constructed a functional theory of international regimes on rational-choice foundations. This theory reaches some of the same conclusions as the Institutionalist position discussed in chapter 1; but it does so on a different basis—indeed, on the premises of Realism itself. Rational, self-interested actors, in a situation of interdependence, will value international regimes as a way of increasing their ability to make mutually beneficial agreements with one another. In chapter 7 I tried to show that this account gained further plausibility by relaxing the assumption of rationality, and that additional insights could be achieved by questioning the premise of egoism as well.

Part III, beginning with this chapter, also seeks to synthesize Realist and Institutionalist perspectives. In this Part, however, I do so not abstractly but by using the concepts of power, interest, hegemony, cooperation, and international regime to understand the international political economy of our own era. Chapter 8 shows the complementarity of hegemony and cooperation in the postwar period: American power helped to create cooperation, partly through constructing international regimes that could organize interstate relations along lines preferred by the United States. Chapter 9, which discusses the decline of hegemonic international economic regimes after the mid-1960s, demonstrates that the theory of hegemonic stability yields some valuable insights about this process; but the argument of this chapter also suggests the inadequacy of this or any other explanation that relies exclusively on changes in power to account for changes in patterns of cooperation. As the theory developed in Part II would have anticipated, international regimes have tended to persist longer than they would have if the theory of hegemonic stability were correct. Chapter 10 shows that the newest major international economic regime linking the advanced industrialized countries—the International Energy Agency (IEA)—performs in a way that is consistent with the argument of Part II, although within a framework established by the structure of world power.

The Argument of This Chapter

Powerful states seek to construct international political economies that suit their interests and their ideologies. But as we have noted, converting resources into outcomes is far from automatic in world politics. Even the highly qualified neo-Realist position adopted in chapter 3, that hegemony can facilitate cooperation, therefore requires an answer to the question of how hegemons translate their resources, both material and ideological, into rules for the system. How does the hegemon construct international regimes that facilitate the "right kind" of cooperation from the standpoint of the hegemon itself? That is, how does hegemonic leadership operate?[1]

This question is posed by Realism's emphasis on power, so I begin my analysis there. But in explaining changes in the world political economy, I emphasize the economic sources of power discussed in chapter 3 rather than military force. Sufficient military power to protect an international political economy from incursions by hostile powers is indeed a necessary condition for successful hegemony. Since World War II the United States has maintained such power, pursuing a strategy of "containment" of the Soviet Union. In the shelter of its military strength, the United States constructed a liberal-capitalist world

---

[1] Fred Hirsch and Michael Doyle characterize hegemonic leadership as involving "a mix of cooperation and control" (1977, p. 27). Klaus Knorr has described a similar process with the term "patronal leadership," referring to a pattern characterized by a "reciprocal flow of benefits and the absence of coercion in the hold that the patronal leader has over his client states" (1975, p. 25). In his terminology, the U.S. establishment of the Marshall Plan "was the act of a patron state" (pp. 25-26). Although I agree with the substance of Knorr's argument, I prefer Hirsch and Doyle's phrase "hegemonic leadership" because it implies that coercion is still an element of control, even though it remains in the background. "Patronal leadership" seems to understate the extent to which a leading power, such as the United States after World War II, needs to dominate others and to expropriate resources. "Hegemonic leadership," when distinguished from imperial rule, conveys the combination of paternalistic redistribution and authoritative control that is the distinctive mark of a system of independent states dominated and led by a single power.

136

political economy based on multilateral principles and embodying rules that the United States approved. American leadership in the world political economy did not exist in isolation from NATO, and in these years each was reinforced by the other. European anxiety that the United States might withdraw its protection provided an incentive, especially for the German government, to conform to American wishes. Nevertheless, at least for the twenty or so years following World War II, what Richard N. Cooper (1972-73) has called a "two-track" system prevailed: economic issues were rarely explicitly linked to military ones in relations between the United States and its allies. American military power served as a shield protecting the international political economy that it dominated, and it remained an important factor in the background of bargaining on economic issues; but it did not frequently impinge directly on such bargaining. Thus, as argued in chapter 3, it is justifiable to focus principally on the political economy of the advanced industrialized countries without continually taking into account the politics of international security. Of course, it would be highly desirable, in another study, to analyze the linkages between economic and security affairs in more detail.

We explore in detail the characteristics of economic power resources in the postwar world, and how their distribution and use changed over time. But to answer our questions about the operation of hegemonic cooperation, we must also think about interests and institutions. Hegemonic leadership does not begin with a *tabula rasa*, but rather builds on the interests of states. The hegemon seeks to persuade others to conform to its vision of world order and to defer to its leadership. American hegemonic leadership in the postwar period presupposed a rough consensus in the North Atlantic area, and later with Japan, on the maintenance of international capitalism, as opposed to socialism or a pattern of semi-autarchic national capitalisms (Block, 1977). This consensus can be viewed, in Gramscian terms, as the acceptance by its partners of the ideological hegemony of the United States. Such acceptance rested, in turn, on the belief of leaders of secondary states that they were benefiting from the structure of order that was being created. There was thus a high degree of perceived complementarity between the United States and its partners. The United States sought to reinforce this sense of complementarity by creating international regimes that would provide specific benefits to its partners as well as reduce uncertainty and otherwise encourage cooperation.

Hegemonic power and the international regimes established under conditions of hegemony combine to facilitate cooperation. Hegemony

137

itself reduces transaction costs and mitigates uncertainty, since each ally can deal with the hegemon and expect it to ensure consistency for the system as a whole. The formation of international regimes can ensure legitimacy for the standards of behavior that the hegemon plays a key role in maintaining. In the areas of money and trade, where their allies' cooperation was necessary, American leaders therefore invested resources in building stable international arrangements with known rules. It made sense for the United States to bind itself, as well as others, in order to induce weaker states to agree to follow the American lead.

American leaders did not construct hegemonic regimes simply by commanding their weaker partners to behave in prescribed ways. On the contrary, they had to search for mutual interests with their partners, and they had to make some adjustments themselves in addition to demanding that others conform to their design. They had to invest some of their power resources in the building of institutions. In so doing, they encountered numerous frustrations. As William Diebold has reminded us, "we have no memoirs called 'my days as a happy hegemon'" (1983, p. 3). It is important not to exaggerate the ease with which the United States could make and enforce the rules. Yet the United States ultimately succeeded in attaining its crucial objectives, if not by one expedient, then by another. Frustrations on particular issues melded into a rewarding overall pattern of hegemonic cooperation. Simplistic notions of hegemony as either complete dominance or selfless, dedicated leadership hinder rather than promote historical understanding.

Although Henry Luce foresaw an American Century, the period of hegemonic cooperation premised on a common commitment to openness and nondiscrimination lasted only about twenty years. This era began in 1947, the year of the Truman Doctrine and the Marshall Plan. It was already fading on some issues by 1963, the year of the Interest Equalization Tax, the first attempt by the United States to protect the status of the dollar against the consequences of the open world economy that it had struggled to create. In oil and trade, the first signs of new selective protectionist initiatives had already appeared. Mandatory oil import quotas were imposed in 1959, and in 1961 the United States secured a Short-Term Agreement on Cotton Textiles, which led eventually to a series of restrictive agreements on textile fibers. On some issues, such as tariff reductions, the 1960s witnessed further liberalization. But by 1971, when the United States broke the link between the dollar and gold, it was clear that something fundamental had changed. Exact dating is arbitrary. In this chapter we focus on the twenty years or so after 1947, and especially on the 1950s, to discover how hegemonic cooperation operated. Whichever date between 1963 and 1971 were chosen, it would still be clear that one of the most important features of American hegemony was its brevity.

At the end of World War II the United States was clearly the leading power in the world political economy, with respect to each of the resources discussed in chapter 3 as essential to hegemony: productivity in manufacturing and control over capital, markets, and raw materials. The United States used many of these resources after the war to gain what Albert Hirschman (1945/1980) has referred to as an "influence effect" of supplying something valuable to another country. Specifically, American influence rested on three major sets of benefits that its partners received from joining American-centered regimes and deferring to U.S. leadership:

1) *A stable international monetary system*, designed to facilitate liberal international trade and payments. This implied that the United States would manage the monetary system in a responsible way, providing sufficient but not excessive international liquidity.

2) *Provision of open markets for goods.* The United States actively worked to reduce tariffs and took the lead in pressing for the removal of discriminatory restrictions, although it tolerated regional discrimination by European countries and permitted the Europeans to maintain temporary postwar barriers during the period of dollar shortage.

3) *Access to oil at stable prices.* The United States, and American companies, provided oil to Europe and Japan from the Middle East, where U.S. oil corporations held sway, and in emergencies such as 1956-57 from the United States itself.

It is conventional to bracket trade and money together as the two crucial areas of the world political economy. American policymakers believed that they needed to build a consistent pattern of rules in international trade and finance. In particular, they thought that their efforts to construct a satisfactory international political economy based on nondiscrimination in trade depended on successful establishment of currency convertibility at stable exchange rates in international finance (Gardner, 1983). Trade and finance are traditionally regarded as the foundations of the Americanocentric world system, in part because in those areas the United States sought to establish international regimes characterized by formal agreements and institutional structures, and in part, I suspect, because until 1973 Americans took stable, cheap energy for granted.

It is less common to expand the trade-money pair to a trilogy including oil. Yet oil has been for decades by far the most important raw material involved in international trade, and it was particularly significant for economic recovery and growth in Western Europe and Japan after World War II. The open, nondiscriminatory monetary and trade system that the United States sought depended on growth and prosperity in other capitalist countries, which in turn depended on readily available, reasonably priced imports of petroleum, principally from the Middle East. In a material sense, oil was at the center of the redistributive system of American hegemony. In Saudi Arabia, and to a lesser extent in other areas of the Persian Gulf, major U.S. oil companies benefited from special relationships between the United States and the producing countries and from the protection and support of the American government. Most Middle Eastern oil did not flow to the United States, but went to Europe and Japan at prices well below the opportunity costs of substitutes, and even below the protected American domestic price. Even though the United States never established a formal international regime for petroleum, oil was of central importance to the world political economy.

During and after World War II the United States sought to construct formal international regimes not only in money and trade but also in oil. All three initial efforts to do so failed, at least in the short run. The United States reacted to the initial weakness of the International Monetary Fund (IMF) and the failure of the British Loan of 1946 by instituting the Marshall Plan, supporting the European Payments Union (EPU), then eventually reconstituting an international monetary regime with the IMF at its center. The United States compensated for the defeat of the International Trade Organization (ITO) by supporting the General Agreement on Tariffs and Trade (GATT). But, in oil, initial defeat at the hands of the Senate led not to a new multilateral accord but to increasing reliance by the U.S. government on the international oil companies and the international regime that they dominated. As we will see, domestic politics constituted a crucial factor affecting this outcome.

Since no international regime with broad membership was established in oil, this issue-area constitutes a challenge to the theories presented in Part II, which imply that a hegemonic power should seek to institute international regimes on an intergovernmental basis as a way of helping to control the actions of other states. Oil is the apparent exception that tests this rule. The fact that American leaders sought such a regime, and were only thwarted from establishing one by the domestic oil industry, suggests that the U.S. government—or at least the executive branch—did indeed have the incentives that the theory predicts. Domestic politics, however, got in the way.

The historical discussion in this chapter begins with money and trade. Then we will consider, in detail, five episodes within the international political economy of petroleum. Four of these involved the international exercise of political influence: American efforts to control Arab oil between 1943 and 1948, which included plans for an Anglo-American Petroleum Agreement in 1943-45; the sterling-dollar oil problem of 1949-50; British and American intervention in Iran between 1951 and 1954, including the formation of the Iranian Consortium in the latter year; and the Emergency Oil Lift Program implemented by the United States in the wake of the abortive Anglo-French invasion of Egypt in 1956. Taken together, these cases demonstrate that the American dominance of international oil was neither an accident nor a product of absent-mindedness, but rather the result of careful strategic planning by both governmental and corporate officials, with the government often taking the lead. Furthermore, the control of oil was a major political resource for the United States in its dealings with Europe, as the aftermath of the Suez crisis showed.

American hegemony in petroleum politics rested on multiple sources of influence, including close political ties with the Saudi monarchy, the capacity to intervene in the domestic politics of Middle Eastern countries, military and technical aid provided to Iran, Saudi Arabia, and other oil-producing countries, the preponderant military strength of the United States in the Mediterranean, and—not least—the continued availability of excess petroleum production capacity at home. There was, however, a ghost at the feast: the shadow cast by the political influence in the United States of its own domestic oil industry. Members of the industry defeated the scheme for an Anglo-American Petroleum Agreement and provided the major stumbling-block to effective use of hegemonic power during the Suez crisis. The most debilitating effects of industry influence were felt through the Mandatory Oil Import Program instituted by the United States in 1959 and maintained until 1973: under the guise of protecting American security, this program "drained America first." We need to understand the origins of this program to understand how, even at the height of American power, the seeds of decay had been planted. The oil import program therefore constitutes our fifth case.

HEGEMONIC COOPERATION IN FINANCE AND TRADE

At a United Nations conference held at Bretton Woods, New Hampshire, in 1944, the United States, Great Britain, and their allies agreed to form an International Monetary Fund (IMF) and an International Bank for Reconstruction and Development (IBRD), later known as the World Bank. The IMF was the institutional center of a new international monetary regime, designed principally by British and American planners led by John Maynard Keynes and Harry Dexter White, that was to facilitate liberal trade and payments in the postwar world. U.S. leaders hoped that establishment of multilateral rules for the world economy—plans were also under way for an International Trade Organization—would make it unnecessary for the United States to provide large and continuing aid, or to intervene frequently to maintain financial equilibrium. Like Newton's deity—which set the celestial machinery in motion but which refrained from interfering in its operation—the United States, having established multilateralism, would return to the background and let the financial system operate smoothly through a combination of markets and international agreement.

Yet by 1947 it had become clear that the European economies were too weak for this vision of easy multilateralism to be realized. Indeed, the harsh winter of 1946-47 raised the specter of European economic collapse. Problems of internal reconstruction were compounded by an acute global shortage of dollars, which threatened to cripple world trade and certainly hampered the ability of U.S. firms to export their goods to countries desperately in need of them. U.S. officials worried about the possibility that economic distress in Europe could lead to attempts at autarchic national capitalism or even communism, both of which would be antithetical to American plans.

Responding to what it saw as a crisis, the Truman Administration changed its policy during the course of 1947 from one of demanding quick sterling convertibility (unsuccessfully attempted in the summer of 1947) on the basis of loans from the United States to provision of billions of dollars' worth of grant aid to Europe, under what became known as the Marshall Plan. This aid was administered by the Economic Cooperation Agency (ECA), which was much more sympathetic to European interests and policies than the Treasury, which had managed the relatively tough provisions of the British Loan of 1946. These new, bold measures overshadowed the young IMF, which "engaged in virtually no exchange operations during the early years of the Marshall Plan" (Gardner, 1956/1980, p. 303).

The United States thus turned from its intention of being a passive, rather tightfisted hegemon—able without much continuing effort to make and enforce rules for a liberal and nondiscriminatory world economy—to becoming an active and relatively openhanded one. Hegemony "on the cheap" no longer seeming realistic, the United States adjusted to European weakness by providing huge resources through the Marshall Plan. By doing so, it provided itself with the political leverage to achieve hegemonic cooperation in an operational sense. That is, the United States could use the influence provided by European reliance on its aid to take the lead in creating and maintaining a new set of post-Bretton Woods rules for the world financial system. Yet these rules had to take account of political and economic realities. As we have seen, they could not simply be imposed by the United States, nor could they simply be established and allowed to implement themselves. On the contrary, maintaining control of the rule-making process required a delicate and continuous combination of intervention and negotiation.

Not only did the American government have to negotiate with the Europeans, it also had to persuade Congress to appropriate the funds that would provide it with the means of influence. In this task it was greatly aided by the clumsiness of Soviet policy under Stalin, since the increasing perception of a Soviet military as well as political threat helped to rally support for President Harry Truman's program in Congress. Historians of various schools have emphasized the importance of the Cold War for the Marshall Plan. Truman is reported to have said that the Marshall Plan and the Truman Doctrine, which began the formal policy of containment, were "two halves of the same walnut" (LaFeber, 1972, p. 53). Later this symbiotic relationship continued as the post-Marshall Plan flow of dollars to Europe was maintained through rearmament programs after the beginning of the Korean War (Block, 1977, p. 107 and pp. 242-43, n. 91).

Along with their plans for a liberal international monetary regime, U.S. officials during World War II had also developed schemes for an International Trade Organization (ITO), which would institutionalize nondiscriminatory trade on a global basis. The first proposals for an ITO were developed by American and British negotiators in 1943 (Gardner, 1956/1980, pp. 103-109) and were nursed, largely by Americans, through a series of protracted and difficult negotiations, culminating in the Havana Conference held in early 1948. At Havana differences appeared on discrimination, on provisions for private capital movement, and on how broad a scope developing countries should have to impose quantitative restrictions on trade (Gardner, 1956/1980, pp. 361-68). Nevertheless, final agreement on the Charter was reached in March of 1948. The proposed ITO was carefully designed not to infringe on delicate issues of state sovereignty, but to be more flexible and ambiguous than a traditional legal system. "The coercive force of

143

the ITO legal system rested almost entirely in an escalated series of normative pressures—at root, the obloquy of having done something wrong," rather than on sanctions as such (Hudec, 1975, p. 30). But the ITO was given a "second-rate funeral," rejected by the U.S. Senate without even a vote (Hudec, 1975, pp. 53-54). American business objected to the lack of a complete ban on new preferences and quantitative restrictions, and to provisions that made allowance for economic planning and state trading (Brown, 1950, pp. 362-75). The U.S. Chamber of Commerce, in April of 1948, had demanded "positive declarations in behalf of the maintenance of private initiative and enterprise in world commerce" (Brown, 1950, p. 370). When such provisions were not adopted, organized American business interests opposed the ITO. As William Diebold says, the ITO was defeated because of "an investment code unwisely asked for by American business and then opposed by the same people" (1983, p. 6). Even at the height of American economic preponderance, resistance to U.S. liberalism by other countries and ideological cross-pressures at home destroyed prospects for what one of its chief architects called a "charter for world trade" (Wilcox, 1949).

Thus, by the end of the 1940s, the monetary and trade regimes designed during World War II were either ignored or in ruins. The IMF was inactive and the ITO was dead. Yet although the institutions envisaged by the wartime planners did not live up to the hopes of their inventors, the United States was able to achieve its essential purposes in other ways. As we have seen, the Marshall Plan provided Europe with dollars and the goods that only dollars could buy. At the same time, other institutional innovations appeared, designed to provide the nondiscriminatory liberalization that had been the goal of the IMF and the ITO.

On the financial side, the United States, led by the ECA, pushed for a European Payments Union (EPU), which was agreed upon in the late summer of 1950. The EPU was an institutional response to the shortage of dollars that was restricting trade and hampering economic recovery: it complemented the Marshall Plan by reducing the need for dollars and increasing the efficiency with which scarce resources were used. The first reaction of governments to the dollar shortage had been some two hundred bilateral agreements negotiated by European countries in the first two years after the war. Although these arrangements were preferable in terms of efficiency to straight barter deals, they distorted trade by virtually requiring bilateral balancing of accounts. A multilateral payments union could improve efficiency by summing up each country's surpluses and deficits vis-à-vis other members of the

144

group and arriving at a single figure. Thus if Germany had a surplus with France but a deficit of equal size with Italy, while France had a similar surplus with Italy, these accounts could be balanced on a multilateral basis, whereas strict bilateral balancing would require distortion of trade patterns (Patterson, 1966, pp. 75-83). In the language of chapter 6, the EPU drastically reduced the transaction costs associated with financing intra-European trade.

The United States proposed the EPU and succeeded in getting it established over British opposition, going so far as to indicate at one point that it was willing to support the EPU with dollars even if several countries opted not to join (Triffin, 1957, p. 166). American enthusiasm for the EPU was accounted for partly by its superior economic efficiency compared to bilateral arrangements, but it was also seen as a way of promoting intra-European trade as a step toward eventual European participation in a liberal world economy. "The EPU was the key element in what was seen as a gradual evolutionary process that would take Europe from bilateralism to full multilateralism" (Block, 1977, p. 100). Although it was a financial arrangement, the importance of trade was underlined by the fact that the EPU was coupled with a Code of the Liberalization of Trade, sponsored by the Organization for European Economic Cooperation (OEEC), which provided for almost immediate elimination of most quantitative import restrictions covering intra-European trade (Mikesell, 1954, p. 130). The United States and its European partners both recognized that trade and payments had to be liberalized together, if this were to be done successfully at all.

In the short term, however, the EPU did not promote liberalization. On the contrary, it legitimated discrimination against American exports, which was encouraged both by the shortage of dollars and the availability of the EPU's multilateral clearing arrangements within Europe. And the EPU provided no guarantees that the European system would dissolve into the global multilateralism that the United States desired. The Treasury Department grumbled about this on the grounds that the EPU would lead to new vested interests that would support a continuation of its controls: "Europe would become a high inflation area, largely insulated from trade with the United States" (Block, 1977, p. 101). Opposition to the EPU was also strong in the IMF (Patterson, 1966, pp. 113-19). But, in the absence of a positive program of their own, the pessimists could not prevail.

Subsequent events justified the confidence of the optimists. The EPU did not foster inflation, and when European economies became strong enough to move toward currency convertibility in the middle of the decade, it was dissolved. On the whole, one authority holds, the EPU and associated trade arrangements "probably did facilitate the movement toward convertibility and nondiscrimination in trade" (Patterson, 1966, p. 111).

The most remarkable aspect of the Marshall Plan and the EPU is that the United States gave up its usual demands for reciprocity. Marshall Plan aid consisted of grants, not loans: the European countries had to get together to ask for the money on the basis of an agreed plan, but they did not have to reciprocate American benefactions. Similarly, the EPU was an agreement made on the basis of faith in the future, rather than in return for a direct *quid pro quo* by the Europeans. In 1950 Europe had little to give except promises of good faith; insistence on a fair exchange in the short term would have meant no agreement at all. So the United States farsightedly made short-term sacrifices—in giving financial aid and in permitting discrimination against American exports—in order to accomplish the longer-term objective of creating a stable and prosperous international economic order in which liberal capitalism would prevail and American influence would be predominant. Perhaps American leaders, like Marshall Sahlins's "stone-age economists" whom we encountered in chapter 7, expected that receipt of unrequited gifts would create "a diffuse obligation to reciprocate" on the part of the recipients. Surely some of them also felt empathy for Europe's plight. Whatever their motivations, American leaders saw that risks had to be run to make progress, but the extent of these risks was limited by the enormous resources at the disposal of the U.S. government. For the foreseeable future, the combination of European need for American military protection and the dollar shortage would give the United States a great deal of continuing leverage over the evolution of European policies. The United States could take the long view precisely because it had the power to shape the future. Awareness of its hegemony was therefore the foundation on which American generosity rested.

It is important to recognize that the U.S. policies put into effect most dramatically with the Marshall Plan in 1947-48, and followed later by the EPU, represented an attempt to achieve long-standing American aims in new ways, rather than an abandonment of earlier policy objectives. As Fred Hirsch and Michael Doyle have pointed out (1977, pp. 31-32):

> The United States—by providing massive additional *financing* and accepting trade and payments liberalization by *stages*—saved rather than abandoned its earlier objective of ultimate multilateralism

in 1947-48. Such a policy was then possible because of the fundamental characteristic of the international political economy of the time: United States leadership on the basis of only qualified hegemony. The strategy, as is well known, was a major success: the moves toward progressive regional liberalization, undertaken by European economies that were strengthened by the aid injections, paved the way for a painless adoption of multilateralism at the end of the 1950s, with the moves to currency convertibility and the ending of trade discrimination against dollar imports.

If there was change in the 1947-48 period, particularly in U.S. willingness to finance European recovery and to tolerate European discrimination against American exports, there was also continuity. After the failure of the U.S. Senate to ratify the ITO, the American government sought to achieve the same nondiscriminatory and liberalizing objectives through the General Agreement on Tariffs and Trade (GATT), which had been envisaged as merely a provisional arrangement until the ITO could be established. GATT had been negotiated and signed in 1947 as a temporary agreement that incorporated the draft Commercial Policy Chapter of the ITO as it then stood, with some differences reflecting the predominant role of the major powers at the GATT conference and the lessened need, as compared with the ITO conference, to make concessions to less developed countries. Owing to its presumed temporary nature, governments only accepted GATT provisions "provisionally," and GATT was not made into a formal international organization. The General Agreement refers neither to GATT as an organization nor to the concept of membership (Dam, 1970, p. 335).

Despite its inauspicious beginnings, GATT was remarkably successful during the 1950s, being transformed from a mere multilateral agreement providing for "joint action" by its Contracting Parties into the centerpiece of a new international trade regime. It remained highly informal, in a successful effort to avoid running afoul of the U.S. Congress's sensitivity to international organizations designed to liberalize trade. Indeed, the spelling of Contracting Parties in capital letters "was to be the sole indication of a collective identity. Every other hint of organizational existence was ruthlessly hunted down and exterminated" (Hudec, 1975, p. 46). GATT proceeded to operate not on the basis of centralized decisionmaking and enforcement, but with the aid of workable informal procedures based on the "sense of authoritative certainty" possessed by key participants. They knew what they had meant when the rules were written, even if the rules themselves were ambiguous! This sense of certainty "gave GATT administrators both the confidence and the community support needed to interpret GATT law in a manner that would bring out the basic policies and objectives underlying the written text" (Hudec, 1975, p. 103). A small but highly competent and imaginative secretariat was created under the leadership of Eric Wyndham White. Except when domestic politics interfered—as, most markedly, in agricultural trade policy—the United States was highly supportive of GATT's efforts to facilitate liberalization.

If the failure of the ITO reflected the difficulties of securing a formal international agreement that could command support in the United States, the success of GATT was indicative of the conditions facilitating successful hegemonic cooperation. GATT had an appropriate institutional design, which stressed reduction of uncertainty and decentralized coordination rather than centralized rule-enforcement. This helped the organization to avoid damaging symbolic struggles about its authority relative to that of member governments. In addition, GATT benefited from the resourcefulness of U.S. officials, the extent of American power, and the value of the ideological consensus that existed among the liberally oriented governments solidly established in Europe after 1947. GATT's effectiveness in the 1950s suggests how hegemonic cooperation can work.

The United States was willing not only to support European efforts at trade liberalization, but to pressure reluctant European governments to go farther, faster. One of the most striking examples of hegemonic leadership for this purpose is provided by American efforts, dating from 1949, to persuade its reluctant European partners to give most-favored-nation treatment to Japan. From the autumn of 1951 onward Japan sought, with American support, to be allowed to join GATT. The struggle was long and difficult: Britain in 1951 even opposed allowing Japan to send an official observer to GATT; in 1953 it was finally agreed that Japan could participate in GATT without a vote; and in 1955 Japan became a Contracting Party. Even then other members that accounted for 40 percent of Japan's exports immediately invoked Article 35, making GATT's nondiscrimination provisions inapplicable to their relations with Japan. For a decade the United States helped Japan persuade other GATT members to disinvoke Article 35; this was accomplished for all major trading partners by the mid-1960s.

American policy was based on a combination of political and economic calculations. If Japan were to prosper, it would need to trade with other industrialized countries; hence American markets must be open to Japanese exports. Given this politically determined necessity, discriminatory restrictions imposed on Japan by other nations would result in a heavier burden placed on the United States: goods not imported by others would have to be absorbed by the American market. Since the United States, as leader, was resolved to keep Japan in the American-led system, it had strong incentives to persuade or pressure its allies into helping out. "Free world interest" combined with U.S. interests to mandate a strategy of liberalization and incorporation of Japan into the European–American political economy (Patterson, 1966, pp. 271-305).

The American campaign against discrimination was rendered ambiguous by the fact that the United States supported the creation of the European Economic Community (EEC) in 1958. The existence of the EEC, of course, entailed discrimination by the Community against exports from outsiders, including the United States. Nevertheless, both for political reasons and because of a belief that European integration would contribute to economic growth and therefore to world trade, the United States endorsed this process. Indeed, at least until the end of the 1950s it was widely believed that the EEC would, on balance, contribute to lower trade barriers, although during the 1960s increasing concern was expressed about the possibility that the European Community would lead as much to protectionism and discrimination as to liberalization (Patterson, 1966, pp. 181-88). Eventually EEC policy, particularly its association agreements with other countries, led to a number of new disputes about discrimination that became increasingly acrimonious in the early 1970s and 1980s under the pressure of economic stagnation and structural changes in world production and trade. But until at least the mid-1960s the American policy of allowing a great deal of scope for European integration, even at the expense of immediate liberalization, seemed to be a clear success.

On the monetary side, the late 1950s and the early 1960s were also years of apparent triumph and high expectations for the future. After 1958 the international monetary regime established at Bretton Woods finally began to operate as it had been meant to by its founders. European currencies became formally convertible into dollars, and the IMF became the central international organization in a par-value international monetary regime. The dollar was linked to gold at a fixed price of $35 per ounce, and the currencies of other countries belonging to the regime were pegged to the dollar at fixed rates of exchange. Exchange rates could be altered, supposedly after consultations in the IMF, but they rarely were (although the requirement of consultation was more avoided than honored). The certainty provided by the par-value system seemed to contribute, along with the GATT-centered trade regime, to the growth of world trade, which was remarkably rapid during this period. Both in money and in trade, the twin American goals of liberalization and nondiscrimination had been achieved, not through simple implementation of the Bretton Woods blueprint, but through an incremental and nonlinear process involving "two steps forward, one step back." In the years after 1958 international economic cooperation flourished within the framework of hegemonic regimes.

HEGEMONIC COOPERATION IN OIL

The major theme of our first four oil cases is the efficacy of American action. The United States had so many resources—economic, political, and military—that it was able to attain its essential objectives even without establishing a formal multilateral regime. In oil, the United States was so predominant that it could implement cooperation on essentially its own terms. Thus a Realist analysis of the search for wealth and power and the role of hegemony in creating rules is fundamental to an understanding of these cases.

A contrast to this emphasis on the American government's power is provided by the importance of domestic politics, which constrained the U.S. government and eventually helped to undercut the material basis for American leadership. This discordant note was first sounded with the failure of the attempt to establish control over Middle Eastern oil supplies through an international regime, under provisions of the Anglo-American Petroleum Agreement. It swelled to a crescendo with the unilateral enactment of Mandatory Oil Import Quotas in 1959, which in the long run eroded rather than bolstered U.S. power. The fragility of hegemonic cooperation—reflected in the fact that it lasted for a score of years rather than for a century—can be accounted for in good measure by the refusal of domestic interests to adjust, or to sacrifice, for the sake of the long-term power position of the United States.

Neither of these themes would come as a surprise to Realist analysts. Despite the degree to which the oil cases conform to Realist expectations, however, the themes of Part II, though muted, are not irrelevant even here. Cooperation as I have defined it took place: it was compatible with hegemony and arose from real or potential discord, which itself stemmed from international economic interdependence. The lack of reliance of the United States on international institutions in the oil area until 1974 indeed shows that hegemony can substitute for international regimes. But the evidence indicates that the U.S.

government had some incentives earlier to form international regimes, although pressures to do so may have been lower than in money and trade. The United States sought in 1944-45 to create what would have amounted to an intergovernmental petroleum cartel with the United States as senior member and Britain as its junior partner. This was only thwarted by domestic opposition. As we will see in chapters 9 and 10, the United States moved to construct a consumers' oil regime after the crisis of 1973-74, which revealed the decline of U.S. power in oil. By then, however, this could no longer be done on its own terms.

Controlling Arab Oil, 1943-1948

Before World War II the United States had sought to secure access by American companies to concessions in areas dominated politically by Britain and France. Under the Red Line Agreement of July 31, 1928, American firms (linked together in the Near East Development Corporation) received a 23.75 percent share in the Turkish Petroleum Company, with concessions in areas now controlled by Turkey, Syria, and Iraq. Within the "Red Line Area," which included the Arabian peninsula, members of the Turkish Petroleum Company (later the Iraq Petroleum Company) were required by the agreement "to refrain from obtaining concessions or purchasing oil independently in any part of what was construed to have been the old Ottoman Empire" (Anderson, 1981, p. 18). This was part of a network of agreements made in the 1920s to restrict supply of petroleum and ensure that the major companies, working together, could control oil prices on world markets.

During the 1930s a number of significant oil discoveries were made. The most important of these for oil markets in that decade took place in East Texas in 1930, but from a long-term international standpoint the most significant find occurred in 1938, when oil in commercial quantities was discovered in Saudi Arabia by the California Arabian Standard Oil Company, or Casoc (later to become the Arabian American Oil Company, or Aramco), a jointly owned subsidiary of Standard Oil of California (Socal) and the Texas Company (Texaco). In 1940 these fields produced only 5 million barrels of oil, but by 1941 both the companies involved and the Saudi monarchy recognized that the area's petroleum reserves might be enormous.

After the United States had become a belligerent in World War II, the question of how to exploit Saudi oil for the war effort became a matter of immediate concern for American military planners. Yet by 1943 concern about future domestic oil shortages, and information about the vastness of Saudi reserves, led civilian officials to pay attention to the problem of how to ensure continued postwar American control of the Saudi concession. At first, American suspicion centered on its close ally, Britain. Casoc executives "became convinced that the British were devising all sorts of schemes to deprive them of their concession" (Stoff, 1980, p. 57). The company "employed the British bogey time and again" in its dealings with the Department of State (Miller, 1980, p. 50). King 'Abd al-'Aziz of Saudi Arabia "subtly fanned those fears to increase his chances for financial support," although "nowhere in the accessible British archives is there any evidence of a British plan in the 1940s to actually displace the American concessionaire" (Anderson, 1981, p. 40).

On the initiative of the State Department, supported by Socal and Texaco, President Franklin D. Roosevelt declared Saudi Arabia eligible for American Lend-Lease assistance in February 1943. Socal and Texaco had proposed, in return for Lend-Lease, that their joint venture, Casoc, would create an oil reserve in Saudi Arabia whose contents would be made available to the U.S. government at prices below those on the world market. Following approval of Lend-Lease, the State Department's Committee on International Petroleum Policy, chaired by Economic Advisor Herbert Feis, proposed the formation of a Petroleum Reserves Corporation. The PRC was to acquire option contracts on Arabian oil. After the State Department made this suggestion, however, Interior Secretary Harold Ickes and representatives of the military services (particularly the Navy) proposed that the PRC directly acquire reserves by purchasing all of Casoc's stock. This plan was approved by Roosevelt in late June 1943.

The Secretary of the Interior and representatives of the military, with the reluctant acquiescence of the State Department, had persuaded the President to create a Petroleum Reserves Corporation that would own huge quantities of Saudi oil. Such a plan was sure to be opposed by major corporations, yet little regard was paid to their interests. The PRC's board of directors was to consist of the secretaries of state, interior, war, and navy, without private-sector participation; the right to manage the reserves was to be allocated not necessarily to Socal and Texaco (although they were to be given preference), but to those companies submitting the best bids. As Anderson comments, "the audacity of the overall plan was possibly reflective of the mood of wartime Washington" (1981, p. 55).

Negotiations between Ickes and the presidents of Socal and Texaco had apparently reached tentative agreement on sale of a one-third interest in Casoc to the government, when pressure was brought to bear by Standard Oil of New Jersey (now Exxon) and Socony-Vacuum (now Mobil). John Brown of Socony indicated that "his company and others in the foreign field didn't like the idea of government competition" (Anderson, 1981, p. 64). Fearing that he would lose a struggle on this issue, and that it would undermine his political position, Ickes broke off his talks with Socal and Texaco, covering his tracks by claiming that these companies had refused to negotiate in good faith with the government.[2] The PRC later attempted to make arrangements for a government-owned pipeline from the Persian Gulf to the Mediterranean, a scheme that was also blocked by competitors of Socal and Texaco (Anderson, 1981, pp. 78-83, 96-102).

Failure of the PRC brought to the fore another idea, which had been discussed in the State Department during 1943 and which Ickes had embraced as well: the negotiation of a petroleum agreement with Great Britain. The heart of the original agreement, worked out in the summer of 1944, was a provision for an International Petroleum Commission, which would have recommended " 'production and exportation rates for the various concessions in the Middle East . . . [to prevent] . . . the disorganization of world markets which might result from uncontrolled competitive expansion.' "[3] In other words, it would have established what amounted to an Anglo-American cartel, fifteen years before the founding of OPEC. The major international firms supported this conception, provided that they would be furnished with immunity from antitrust prosecution; if it granted this exemption, the government would be achieving for them what they had long sought in world markets through informal collusion and more or less secret agreements. The proposed petroleum agreement was a bold plan for a formal international oil regime dominated by the United States. The fact that it could have been used as a device to exploit poorer and weaker states—consumers as well as producers of oil—reminds us that cooperation is not necessarily benign.

The proposal for an Anglo-American Agreement had to be submitted

[2] Ickes managed to confound a generation of historians about the reasons for the collapse of his negotiations with Casoc, by not only lying to Congressional committees but by altering the minutes of relevant government-industry meetings and even including an incorrect account in his "secret diary," later published. Anderson (1981, pp. 56-67) shows on the basis of Ickes's personal confidential diary (not designed for publication) that it was Ickes who broke off the negotiations under pressure from Socony and other oil companies. For a brief discussion, see Keohane, 1982c.

[3] Anderson, 1981, p. 95, quoting a memorandum by John A. Loftus of the Petroleum Division, Department of State, November 9, 1944.

to the Senate as a treaty, owing to insistence on that point from the outset by members of the Foreign Relations Committee. There it came up both against a formidable coalition of interests and against mainstream American ideology. The plan for an intergovernmental cartel "ran counter to the vested interests of the American independents, the antitrust philosophy of the Department of Justice, the laissez-faire ideology of a remnant of New Deal opponents, and State's own longstanding practice of not supporting one domestic interest group over another" (Anderson, 1981, p. 96). Furthermore, the scheme ran afoul of a fierce bureaucratic battle for the control of oil policy between Harold Ickes and the dominant forces in the State Department, and suffered from the aftermath of the intense controversy engendered by the Petroleum Reserves Corporation scheme.

The interests of independent domestic oilmen were particularly threatened. They feared that "the pact might open the American market to cheap foreign petroleum" (Krasner, 1978a, p. 204). Despite the frequent denials of this intent by government officials, the apprehensions of the oilmen were justified: an essential purpose of the agreement was to reduce the drain on Western Hemisphere oil reserves by developing Middle Eastern resources for marketing in Europe, and perhaps even in the United States. As Acting Petroleum Advisor James Sappington wrote on December 1, 1943, for security reasons "It was advisable that Middle Eastern oil be developed to the maximum and that supplies in this hemisphere be . . . conserved." He even remarked that "if Middle Eastern oil should enter the United States to meet the postwar need for oil imports, the result should be a further conservation of the reserves" of the Western Hemisphere.[4]

Opposition to the 1944 draft took institutional expression with a demand for radical revisions formulated in December by the Petroleum Industry War Council, representing the industry. In conjunction with the opposition of Senator Tom Connally of Texas, Chairman of the Foreign Relations Committee, this demand led the State Department to withdraw the agreement for reconsideration. It was eventually renegotiated with the industry, and then with the British, to meet industry objections. The resulting agreement, renegotiated under Ickes's

---

[4] "Memorandum on the Department's position," folder "Petroleum Reserves Corporation Activities, 7/3/43–1/1/44," box 1, records of the Petroleum Division, Record Group 59, National Archives (cited by Anderson, 1981, p. 78, n. 27). The head of the Petroleum Division in 1945, John A. Loftus, expressed similar views to those of Sappington. See Loftus memo, May 31, 1945, National Archives, decimal file 1945-49, Box no. 5849, file no. 841.6363/5-3145.

leadership, would have restricted the role of the International Petroleum Commission to the preparation of reports and estimates, excluded the U.S. industry from regulation, and relied entirely on voluntary compliance. As a result, the State Department became lukewarm
toward the agreement. State was strong enough to delete the antitrust
immunity clause, over Ickes's resistance; but this change meant that
the major international companies now lost interest in it. Thus the
agreement was rendered virtually meaningless by renegotiation. By
late 1944 or early 1945 the precarious pro-agreement coalition of
Ickes, the State Department, and the international oil majors had
collapsed under pressure from the domestic industry. Only the shadow
of a public international agreement remained. This "orphan," as one
State Department official characterized it in 1946 after Ickes's departure from the government, was never ratified by the Senate.[5]

The United States had failed to secure Saudi oil through direct
government ownership or to achieve broader control over Middle
Eastern petroleum through an Anglo-American agreement. Initiative
thus passed to the companies, supported by the Department of State.
In 1946 Socal and Texaco found themselves with prolific oil fields in
Saudi Arabia and a joint venture, now named Aramco, operating there
with a skilled production team; but they also faced large demands for
capital and uncertain markets for the huge quantities of oil that could
be produced. Standard Oil of New Jersey, by contrast, was chronically
short of crude and concerned about being excluded from the richest,
lowest-cost concession in the world. Moved by the business conser-
vatism of their leaders, and over the strenuous objections of other
company officials (at least in Socal), Socal and Texaco decided, in
early 1946, to invite Jersey to purchase a share in Aramco. Eventually,
Socony was also asked to participate, and arrangements were made
for a 30 percent purchase in Aramco by Jersey and a 10 percent
participation for Socony.[6]

[5] This account follows Anderson (1981) rather than Miller (1980) or Stoff (1980),
for reasons given in Keohane, 1982c. The "orphan" phrase, which appears in a memo
of February 1946 from Clair Wilcox to Will Clayton, is cited by Stoff, p. 193, and
Anderson, p. 130.

[6] The issue of which corporation took the initiative was obscure in the literature until
the publication of Anderson's book. It has long been known that high executives of
Socal opposed the deal, on the grounds that Saudi oil would allow the company to
expand rapidly at the expense of competitors if the latter were not allowed into Saudi
Arabia. The staff of the Federal Trade Commission (U.S. Senate, 1952) and a Senate
subcommittee on multinational corporations (U.S. Senate, 1975) both claimed that

Yet to consummate this deal it was necessary somehow to nullify the restrictions of the Red Line Agreement of 1928, which required that the partners in the Iraq Petroleum Company (IPC) only produce or purchase oil within the Red Line area through the IPC. By 1946 the IPC companies were Anglo-Iranian (23.75 percent), Shell (23.75 percent), Companie Françaises des Petroles (23.75 percent), Socony (11.875 percent), Jersey (11.875 percent) and the Gulbenkian interests (5 percent). Socal and Texaco, not being members of the IPC, were not restrained from producing in Saudi Arabia, but Socony and Jersey were. For these companies to join Aramco would constitute a violation of the Red Line Agreement.

The story of how Jersey and Socony maneuvered to dissolve the Red Line Agreement is a fascinating tale of international legal intrigue. In early negotiations, Shell assured the American companies that it would participate in drafting new arrangements for IPC, and Jersey placated Anglo-Iranian with an agreement to purchase large amounts of Iranian and Kuwaiti oil from it, over a twenty-year period, and to construct a new pipline (never built) from Abadan to the Mediterranean. Companie Françaises des Petroles (CFP) and Gulbenkian posed more serious problems. Fortunately for the American companies, however, during World War II CFP and Gulbenkian had operated within Nazi-controlled territory and had in 1940 been construed by a distinguished British barrister as having become "enemy aliens," thus rendering the Red Line Agreement null and void. This served as a sufficient pretext in 1946 for Jersey and Socony to argue that the agreement was legally dissolved and to open negotiations for a new agreement free of the restrictive clauses of the earlier one.[7]

Not surprisingly, CFP objected strenuously. Not only were its leaders presumably insulted by being labeled "enemy aliens" as a result of the defeat of France; they feared that the effect of the Aramco deal

---

negotiations were initiated by Jersey and Socony. John Blair (1976, p. 39) even went so far as to suggest that Socal sold its share because the Rockefeller family, which also controlled Jersey and Socony, put its interests above those of the corporation itself. Anderson's evidence (1981, pp. 144-45) that it was Socal and Texaco that took the initiative, moved by the risk-avoidance preferences of their top executives, refutes these speculations.

[7] The essentials of this story are in Anderson, 1981, ch. 5. See also U.S. Senate, 1952; U.S. Senate, 1974b, appendix 2; U.S. Senate, 1975, ch. 2; and Blair, 1976. For the draft contract between Jersey and the Anglo-Iranian Oil Company, see National Archives (Record Group 59, Box 4231, file no. 800.6363/1-2847), material dated December 20, 1946, with a covering letter from a Jersey official to the head of the Petroleum Division of the Department of State, indicating that this contract was the basic document in the transaction.

would be to reduce production from Iraq, where CFP shared an interest. CFP therefore sought participation in Aramco itself, along with Jersey and Socony. In addition, the French government protested strongly, holding the U. S. government responsible and threatening to take direct action in France against Jersey in retaliation for its actions.[8]

CFP's demand for participation in Aramco was blocked by King 'Abd al-'Aziz of Saudi Arabia, who declared that he would not agree to the sale of any part of Aramco to a non-American firm (Anderson, 1981, p. 155). Nevertheless, the State Department, which had been following the intercompany negotiations closely, recognized the seriousness of French protests. In February 1947 Paul Nitze, Deputy Director of the Office of International Trade Policy, suggested that the issue could be resolved without dissolving the Red Line Agreement and antagonizing the French, if Jersey sold its interest in IPC to Socony and entered Aramco alone.[9] Jersey and Socony, however, rejected this proposition.

The terms worked out among the IPC members dissolved the Red Line Agreement but gave the French the right to draw larger shares of oil from IPC production than their proportionate holdings in IPC would have allowed and involved a commitment by Jersey and Socony to support increased IPC production. Protracted negotiations took place with Gulbenkian, who reportedly told John C. Case of Socony that he simply would not respect himself unless he "drove as good a bargain as possible." Gulbenkian's ace in the hole was the fact that he had filed suit in London, threatening to open the complex affairs of IPC to the public; the day before arguments were to begin, the suit was settled out of court.[10]

---

[8] See dispatches of January 14 and 20, 1947, from the Embassy in London to the State Department (Record Group 59, Box 4231, file no. 800.6363/1-1447 and 800.6363/1-2047).

[9] Memo from Paul Nitze to Will Clayton, February 21, 1947 (National Archives, Record Group 59, Box 4231, file no. 800.6363/2-2147).

[10] Anderson, 1981, p. 159. The Church subcommittee alleged in 1975 that "although Exxon and Mobil eventually reached an IPC settlement the French never forgave the Americans for keeping them out of Saudi Arabia" (U.S. Senate, 1975, p. 55). No evidence, however, is adduced for this assertion, and no trace of it appears in Anderson's account. Indeed, certain pieces of evidence suggest the contrary. The Embassy in London reported on March 14, 1947, that the French seemed to like the idea that they could purchase more than their regular quota of oil from the IPC (Record Group 59, Box 4231, file no. 841.6363/3-1447). On May 29, 1947, the Embassy reported satisfaction in London and said that "the only cloud on the I.P.C. horizon at the moment is the difficulty the major partners are having with Gulbenkian" (Record Group 59, Box 4231, file no. 800.6363/5-2947).

This episode illustrates several important points about hegemonic cooperation. First, although cooperation in the sense of mutual policy adjustment was eventually achieved, the process of achieving it was certainly not a harmonious one. Cooperation arose from the reality and prospect of discord. Second, the difficulties of cooperation in this case reflect in part the absence of agreed-upon institutions to establish a framework for bargaining. Indeed, the desire of the United States and of U.S. companies to destroy the old regime of the IPC led to the struggle in the first place.

The eventual success of U.S. attempts to control Arab oil also illustrates the fact that hegemony was a real phenomenon, even if American officials, continually seeking to solve more and more difficult problems, often had trouble achieving their objectives. The negotiations with Britain for an Anglo-American Petroleum Agreement were not as difficult as the internal bargaining within the United States. In the Red Line negotiations, the British, French, and Gulbenkian could all be brought to agreement through a combination of threats to break the old arrangements and promises to pay off partners who would cooperate in the desired restructuring of Middle Eastern holdings. Hegemonic cooperation as we have defined it occurred, although no formal international regime was brought into being.

The compatibility of hegemony and cooperation indicates once again that international cooperation does not depend on substantive equality among states. To emphasize the "inequality of nations" (Tucker, 1977) is not to foreclose prospects for mutual adjustment of policy, although it does imply that different, and unequal, adjustments will be made by the powerful and by the weak. Indeed, it could be argued that cooperation in the postwar period depended on the prior establishment of U.S. dominance. This was true in oil. After the brusque actions of American companies and the American government to abrogate the Red Line Agreement had ensured American supremacy in Saudi Arabia, the United States deigned to assure Europe that it would receive ample oil supplies, at least as long as European governments continued to defer to U.S. leadership. Likewise, in financial and commercial policy, the United States had ensured its predominance over Britain before it switched to providing positive incentives for cooperation through the aid programs of the Marshall Plan. Britain's reserves were kept within a range sufficient to allow it to finance its wartime purchases, but too small to give Britain financial independence after hostilities had ceased, and strong efforts were made to persuade Britain to agree to dismantle the discriminatory trade barriers that had been erected during the 1930s (Kolko, 1968, pp. 280-94). American pres-

sure continued after the war, most notably in connection with negotiations for the British Loan of 1946 (Gardner, 1956/1980, pp. 188-
207). As in petroleum policy, establishment of dominance preceded
the distribution of economic benefits.

The frustrations that faced American policymakers in the oil issue-
area resulted less from the efforts of other countries than from the
nature of American politics and society. This did not mean that the
ultimate objective of securing Arab oil supplies had to be abandoned—
on the contrary, it was achieved—but rather that the vehicles for U.S.
policy had to be adapted to the realities of American society. Plans
for government ownership, or for intergovernmental control of production and prices, were abandoned in favor of support for the expansion of private corporations abroad and for their transnational
political strategies. The nature of hegemonic cooperation in oil—*ad
hoc* rather than highly institutionalized—was shaped both by the opportunities abroad for extension of national power and expropriation
of wealth and by the constraints engendered by capitalism and pluralist
politics at home.

The Sterling-Dollar Oil Problem

Even during the war the British government anticipated a shortage
of foreign exchange in the postwar years and insisted, in negotiations
on a petroleum agreement, on "the right of each country to draw its
consumption requirements, to the extent that may be considered necessary, from the production in its territories or in which rights are
held by its nationals."[11] In 1949 Great Britain decided to take such
measures to save on dollar costs by discriminating against American-
owned oil companies, contrary to agreements reached between the
British government and U.S. companies in the 1920s and 1930s. British
measures not only affected imports into the United Kingdom but also
reduced sales of American firms in countries such as Argentina and
Egypt, with which Britain made barter agreements, providing oil in
return for other goods. The British government in addition, in the
spring of 1949, ordered British bankers

to refuse to transfer funds in payment for American-supplied oil
from sterling balances in London of countries outside the sterling

[11] Memorandum, "The Petroleum Division," October 1944, p. 35 (Box 48, Harley
Notter files, National Archives, Record Group 59. Cited in Anderson, 1981, ch. 3, n.
73.

area. Consequently, such countries as Finland, Sweden, Norway and Denmark, which were so short of dollars as to require that all or part of their oil needs be purchased with sterling, were unable to draw on their sterling balances in the United Kingdom to pay for imports supplied by American companies. Consequently, they had to buy sterling oil (Larson et al., 1971, p. 706).

The U.S. companies protested, claiming that Britain's actions were meant less to save dollars than to strengthen the position of British companies in the world oil industry at the expense of their American competitors (Brown and Opie, 1953, p. 226; Larson et al., 1971, p. 707; Anderson, 1981, ch. 6). The glut of oil that had emerged, at current prices, made it impossible for the companies to sell all the pertroleum they could produce; so the Americans' loss was the British firms' gain. Furthermore, a cutback in markets for American-owned Eastern Hemisphere oil was seen in the State Department as having ominous implications for America's security interests.

The situation raises serious security, political and economic problems in view of the fact that the foreign oil concessions, refining and marketing facilities and organizations of American oil companies depend upon the maintenance of foreign market outlets. If the American oil companies producing abroad are faced with the shrinkage in the market for their output they must necessarily curtail production. If the American companies are forced to cut back production at the same time the British companies are expanding their output, the former are placed in a difficult political and financial position which may in turn prejudice U.S. national security interests.[12]

An internal State Department memo in December focused directly on the implications of British policy for the U.S. position in Saudi Arabia:

Loss of one-quarter annual revenue might stalemate Saudi Arabia progress while neighboring states advance, jeopardizing the unique cooperation and friendship now existing between U.S. and Saudi

[12] Memorandum of Conversation of a meeting called by Paul Nitze of the Bureau of Economic Affairs, Department of State, on April 9, 1949, "to discuss the major aspects of the dollar-sterling oil problem and the views thereon of the interested offices of the Department" (Record Group 59, Box 4232, file no. 800.6363/4-949).

Arabia. Western orientation of Saudi Arabia, which counters Arab reaction to Western support of Israel, would suffer.[13]

Not everyone in the American government saw the national interest and the interests of the Aramco partners as so closely linked. Oil was selling at several times its cost of production, yet neither the American nor the British companies were seriously considering reducing prices further as a response to stagnation in demand. The British financial situation was much more serious than the plight of already wealthy American oil companies.

The important interests of the United States would not be served if the dollar and other economic drain on the British is maintained at anywhere near the present or projected levels. $710 million in fiscal 1950 and well over $600 million in 1953 seems [sic] an impossible drain for anyone to contemplate. The absolute maximum savings of dollars and economic resources on the sterling area's oil accounts are [sic] desperately needed in view of Britain's present balance of payments and budgetary positions and the uncertain outlook for future ECA [Economic Cooperation Administration] appropriations. . . . It would sound very badly to have it publicized that the Government imposed serious burdens on the British economy, thereby nullifying part of the U.S. foreign aid program, in order to win for the five big American oil companies in the Persian Gulf the unique privilege denied to all American farmers and other American businesses of selling for sterling in third countries, on the ground of threat to the U.S. national interest, when the companies are selling Persian Gulf oil at a price between three and five times the costs of its production.[14]

The problem was essentially one of adjustment costs. Who should have to pay the costs of adjusting to a slacker oil market? Different

[13] "Working Paper, Near East Conference," December 20, 1949, p. 4 (box 2, records of the Petroleum Division, Record Group 59). Anderson also refers to this working paper, considering it as expressing "the basic State Department position for the duration of the 'dollar oil' crisis" (1981, ch. 6, p. 186, n. 94).

[14] Personal memo of George Eddy of the Office of International Finance, Treasury Department, mentioned in a memo from Eddy to Henry Labouisse in the State Department on December 16, 1949 (Record Group 59, Box 4232, file no. 800.6363/12-1649). Eddy's personal memo had somehow fallen into the hands of the British, who were using it in their arguments with the American government. Raymond Mikesell, in the Department of State, also criticized high oil price policies: "I hope that some consideration will be given to the consumer, who thus far has been the forgotten man in this picture! " (Record Group 59, Box 4232, file no. 841.6363/7-649 CS/RA).

possible outcomes were associated with different patterns of adjustment:

1) Intense price cutting could have taken place, sharply reducing
the cost of imported oil in Europe and elsewhere. This would have
continued a trend encouraged by the ECA, which exerted significant
downward pressure on prices, leading to a fall in the per barrel "company take" in the Middle East from $1.52 in 1948 to $1.14 in 1949
(Brown and Opie, 1953, pp. 227-30; Maull, 1980, p. 211).

2) The United States could have accepted greater oil imports, thus
reducing excess supply on world markets, at the expense of U.S. *domestic* production. American independent firms would have borne
much of the cost of adjustment.

3) Great Britain could have withdrawn its restrictions on American
companies' operations. In this case, the burden of adjustment would
have fallen chiefly on the British economy, since the dollar drain would
not have been reduced.

4) The United States and Britain could have *jointly* forced adjustment costs onto others by requiring purchasers of oil outside the United
States and Britain "to pay at least the dollar cost in dollars of the oil
supplied." This was the essence of a plan presented in November 1949
by W. L. Faust of Socony. His was a proposal for a duopolistic regime,
which would extract resources from countries other than the United
States and Britain for the benefit of U.S. and British oil companies.
As the U.S. Counselor for Economic Affairs in London noted, "of
course, many consumers would object, but if all American and British
oil were marketed in this pattern they would have no alternative but
to accept it." Nitze argued similarly that "it may be desirable for the
Governments of U.S. and U.K. to attempt to regulate, on a formal or
informal basis, the production and flow of oil products. Competition
in the usual sense is unlikely, and probably undesirable."[15]

5) Great Britain could have permitted U.S. companies to sell oil for
sterling outside the sterling area, only converting into dollars the dollar

[15] The quotes all come from documents in the National Archives of the United States
(Record Group 59, Box 4232): 1) Memorandum of Conversation of meeting between
B. Brewster Jennings, President, Socony-Vacuum Oil Company, Inc., and various members of the Department of State staff, December 21, 1949 (file no. 841.6363/12-2149);
2) letter of December 2, 1949, from Don C. Bliss, Counselor for Economic Affairs of
the U.S. Embassy in London, to Henry R. Labouisse, Jr., Office of British and Northern
European Affairs, Department of State (file no. 800.6363/12-249); and 3) Memorandum
of Conversation of a meeting called by Paul Nitze of the Bureau of Economic Affairs,
Department of State, April 9, 1949, cited above in note 12.

cost of that oil: "unconverted pounds would be used by United States oil companies to purchase goods and services from the sterling area." This arrangement would have removed the discrimination against American firms vis-à-vis British firms while, according to Caltex (a Socal-Texaco joint venture) and American officials who supported its scheme, not increasing the dollar drain on Britain beyond what would be incurred by *British* companies increasing their production abroad.[16] This was an attempt to divide the adjustment costs between American and British firms, since the latter would lose the competitive advantages conferred on them by discriminatory British measures. Costs of adjustment would also be shared by American exporters of nonoil products, which would be discriminated against by the restrictions on the American oil companies' ability to purchase goods for dollars. As a tactic, it was clever because it took the avowed British purpose of protecting its currency reserves literally while devising measures to achieve this goal that would not also give British oil companies government-created advantages over their American counterparts.

The first three solutions were vetoed by the powerful actors on whom adjustment costs would have fallen. Neither the companies nor the governments wanted to solve the problem of an oil glut by adopting the first course of reducing prices. The firms' reasons for rejecting this solution are obvious. On the government side, Britain did not use sterling devaluation, in 1949, to encourage British companies to undersell U.S. firms or to prevent British companies from increasing their profits from oil for which costs were incurred in sterling. British officials were presumably worried about the effects of lower prices on oil company profits (which were shared by the government through its partial ownership of British Petroleum), as well as the impact of lower profits on Britain's balance of payments. Those American officials concerned with Saudi Arabia and other producing countries would not have been happy with the prospective effects of lower oil prices on relations with these states. The second solution, acceptance of more imports by the United States, ran into the same problem as the Anglo-American Petroleum Agreement: resistance by U.S. domestic producers. "A solution on this basis would be strongly opposed by U.S. independent producers, and it would probably not permit nearly

[16] For the quotation and the argument, see a memo to Ambassador Childs from R. Funkhouser, "Background on Current U.S.-U.K. Oil Talks" (National Archives, Record Group 59, Box 4232, no file number, no date). It appears to have been written in September 1949.

as large an expansion of U.S. output in the Middle East as U.S. companies have been planning."[17] The third possibility, withdrawal of all restrictions, was staunchly resisted by Britain.

The other two schemes would have shifted adjustment costs away from immediately involved powerful actors. In its proposal for the U.S.–British condominium, the Faust Plan resembled the Anglo-American Petroleum Agreement of 1944. According to a recent account, this proposal was unattractive to the British government because Britain "retained a political interest in maintaining a viable sterling area" (Kapstein, 1983, p. 16). The United States had similar reservations, since many of these peripheral countries had become U.S. clients. Transferring part of the dollar crisis to other oil-consuming countries meant increasing the burden on U.S. foreign aid to these states. Furthermore,

> The "third" indicative countries, faced with paying a portion of the cost of petroleum in dollars, might demand similar treatment for their own exports of other commodities. . . . If this pricing policy became common we would be introducing an additional complicating element in international trade that seems clearly undesirable. Our general policy is in the opposite direction; for example, in our work on European integration our objective is to avoid the need for dollar settlements.[18]

Although the great sympathy within the U.S. executive branch, and in the Congress, for the oil companies seems to have prevented the government from rejecting the Faust Plan out of hand, the Caltex proposal (solution 5) was more congenial because it did not involve third-party complications and resulting threats to broader American interests. Thus by December 1949 the Caltex proposal had essentially become the basis of the U.S. position.

> After extended interagency discussion, the U.S. Government has proposed to the British that American companies be allowed to sell part of their production to third countries against sterling payment. U.S. companies would be allowed to convert into dollars

---

[17] Memo from Paul Nitze of the Bureau of Economic Affairs to the Secretary of State, April 27, 1949 (Record Group 59, Box 4232, file no. 800.6363/4-2749).

[18] Memo from Mr. Rosenson of the State Department Monetary Affairs Staff to Henry R. Labouisse, Jr., Office of British and Northern European Affairs (Record Group 59, Box 4232, file no. 800.6363/12-1349), December 13, 1949.

an amount equal to dollar outlays British companies would have to make to replace equivalent existing U.S. production capacity.

Acceptance of this proposal by the British would have ended the discriminatory advantages that British companies were then, according to the United States, gaining as a result of British government policy and would have protected American firms from unfair British competition.

British companies are expanding at rates double normal estimates of increased demand and using surplus oil to displace United States oil through currency and trade restriction rather than through competitive actions such as price reductions, superior products, efficiency, etc.[19]

Yet the British government not only failed to accept this proposal but, in December 1949, imposed new restrictions requiring affiliates of American companies to buy oil for import into the sterling area from British and British–Dutch companies rather than from American-owned firms (even members of their own group). "An American owned affiliate thereafter could import oil from sources owned by American companies only insofar as the volume of oil required to meet its needs was beyond what the companies having sterling status could supply. Jersey oil thus became marginal in its most important Eastern Hemisphere markets" (Larson et al., 1971, pp. 706-707).

The American companies responded to this attack on their interests both by pressing the U.S. government to intervene more vigorously on their behalf and by entering into direct negotiations with the British government. In January 1950 Tom Connally, then Chairman of the Senate Foreign Relations Committee and a leading spokesman for Texas petroleum interests, advocated a cutoff of all Economic Cooperation Administration assistance to Britain. This was not done, but the ECA did suspend assistance to projects for expanding the British oil industry.[20] In April the State Department "presented a note to the

[19] This quotation and the previous one both come from Working Paper, Near East Conference, December 20, 1949 (Record Group 59, Box 4232, no file number), pp. 1 and 3.

[20] Brown and Opie, 1953, p. 226. Within ECA, Walter Levy, ranking petroleum officer, had pointed out as early as February 1949 the difficulties posed for American companies by ECA plans to finance refinery construction in European countries by European firms. See National Archives, Record Group 59, Box 4232, file no. 800.6363/2-1048, for memo by E. L. McGinnes, Jr., on meeting of International Petroleum Policy Committee, February 10, 1949.

British Government insisting on the right of United States companies to trade anywhere in the sterling area."[21] Having secured the support of the U.S. government, some of the companies negotiated successfully with Britain.

Jersey's Howard Page finally negotiated a complicated but satisfactory settlement directly with the British treasury in May 1950. The British agreed to end gasoline rationing, and Jersey undertook to supply all of the additional gasoline required by its British affiliates with payment in sterling. Instead of remitting profits to the United States in dollars, Jersey would use the sterling proceeds to purchase needed goods and equipment manufactured in Britain. Along with a series of similar agreements worked out by Page in 1950 and 1951, this arrangement essentially solved the dollar oil problem (Anderson, 1981, pp. 186-87).

A key condition in the background facilitating this solution was provided by the economic boom that took place after the Korean War broke out in June of 1950. Increased economic activity quickly eliminated the oil surplus and improved Britain's balance-of-payments position. The outbreak of the Korean War, by stimulating rearmament and preventing a recurrence of serious recession, removed the economic difficulty of oversupply that had created the issue in the first place.

The sterling-dollar oil problem illustrates how discord can arise from interdependence, and in particular from efforts of governments to shift the costs of adjustment onto others. It also illuminates once again the process by which discord, with its political pressures, may lead eventually to cooperation on terms that are affected by the intensity of actors' preferences as well as by their power. The fact that British preferences were so intense imposed constraints on the exercise of U.S. power, and therefore made the outcomes of hegemonic cooperation in this case less asymmetrical than they were in the Red Line Agreement episode. As the theoretical arguments of Harsanyi and March discussed in chapters 2 and 3 would have anticipated, it is impossible to predict accurately outcomes of bargaining merely on the basis of the tangible power resources at the disposal of each side. Although the United

[21] Kolko and Kolko, 1972, p. 461. In a meeting held in December 1949 a Socony representative had "emphasized that the oil companies were convinced that they would be unable to get anywhere with the British unless and until the State Department took a firm position with the British and insisted that a settlement of the matter be reached." Memorandum of Conversation, Department of State, Record Group 59, Box 4232, file no. 841.6363/12-949, December 9, 1949, p. 2.

States could change the rules governing oil concessions in Arabia, it could not exert such easy dominance on issues where British interests were intimately involved and which Britain could in the first instance control through authoritative government action.

The incident also indicates the combination of pursuit of narrowly defined self-interest and concern for alliance management that characterized U.S. hegemonic leadership. The State Department came to the aid of powerful American firms that were being discriminated against; but the desire of the U.S. government to rebuild a liberal-capitalist world political economy inhibited the government from pushing the oil companies' case too hard, or from accepting schemes to force adjustment costs onto countries other than Britain or the United States itself. The sterling-dollar oil controversy illustrates once again the proposition that many of the constraints on a hegemon derive not from lack of power but from the ambition to construct a world order that power makes possible. Seeking to build its own world system, the United States had to be concerned not only about the effects of its own actions on its partners, but also about the effects on third parties of any bilateral deals that it might make. The nets of interdependence cast by a hegemon also entangle itself.

Iran, 1951-54: Intervention and the Consortium

Before and during World War II Britain dominated the oil-producing areas of Iran. The Anglo-Iranian Oil Company (AIOC), which was entirely owned and controlled by British interests, profited immensely from its monopoly of Iranian oil production. By 1950 its net profits were over 33 million pounds sterling, about double its payments for that year to the Iranian government (Shwadran, 1955, table 1, pp. 162-63). In 1950 the Iranian government sought to renegotiate the concession with AIOC, and the United States sought to persuade company officials to accept the 50/50 profit-sharing arrangements that were becoming standard between American companies and host countries. But AIOC refused, and the agreement that was finally reached between the company and the government of General Ali Razmara was so strongly opposed by the Iranian parliament (the Majlis) that it was withdrawn without a vote in December 1950. By early the following May the nationalist Mohammed Mossadegh was premier and Iran had decreed the nationalization of AIOC (Rubin, 1980, pp. 42-53).

AIOC remained intransigent, supported by the British government. The United States first attempted to mediate the dispute. Later, as turmoil in Iran increased and the Soviet-oriented Tudeh Party gained strength, the U.S. Central Intelligence Agency put into action a plan designed to overthrow Mossadegh and put the Shah, who had been deprived of all effective influence on the government, back into power. Aided by thugs whose services were secured with CIA funds, the Iranian army deposed Mossadegh and restored the Shah, who had fled briefly to Italy during the disturbances, to his throne. As a result of this American-sponsored revolution, the old political institutions of Iran were either destroyed or reduced to only symbolic importance, as the Shah became an absolute monarch (Rubin, 1980, pp. 54-94).

This intervention still left the problem of how of restore oil production on terms acceptable to the Shah's government. Iran demanded that U.S. companies be involved in any new arrangement, since Iranian nationalism made it politically impossible to return to a wholly British concession. The State Department therefore arranged a consortium, in which American firms received a 40 percent share of the Iranian operation, with AIOC retaining 40 percent, Shell receiving 14 percent, and CFP, the French company, 6 percent.

As in other cases of American hegemonic leadership, negotiating with the oil companies was in many respects as difficult as dealing with foreign governments. First, the five major U.S. international companies invited to join the consortium professed reluctance to do so, whether genuinely (owing to fear of disrupting delicate oligopolistic arrangements, threatened by oversupply, for keeping oil prices high) or as a way of wheedling additional concessions from the American government.[22] To facilitate agreement by the companies, the State Department successfully urged President Truman in January 1953 to downgrade a pending criminal antitrust suit against the majors to a civil proceeding, and the Department of Justice ruled a year later that American firms' participation in the consortium would not constitute an illegal restraint of trade (U.S. Senate, 1974a; Krasner, 1978a, pp. 125-26).

Original plans for the involvement of only five major U.S. companies

---

[22] George W. Stocking expresses skepticism about the companies' show of reluctance: "it is not clear why they should have been [reluctant]. Iranian oil could not re-enter world markets without causing readjustments in oil commerce, and it would seem more compatible with the interests of existing marketers that they share in control of the process. Moreover, they were not a group that had hitherto evidenced an unwillingness to share in virtually riskless but highly profitable oil ventures" (1970, p. 157). This ambiguity illustrates a more general point: in any bargaining situation, strategically oriented actors will be willing to conceal their true preferences if doing so provides them with an advantage. Thus it is difficult to be confident about which parties made more concessions, without access to confidential internal documents of participants detailing their true positions prior to negotiations.

had to be altered at the insistence of a group of eight independent American companies, which wound up with a total of 5 percent of the Iranian concession. These firms, at least, were not reluctant to admit their desire for access to cheap Iranian crude.

For the additional members of the Iranian Consortium, their minor share proved an exceedingly profitable investment and the prospectus which had been drawn up by a large firm of chartered accountants showed clearly for all concerned to see that even after the compensation payable to Anglo-Iranian any stake in that venture was like getting a "license to print money" (Stocking, 1970, p. 158, quoting Frankel, 1966, pp. 95-96).

The Iranian episode illustrates the variety of instruments at the disposal of the U.S. government. The State Department became involved late in a dispute between Britain and Iran whose origins it could not control, but the United States was nevertheless able, through political intervention and its links with the Iranian military, to bring about a revolution in Iranian politics. It then secured the establishment of a new oil consortium that provided American companies with 40 percent of Iranian production for a relatively small outlay of funds. Political, military, and economic resources were used in combination with one another. The hegemonic combination of expropriation and control on the one hand and cooperation (with allies, whether long-standing or created for the occasion) on the other was never clearer. The remarkable part of the trick was that the American government, and American firms, profited immensely while appearing to be reluctant to become involved and only to be doing so to aid in reconciliation, economic development, and the provision of public order. Hegemonic leadership was never more rewarding than this!

The limits on American freedom of action were largely set by its own oil companies. To pursue its strategic goals, the U.S. government had to make concessions on antitrust enforcement: firms would act as instruments of government policy, but they would not do so "for free." The State Department also had to include independents in the consortium. External strength was once again combined with relative weakness at home.

The Emergency Oil Lift Program, 1956-57

In July 1956 a series of disputes erupted between Egypt on the one hand and the United States, Britain, and France on the other. On July 19 the United States withdrew its offer to contribute $56 million toward financing the Aswan Dam; one week later Egypt nationalized the Suez Canal. This action led to an international crisis, the climax of which involved the invasion of Egypt by Israeli, British, and French forces in late October and the collapse of that invasion under pressure from the United States as well as the resistance of Egypt and threats from the Soviet Union. As a result of the military actions, the Suez Canal, which at that time was the main route for oil shipments between the Persian Gulf and Europe, was suddenly blocked, leading to a potentially severe oil shortage in Europe (Engler, 1961, pp. 260-63; Johnson, 1957; Klebanoff, 1974, especially p. 119). The reaction of the U.S. government to this crisis provides a clear illustration of hegemonic cooperation. The United States used its great economic and political resources, and its links with major oil companies, to cope successfully with the oil shortfall and achieve its own political purposes in the process.

Immediately following nationalization of the Suez Canal, the United States established a Middle East Emergency Committee (MEEC), under the provisions of the Defense Production Act of 1950. The MEEC was composed of fifteen major U.S.-based oil companies. These companies declared that they could not devise detailed alternative tanker schedules for a crisis whose characteristics were still unknown; but they established the organizational structure of the MEEC and acquired the requisite antitrust waivers from the government to allow them to coordinate among themselves. Planning was left to the companies; the role of the government, according to the director of the Office of Defense Mobilization, was to encourage voluntary agreements among the companies and to exempt them from antitrust legislation.[23] In September the British, Dutch, and French governments sponsored the establishment of a parallel committee composed of the major European-based oil companies—Shell, British Petroleum, and CFP (OEEC, 1957, p. 21).

In response to the British–French–Israeli invasion of Egypt, the United States suspended the operations of the MEEC, which did not meet again until December 3, 1956 (Engler, 1961, pp. 261, 307; U.S. Senate, 1957, pp. 2543-48). The U.S. government sought to use the threat of an oil shortage as one of a number of measures designed to induce Britain and France, during November, to withdraw their troops from Suez. By the end of November U.S. actions were clearly having the desired effects, and it seemed to American leaders that further pressure

[23] Testimony of Arthur Flemming, Director, Office of Defense Mobilization, in U.S. Senate, 1957, p. 12.

on the Europeans was unnecessary and would weaken the Atlantic alliance. President Eisenhower ordered reactivation of the MEEC to permit it not only to arrange tanker schedules but to enter into arrangements on a collective basis with the Organization for European Economic Cooperation (OEEC), in order to plan properly for oil allocations. The Oil Committee of the OEEC established a Petroleum Industry Emergency Group from the industry (involving U.S. as well as European companies), which advised the Oil Committee on procedures for allocation of scarce oil supplies among the European countries.[24] The United States insisted that the OEEC rather than the United States itself or the companies take the responsibility for allocating oil by country. One reason for this demand was to deflect Arab criticism of the United States, which, it was feared, would be more intense if America took a more direct role in petroleum allocation.[25]

Yet the United States played far from a passive role. It urged the OEEC to take immediate action to allocate supplies on a pro rata basis; and the MEEC reinforced the pressure to do so by deciding on December 28 not to cooperate on allocation arrangements in Europe without an OEEC decision, which was eventually forthcoming on January 7. Meanwhile, the MEEC approved tanker schedules allowing more efficient shipments of crude oil and refined products from Venezuela and the United States to Europe, replacing in good measure the long haul around the Cape of Good Hope for oil from the Persian Gulf (U.S. Senate, 1957, p. 1983).

During the early phase of the crisis—between the closure of the canal and early January—the problem was essentially one of transportation: "not one of a shortage of oil but a shortage of the means of bringing it to Europe" (OEEC, 1958, p. 33). If normal tanker patterns had been maintained, Europe would have received only about 60 percent of its estimated needs. Yet reallocation of tanker patterns was remarkably easy; indeed, even before the MEEC was reactivated, international oil companies had increased their shipments from the United States to Western Europe from an average of 50,000 barrels per day to 370,000 barrels per day and had increased the flow of oil to Europe by a further 224,000 barrels per day by increasing shipments

[24] U.S. House of Representatives, 1957, pp. 111-13; U.S. Senate, 1957, p. 595. Eisenhower declared on November 30, 1956, that "the contemplated coordination of industry efforts will insure the most efficient use of tankers and the maximum availability of petroleum product." *Public Papers of the President*, 1956, p. 902.

[25] For discussions of relations between the MEEC and the OEEC, see U.S. Senate, 1957, pp. 1884-1931, 2451-52, 2538-49, and 2583-89.

from the Caribbean and diverting Middle Eastern crude from the United States to Europe (OEEC, 1958, pp. 29-34).

The more serious problem after the beginning of January was not tanker availability but the supply of crude oil. Increases in shipments from the United States were accomplished largely by drawing down stocks, which could not continue indefinitely. But the Texas Railroad Commission, which controlled production in Texas, refused to increase allowable production in January, and only increased it slightly in February, despite the European crisis. The Commission sought higher oil prices—an increase of 12 percent did take place in early January— and feared a later oil glut if supply were increased too rapidly. Independent Texas producers far from the coast opposed the supply increase because their output was effectively limited by transportation problems and because they would benefit from higher prices. Furthermore, Europe needed heavy crude oil for heating, but U.S. producers feared that as a consequence of increasing shipments of heavy crude to Europe they would be stuck with large supplies of gasoline, which would depress the U.S. market. Thus there was what the *Oil and Gas Journal* called a "transatlantic feud" between the United Kingdom and the Texas Railroad Commission. The Commission wanted the United Kingdom to end gas rationing and purchase gasoline from the United States in return for increased Texas production. European foreign offices were pressuring the State Department for increased production, and the Assistant Secretary of the Interior was calling for increased U.S. production; but the state regulatory agencies dragged their feet.[26]

Finally, President Eisenhower took a direct hand in the matter. In his presidential news conference of February 6. 1957, the following colloquy took place:

> *William McGaffin, Chicago Daily News:* The United States has been lagging on oil deliveries to Western Europe, one reason being that the Texas Control Board has not okayed a step-up in production in Texas. According to latest reports, Great Britain is down to about two weeks' oil supply. What do you intend to do?
>
> *President Eisenhower:* Well, of course, there are certain powers given to the President where he could move into the whole field of state proration. I think the federal government should not disturb the economy of our country except when it has to. On

[26] *Oil and Gas Journal,* January 21, 1957, p. 74; February 4, 1957, p. 80. See also the *Economist* (London), January 12, 1957, pp. 113, 133.

the other hand, I believe that the business concerns of our country, the people that operate the tanker lines, the people that produce the oil, and all the other agencies, including those of the proration boards, should consider where do our long-term interests lie. Certainly they demand a Europe that is not flat on its back economically. . . . Now all of this oil must flow in such a quantity as to fill up every tanker we have operating at maximum capacity. And if that doesn't occur, then we must do something in the way, first, I should say, of conference and argument and, if necessary, we would have to move in some other region or some direction, either with our facilities or with others. But it must be done (*Public Papers of the President*, 1957, p. 124).

Faced with this barely veiled threat of federal action, the Texas Railroad Commission shortly thereafter increased the allowable production for March by 237,000 barrels per day over the February figure, to a point that was 380,000 barrels per day over pre-Suez levels. The big international firms favored the increase, and independents were now willing to go along because stocks had been reduced and prices had been raised during the first two months of the year (*Oil and Gas Journal*, February 25, 1957, p. 78).

Once the increase had been put into effect, the crisis evaporated quickly. With a mild winter, and more Gulf of Mexico oil available, drains on stocks were arrested from February onwards; tanker schedules were cancelled on April 18, 1957, and the activities of the MEEC and its European partner organizations were effectively ended by May (OEEC, 1958, p. 38).

The Emergency Oil Lift Program illustrates hegemonic cooperation at its apogee. The United States was able not only to stop the British–French–Israeli invasion of Egypt but, in the wake of the episode, to induce European governments to decide on oil allocations. The U.S. government used its own oil companies, with their tanker fleets, and its unused petroleum capacity at home, to supply Europe adequately with oil during the winter. After the beginning of December 1956 policy coordination between the U.S. government and the multinational companies, between U.S. and European companies, and between the U.S. and European governments took place relatively smoothly. The United States controlled immense resources that it could redistribute at little cost to itself and was therefore able to extract deference from the Europeans. In return, the United States made adjustments in its own oil production arrangements.

These adjustments, however, encountered resistance from domestic petroleum producers and their political allies. As with the Anglo-American Petroleum Agreement, it was neither foreign governments nor the major international companies but the domestic independents that constituted the major stumbling-blocks to federal government plans. Federal-state policy coordination was so difficult that it required a threat of drastic action to achieve the desired results; U.S.–European coordination was easy by comparison. Successful cooperation abroad to cope with interdependence required decisive political action at home.

Mandatory Oil Import Quotas, 1959-73

Imports of crude oil into the United States almost tripled between 1948 and 1957, leading to demands for protection from the domestic oil industry and from coal producers and mining unions. In 1957 the Eisenhower Administration instituted a voluntary oil import control program, but this quickly proved unworkable. In March of 1959 a presidential proclamation, issued under the authority of the Trade Agreements Extension Act of 1954, established a mandatory quota program, which was administered through a set of increasingly complex regulations by the Oil Import Administration of the Department of the Interior. This program, which remained in effect until 1973, raised domestic oil prices above the world market price and therefore encouraged U.S. domestic production while discouraging imports, which rose much more slowly between 1959 and 1970 than they had in the previous eleven years. Imports accounted for 2.4 percent of total domestic demand in 1948, 16.5 percent in 1959, and 21.9 percent in 1970 (Bohi and Russell, 1978, table 2.1, pp. 22-23).

After 1970, however, American domestic production fell, while demand continued to increase. Although the quota program had always been riddled with exceptions, after 1970 these increased dramatically as its administrators loosened regulations to prevent supply shortages, or dramatic price increases in an inflationary period, at home. By 1973 as much as 35.5 percent of domestic demand was supplied by imported oil. In April of that year the Mandatory Oil Import Program was replaced by a system of license fees, which were sufficiently low that "by early 1973, the importation of petroleum had returned to its pre-1957 regulatory status" (Kalt, 1981, p. 8).

Although the mandatory quota program was justified publicly on the grounds of protecting U.S. national security, it seems clear that the principal motivation of its chief proponents was to protect the domestic oil industry and the coal industry, whose prices had to be consistent with the price of residual fuel oil. Advocates of the quota in Congress were led by independent Southwestern oil producers and Eastern coal interests; the major companies were divided (Bauer, Pool, and Dexter, 1963/1968, pp. 30-39). President Eisenhower and many of his top officials had doubts about the security implications of the proposals. Clarence Randall, Chairman of the Council on Foreign Economic Policy, declared that restricting oil imports could not be justified "on grounds of security or those of economic policy":

> Ostensibly, the program is based upon national security, but if domestic petroleum reserves are required for our defense in war, or our recovery after war, I do not see how we advance toward the objective by using up our existing reserves (memo of December 26, 1958, quoted by Barber, 1981, p. 247).

Attorney General William P. Rogers severely criticized the report on which the final proposal for import quotas was based. Eisenhower himself expressed concern about the effect of quotas on depletion of American domestic reserves and lamented the "tendencies of special interests in the United States to press almost irresistibly for special programs like this" that were in conflict with liberal trade (Barber, 1981, pp. 237, 251). Yet the Administration feared that inaction would lead to Congressional restraints that would provide less leeway for administrative flexibility than a presidential directive.

The Mandatory Oil Import Program was a special interest action, supported by the independent producers—not the international majors—and their allies. Indeed, in the design and administration of the program, "virtually every controversy was resolved against the best interest of the original major company importers" (Bohi and Russell, 1978, p. 17). As predicted by Eisenhower and Randall, the program did deplete domestic petroleum supplies. But evaluating its impact on U.S. national security is more complicated than merely concluding that the program "drained America first."

Throughout the 1960s the quota system kept imports from rising as fast as they otherwise would have. Bohi and Russell (1978) estimate that, under free trade, imports would have constituted 61 percent of consumption in 1970, compared with actual figures of 14.6 percent in 1970 and 35.5 percent in 1973. Thus, as compared to free trade, the quota program meant that the effects of a disruption in the flow of foreign oil would have been less with the quota than without it; perhaps it could be argued that this improved the American position in 1967, when a brief and ineffectual embargo was attempted by some Arab producers after the June War. When the 1973 Arab embargo occurred, the quota meant that extent of adjustment required for the

United States, and the magnitude of the increases in oil prices required, were less than they would have been under free trade. In short, the United States was less *sensitive* to a disruption as a result of the quota.

From a political standpoint, however, the key issue is not merely the economic sensitivity of the United States to a disruption, but its *vulnerability*: that is, how effectively could altered American policies, in the wake of a crisis, make available sufficient quantities of petroleum for the United States and its allies (Keohane and Nye, 1977, p. 15)? An analysis of this question for the years after 1973 is less favorable to the quota policy. The depletion of U.S. reserves meant that even over a seven-year period, during which world oil prices increased tenfold, U.S. production of crude oil *fell*. Imports rose by over 10 percent in terms of volume (IEA, 1982a, p. 376).

The costs of the quota program are even clearer when compared with those of other programs that could have been adopted to achieve energy security. It has been estimated that replacing the quota system by a tax on consumption set to make the average price of oil during the 1960s the same as it actually was would have reduced domestic oil production by about 40 percent by 1969. Imports would have risen sharply, but the increased sensitivity produced by this shift could have been counteracted by emergency storage and standby production capacity, paid for with the proceeds of the tax. The total resource cost would have been about the same as that of the import quota program, and more reserves would have remained in the ground for use when the "seven lean years" came. A combination of a tariff plus storage and standby capacity could have been even more cost-effective (Bohi and Russell, 1978, pp. 324-28). Such measures would have depleted U.S. reserves more slowly, while retaining the capacity to respond to an embargo.

The Mandatory Oil Import Program was not necessarily worse from a security point of view than free trade in oil. Under free trade, there would have been more oil in the ground, but not all of it would have been available, both for physical and economic reasons. Furthermore, if the consumerist critics of "big oil" in the 1950s and 1960s had succeeded in securing cheaper petroleum, consumption would have risen and overall dependence might have been even higher. Yet a better American oil security policy than the Mandatory Oil Import program could surely have been devised, as President Eisenhower was well aware.

The Mandatory Oil Import Program does not constitute an effort at cooperation. On the contrary, it was a unilateral substitute for international agreements that would have required greater adjustment by the United States. As such, it reflects the domestic political constraints that inhibited even hegemonic cooperation at the height of American preponderance. Compared to hypothetical superior policies, the Mandatory Oil Import Program helped to undermine the power of the United States, as domestic oil supplies were depleted. Thus the effects of this program, as we will see in the next chapter, made it more difficult to maintain patterns of hegemonic cooperation in the 1970s than it could have been, since the United States possessed a smaller margin of surplus resources to be exchanged for deference and new, post-hegemonic modes of cooperating had not yet had time to emerge.

CONCLUSIONS

The United States did indeed follow a strategy of hegemonic leadership during the 1950s. America was not able simply to dictate terms to the world, but it had multiple ways of providing incentives to others to conform to its preferences. In trade and money the United States supported formal international regimes, while in oil it backed the more narrowly based, company-run regime and engaged in independent action when that seemed necessary. In the short to intermediate term, this strategy worked: the cooperation that it fostered aided the economic and political recovery of Europe and Japan, and maintained the alliance solidarity that the American government sought during the Cold War. In the longer run, however, its success was thwarted, since it neither institutionalized an international regime that might have coped with rising threats to the security of European, Japanese, and, increasingly, American oil imports, nor did it maintain a strong resource base for the exercise of American power.

The story of hegemonic cooperation stimulates reflections on three more general problems in the analysis of international political economy: the relationship between power and interdependence; the problem of maintaining hegemony; and the nature of connections between hegemony on the one hand and international regimes and cooperation on the other.

At one level, these twenty years could be described in terms of the growth of "complex interdependence," involving growing transnational, intergovernmental, and transgovernmental relationships among the advanced capitalist countries (Keohane and Nye, 1977, ch. 2). Force was banished as a direct, explicit means of influence among their governments, and the connections between domestic political economy and international political economy were close, as illustrated

177

by the Emergency Oil Lift Program of 1956-57. Yet it would be mistaken to infer from these patterns of interdependence that power had been eliminated from international political economy. On the contrary, complex interdependence, and the relatively benign attention that the United States gave to the political economy of Western capitalism, rested on American industrial and financial dominance, as well as on American political and military power. The Cold War legitimated U.S. leadership, but the ability of the United States to carry out its strategy of redistribution depended on its own previous measures to control and exploit oil supplies abroad as well as to ensure the central position of the United States in multilateral trade and monetary regimes. As we have seen, the United States was less accommodating when it was seeking to establish its position of dominance than it later became after that position was secure. In each issue-area, the redistributive phase of U.S. hegemonic leadership—aid, acceptance of trade discrimination, and oil shipments to Europe—followed the establishment of American control over the essential power resources and rules involved.

During the war American planners had overestimated British capabilities and had followed a tough line toward the United Kingdom to ensure that the United States could secure the rules that it wanted in the postwar system. The restrictions imposed by the United States, through Lend-Lease, on British wartime reserves, and the stringent terms of the loan granted to Britain in 1946, reflected this aim. Only when British weakness had been revealed in 1947 was there a decisive change toward a redistributive policy in which the United States exchanged tangible benefits for political influence. Once the dominance of the United States had become clear, it became appropriate to shift from a vigorous policy of breaking down trade barriers and asserting control over oil resources to one of providing support for rebuilding European economies, temporarily accepting discrimination against American exports, and assuring America's allies secure and reasonably priced access to oil from the Middle East and, when necessary, the Western Hemisphere as well.

The second issue raised above is the problem of maintaining hegemony. To be successful in the long term, a hegemonic strategy must recreate the conditions for its own existence. Pursuit of a strategy must generate strength, or hegemony will eventually collapse. Any strategy of hegemonic leadership must therefore seek to maintain the national base of resources upon which governmental influence and leadership rest. From this perspective, the failure of U.S. foreign policy lay not in American leaders' attitudes toward international cooperation, but

178

in their inability to implement their preferred policies in the face of domestic political constraints. Special interests prevented both the formation of an international regime for oil and the closely related implementation of farsighted strategic policies of conservation, which officials of the State Department during the war were perceptive and public-spirited enough to envisage and support. The later imposition of mandatory import quotas further accelerated the exhaustion of American petroleum resources and therefore U.S. power resources in the world political economy. The decline of American hegemony was foreshadowed in 1945, with the defeat of the Petroleum Agreement, even before the policy of hegemonic leadership had been implemented.

Thus the United States contracted a disease of the strong: refusal to adjust to change. Small states do not have the luxury of deciding whether or how fast to adjust to external change. They do not seek adjustment; it is thrust upon them. Powerful countries can postpone adjustment. The stronger they are, and the less responsive they have to be to other countries, the longer it can be postponed. For Spain in the sixteenth century, discoveries of bullion in America had disastrous effects; for Britain in the nineteenth century, the existence of the Empire, into which it could retreat, fatally delayed an effective national reaction to industrial decline. The overwhelming economic superiority of the United States during the 1950s, reinforced by the deference that it received as the head of a Cold War alliance and its failure to join an international regime that might have exerted some pressure on it, allowed it to permit domestic interests to accumulate privileges. Since hegemons do not face the external constraints that prevent smaller countries from succumbing to demands of internal special interest groups, they seem to be particularly subject to the sclerotic tendencies that Mancur Olson, Jr., has recently emphasized as a source of economic decline (Olson, 1982; Kindleberger, 1983).

America's strategy of hegemonic leadership, finally, shows that hegemony and cooperation are often complementary rather than incompatible. Amercian hegemony coexisted easily with extensive cooperation: mutual adjustment of policies took place, perhaps to an unprecedented extent among independent countries in peacetime, during the years after World War II. The monetary and trade regimes built in the 1940s and 1950s rested on mutual interests as well as on American power; so did the U.S.-controlled redistributive arrangements for oil. The fact that the United States was so superior to its trading partners in competitive terms meant that it could afford to help rebuild Europe without continually worrying about the consequences for American business, although the restrictions placed on aid to the European oil industry during the sterling-dollar oil controversy indicate that where competitors were strong, the U.S. government was concerned about the fortunes of its own companies. Presumably the willingness of the United States to provide certain collective goods such as monetary stability was enhanced by its size, which increased the absolute value of the benefits that it received from their provision even without compensation from "free riders" (Olson and Zeckhauser, 1966)

Yet one of the striking things about the postwar period is that many of the most important goods that the United States provided were not collective at all. Loans and oil supplies could be distributed to selected recipients; countries that did not behave in ways regarded by the United States as acceptable could be excluded. The principle of reciprocity in trade policy meant that countries refusing to abide by GATT rules and to liberalize their practices could be prevented from enjoying access to the huge American market on favorable terms. Much of what the United States did—providing tangible benefits and receiving influence over the pattern of rules in return—was arranged in ways designed to avoid rewarding free riders. To take another example, the Emergency Oil Lift Program of 1956-57 was clearly conditioned on compliance by potential recipients with U.S. policy in the Middle East.

Perhaps the most important collective good provided by the United States during its period of hegemony was the increased certainty about future patterns of behavior that hegemony brought. As argued in Part II, uncertainty reduces willingness to make agreements in world politics. Often simultaneous exchanges cannot be made: one party has to accept political or economic "credit" in return for benefits that it confers. Since no legal system exists that can enforce eventual repayment against strong independent states, there is always uncertainty about whether these "debts" will be repaid, and their value is therefore discounted. Hegemony tends to reduce such uncertainty in two ways. The hegemon is likely to be more willing to enter into agreements in which it makes initial sacrifices for future gains, precisely because it expects to have considerable control over the behavior of its partners in the future: it can make life difficult for them if they fail to live up to their obligations. The smaller states, at the same time, know that the hegemon is likely to enforce a general pattern of rules. They may therefore be more willing to deal both with the hegemon—because, to the rule-maintainer, precedents and reputation are so important that cheating and double-crossing strategies are costly—and with other countries, since these states may be kept in line by the dominant power. Hegemony therefore provides what otherwise has to be constructed more laboriously through multilateral international regimes: standards for conduct, information about others' likely patterns of behavior, and ways of providing incentives to states to comply with rules. These effects of hegemony may be reinforced by international regimes, but when hegemony is sufficiently onesided, as in petroleum, formal intergovernmental regimes do not appear essential. As Realists emphasize, the operation of international institutions is conditioned by the distribution and exercise of power. Yet if hegemony can substitute for the operation of international regimes, it follows that a decline in hegemony may increase the demand for international regimes. Although this by no means guarantees that international regimes will appear in response to governments' need for them, it does suggest that, after hegemony, regimes may become potentially more important as means of limiting uncertainty and promoting mutually beneficial agreements.

· 9 ·

THE INCOMPLETE DECLINE OF
HEGEMONIC REGIMES

As we saw in the last chapter, U.S. hegemonic leadership fostered a pattern of asymmetrical cooperation, in which the United States made some adjustments to the needs of its allies and partners while imposing other adjustments on them. By the early 1950s these patterns of cooperation were institutionalized in formal international regimes to help regulate international monetary relations and trade in manufactured goods; in oil, informal arrangements were constructed by the United States and major international oil companies to ensure Western and Japanese access to Middle Eastern oil at prices that were highly remunerative to the companies. In part, cooperation among the advanced industrialized countries reflected the complementary interests of the United States and its partners. Given the desire of European and Japanese governments to achieve rapid economic growth with democratic political institutions and capitalist economies, they had good reasons to join the Americanocentric system.

These complementarities of interest were not entirely natural. On the contrary, American leaders worked energetically to ensure that the ruling coalitions in power in Europe and Japan sympathized with the principles that the United States espoused for the world political economy. The United States provided many positive incentives to Europe and Japan. The American government could give aid to Europe and Japan without worrying that this would lead either to a weak dollar or to severe foreign competition for American industries. European and Japanese governments, committed to both democratic politics and membership in the capitalist world economic system, relied on the United States for military protection; and on economic issues they realized that they had to reach accommodations with the United States if they were to recover from wartime destruction.

As the U.S. share of the advanced industrialized countries' material resources fell, American policies changed and the regimes set up in the 1940s and 1950s began to decay. This is, of course, what would have been predicted by the theory of hegemonic stability, discussed in chapter 3. In analyzing this process, the present chapter provides evidence for two propositions discussed in chapter 3: that hegemony facilitates cooperation, and that the decline of hegemony is likely to put hegemonic regimes under stress.

Nevertheless, it would be mistaken to infer from this evidence that cooperation is impossible without hegemony. We have seen in Part II that there are strong theoretical reasons for believing that hegemonic cooperation, which relies on a dominant power making rules and providing incentives for others to conform with those rules, does not constitute the only possible form of international cooperation. The argument that nonhegemonic cooperation can occur is supported by the evidence in this chapter that the decline of cooperation was not complete. Some cooperation persisted in money and trade, within the framework of altered international regimes. In petroleum, a bifurcated pattern emerged, with the Organization of Petroleum Exporting Countries on one side and the oil-importing countries of the OECD, centered on the International Energy Agency, on the other. Although the character of international regimes changed in all three areas over the twenty-year period, in some cases dramatically, the persistence of attempts at cooperation is as marked as the decay of the old regimes.

Taken as a whole, the argument of this chapter emphasizes the importance of the key puzzle of this book. How cooperation can take place without hegemony is an important and vexing question precisely because there is evidence that the decline of hegemony makes cooperation more difficult. Multilateral institutions must furnish some of the sense of certainty and confidence that a hegemon formerly provided. Yet evidence that important elements of the monetary and trade regimes persisted as hegemony waned suggests that international regimes may be adaptable to a post-hegemonic era rather than be doomed to complete collapse.

This general theme is supported by the detailed analysis of this chapter, which shows that the theory of hegemonic stability provides some insights into changes that have taken place in postwar international economic regimes, but that it is not entirely adequate to explain these changes. If the theory of hegemonic stability were wholly wrong, there would be no reason to expect that the demise of hegemony would make any real difference in prospects for cooperation. If the theory were entirely correct, there would be no hope for post-hegemonic international regimes. Either way it would be pointless to focus on how cooperation could take place "after hegemony." The contention of this chapter that the theory is partially valid means that the puzzle of post-hegemonic cooperation is significant for an understanding of the contemporary world political economy and for policy, as well as for theory.

183

This chapter critically assesses how well the theory of hegemonic stability accounts for changes in international economic regimes between the mid-1960s and early 1980s. My emphasis will be more specific than in chapter 3, focusing on particular changes that took place in the international regimes for money, trade, and oil. In these areas, some forms of cooperation declined, but others have persisted and a few cooperative innovations have occurred. My conclusion is that, as a "first cut" at the problem, the crude theory of hegemonic stability makes a contribution by pointing to the importance of material power, yet it does not provide a general causal explanation of the changes that we observe. Cooperation seems also to depend on expectations, on transaction costs, and on uncertainty, all of which can be affected by international regimes. Despite the erosion of American hegemony, discord has not triumphed over cooperation; instead, they coexist. This phenomenon, which could not be explained by hegemonic stability theory alone, is comprehensible when we combine this theory's emphasis on power with the functional theory of international regimes discussed in Part II. The functional theory, it will be recalled, stresses how international institutions change rational calculations of interest and facilitate mutually advantageous bargains among independent states; it also emphasizes the greater ease of maintaining existing regimes than of creating new ones. From this perspective, the international regimes constructed in the era of American hegemony are invaluable for post-hegemonic cooperation. We need to understand their evolution in order to adapt them to contemporary power realities.

CHANGES IN INTERNATIONAL ECONOMIC REGIMES

In the mid-1960s the international monetary regime—that is, the arrangements governing balance-of-payments financing and adjustment—was explicit, formally institutionalized, and apparently stable. Governments belonging to the IMF were required to maintain official par values for their currencies, which could be changed only to correct a "fundamental disequilibrium" and only in consultation with the IMF. Between the resumption of *de jure* convertibility for major European currencies at the end of 1958 and the British, French, and Canadian devaluations of the late 1960s, these rules were followed rather closely; parity changes for major currencies were few and minor. By the mid-1960s, however, signs of stress were appearing: American leaders had expressed repeated concern about gold outflows and had devised a variety of ingenious, if somewhat ephemeral, expedients to improve official U.S. balance-of-payments statements and to provide

184

for cooperative actions by central banks or treasuries to counteract the effects of destabilizing capital flows. The Interest Equalization Tax, introduced by the United States in 1963, was supposed to protect the dollar by reducing incentives for American investors to purchase foreign securities (Bergsten, 1975; Cohen, 1977; Eckes, 1975; Hirsch, 1967).

The trade regime of the mid-1960s, centered on GATT, was based on the principles of reciprocity, liberalization, and nondiscrimination. Partly reflecting its success, world trade had increased since 1950 at a much more rapid rate than world production. Furthermore, tariff liberalization was continuing: following passage of U.S. authorizing legislation in 1962, preparations were going forward for what would become known as the "Kennedy Round," which resulted by mid-1967 in substantial tariff reductions on a wide range of industrial products. Yet, despite its obvious accomplishments, the GATT trade regime in the mid-1960s was already showing signs of disarray. Tolerance for illegal trade restrictions had grown, and few formal complaints were being processed. What one observer called the "general breakdown in GATT legal affairs" (Hudec, 1975, p. 256) was already under way.

These international regimes for trade and monetary relations were highly institutionalized, with explicit rules and widespread membership. In oil, arrangements were less explicit and less comprehensive, since the rules and practices had not been agreed upon at international conferences but had been constructed largely by the major oil companies, supported by the U.S. and Britain and acquiesced in, increasingly grudgingly, by the still weak producing countries. There was no global international organization monitoring state behavior. Thus, on a strict construction of what qualifies as a regime, it would be questionable that an international oil regime still existed by the mid-1960s. Nevertheless, informal principles, norms, rules and procedures remained, around which actors' expectations converged. It is therefore not stretching the word too far—although perhaps it is reaching its limit—to call the oil arrangements a regime.[1]

---

[1] As noted in chapter 8, the oil regime of the 1950s was not a formal intergovernmental regime. But its principles and norms created practices and expectations, so it was a genuine regime nonetheless. These principles and norms were created and implemented by a few international companies and the U.S. and British governments. By the early 1970s the regime had clearly broken down. The injunctions applying to oil during the period of transition in the mid-1960s were quite informal and loose, as compared to those in the monetary and trade regimes; yet, in contrast with the situation in oil after 1973, it is their relative clarity and coherence that stand out. It is useful to describe the arrangements of the mid-1960s as a regime, albeit a weak one, to highlight contrasts with what would come later and to facilitate comparisons with money and trade.

Power relations in this regime were highly asymmetrical. The major companies possessed superior information about oil markets and technology; in addition, they retained financial resources and capabilities in production, transportation, and marketing that the producing countries could not match. When they were threatened with nationalization and revolution, the companies could turn to the American and British governments for aid. From the perspective of the 1980s, some of the vulnerabilities of the regime seem evident. Formerly domestic firms were entering the international arena in the 1960s, reducing the dominance of the "seven sisters," as the largest companies were called; and the governments of producing countries were becoming more sophisticated as their elites became more assertive and demanding. Yet, for the time being, the companies still appeared powerful. As Louis Turner comments: "Whatever the weakness of company defences which is apparent in retrospect, the host governments did not realize it at the time. Their knowledge of the complexities of the industry was scanty, their experience of serious bargaining with the companies was limited and their awe of the companies was great" (1978, pp. 94-95).

By 1983 great changes had taken place in all three of these international economic regimes. Let us look at these changes in some detail.

The International Monetary Regime

The rules of the international monetary regime established at Bretton Woods had been first bent, then broken, and finally abandoned. The pegged-rate regime devised at Bretton Woods, with the dollar linked to gold at a fixed price, had been renounced by the United States in 1971, and its jerry-built successor cobbled together at the Smithsonian Institution in December of that year had collapsed by early 1973. After 1973 major currencies or currency blocs floated against one another, their values affected both by market forces and by frequently extensive governmental intervention. In 1976 agreement was reached on amendments to the IMF Articles of Agreement; yet this did not return the world to stable international exchange rates or multilateral rule-making, but merely provided for vaguely defined "multilateral surveillance" of floating exchange rates. Exchange rates have fluctuated sharply. Even the dollar has displayed large fluctuations, while other currencies have varied even more. As compared to its parity before June 1970, the effective exchange rate of the dollar had declined by almost 20 percent in early 1975. By the end of 1976 it had strengthened by about 10 percent, only to fall back by early October 1979 to a level about

20 percent below the pre-June 1970 rate. By 1983 it had risen to a point above that of 1970.[2]

Yet despite the fact that explicit, well-defined rules and procedures governing international monetary relations have practically vanished, there has been continuity in regime principles. First, what John Ruggie has called "embedded liberalism" persists: that is, arrangements facilitating international transactions are "embedded" in acceptance of the domestic welfare state. In the event of conflict between the two, the international system must accommodate demands by powerful states to manage their own economies consistently with their social-welfare goals (Ruggie, 1983b; Hirsch, 1978). Second, as Benjamin Cohen argues, "there has been a strong element of continuity" in the principles underlying the regime governing balance-of-payments financing: "In its maintenance of a balance of recognized rights and obligations for deficit countries, the financing regime remains very much the same as before" (1983, p. 333). Finally, respect for the principle that national policies may properly be subjected to international scrutiny continues, even if effective measures to bring international influence to bear on national policies are not implemented. The procedures for multilateral macroeconomic surveillance in conjunction with the IMF, agreed upon at Versailles in 1982 and reaffirmed at Williamsburg in 1983, attest to the legitimacy of this principle (De Menil, 1983, p. 37; *New York Times*, May 31, 1983). Such declarations are, of course, largely symbolic; but even vague principles provide some basis by which states can judge, as well as monitor, others' behavior. International monetary cooperation in the early 1980s is certainly less institutionalized than it once was, and the rules are less clear; but the degree of discord is probably no greater than it was in the years between 1968 and 1971, though more acute than in the years before the British devaluation of 1967.

The Trade Regime

Tariff levels were lower in 1983 than in the mid-1960s, as a result of two major tariff-cutting negotiations: the Kennedy Round, concluded in 1967, and the Multilateral Trade Negotiations, or "Tokyo Round," which was completed in Geneva in 1979. Trade issues, however, are no longer reducible to tariff issues. As Raymond Vernon has put it (1982, p. 503):

[2] *World Financial Markets*, February 19, 1975; January 1977; October 1979; May 1983.

With tariffs reduced to tolerable levels, the ascendant problems in the 1970s included the proliferation of public subsidies in all their obvious and subtle forms: governments' demands on selected enterprises (usually foreign owned) in their territories that the enterprises should limit their imports and increase their exports, the procurement practices of state entities, and the unilateral application of quotas by importing countries.

Between the mid-1960s and early 1980s the regime became less effective. National controls on trade, often under the guise of industrial policy, proliferated for a wide variety of other manufactured goods (Bressand, 1983). The proportion of trade covered by governmental controls rose sharply in the 1970s. Admittedly, ways were often found around these controls by ingenious producers in the newly industrializing countries (Odell, 1980; Yoffie, 1983) or by multinational enterprises (Vernon, 1982, p. 482). In the United States, liberalism remains strong and the executive branch has sought, sometimes effectively, to resist protectionist pressures (Goldstein, 1983). Nevertheless, most observers would have agreed with the Managing Director of the IMF when he declared at a GATT ministerial meeting in November 1982 that "pressures for the adoption of protectionist measures have intensified" and that "these pressures threaten to fragment the world economy" (IMF *Survey*, November 29, 1982, p. 369).

The extent of these pressures was evident at the ministerial meeting itself. Severe disagreements led the gathering to be extended for two days so that a consensual statement could be laboriously worked out. This statement recognized that "the multilateral trading system is seriously endangered" and that "protectionist pressures on governments have multiplied, disregard of GATT disciplines has increased, and certain shortcomings in the functioning of the GATT system have been accentuated" (GATT *Focus*, December 1982, p. 2). Yet despite their recognition of the severity of the problems, the ministers only managed to respond to them with general statements in support of the regime and with authorization of further studies and negotiations.

To a considerable extent, members of GATT still subscribed in the early 1980s, at least nominally, to the principles of nondiscrimination, liberalization, and reciprocity, though all of these principles had been modified for the less developed countries by the acceptance in 1970 of a Generalized System of Preferences (GSP). Quite apart from arrangements made with regard to the less developed countries, the principle of nondiscrimination was under especially strong pressure. Some of the codes adopted at the Tokyo Round permit discrimination

188

against nonadherents. So-called voluntary export restraints have proliferated, in effect leading to discrimination against exporters subject
to them. For instance, the United States forced Japan to agree to such
restraints on its auto exports to the U.S. in 1981, without imposing
similar restrictions on European producers. By 1983 well over 40
percent of Japan's exports to the European Community were restricted
by measures that violated the letter or the spirit of GATT rules (*Economist*, November 26, 1983, p. 52). According to some observers, the
EEC has been less inclined than the United States to make sure that
its protectionist measures conform to the formal provisions of GATT
(Vernon, 1982, p. 496).

Despite the pressures facing the trade regime, dire warnings uttered
in the early 1970s that it might collapse—warnings uttered chiefly by
liberals who hoped thereby to ward off this outcome—have not come
true, although such predictions have seemed increasingly credible. Two
close observers of the regime could, in 1983, emphasize its continuous
evolution over three and a half decades (Finlayson and Zacher, 1983),
and another student of trade concluded that the evolution of the trade
regime was, "for the most part, consistent with its longstanding norms."
Changes were more evident in "its rules and shared expectations, in
major states' conformity to the rules, and in the sectorally differentiated treatment of traded goods" (Lipson, 1983, p. 268). Thus the
pattern in trade was a mixed one of incremental protectionism combined with the maintenance of a basic liberalism. The situation still
resembled Prisoners' Dilemma, as discussed in chapter 5, in which
common interests are recognized by all but are difficult to promote
through collective action, although some major political interests were
beginning to question liberalism itself, as they had in the 1930s. If
those questions about liberalism should turn into opposition to cooperation, the situation would be transformed from Prisoners' Dilemma into one with less potential for cooperation (Oye, 1983b).

It is all too easy, in assessing cooperation in trade, to confuse it
with liberalization or nondiscrimination. But this would be to conflate
two very different phenomena. Liberals see them as conjoined—and,
in fact, it seems true that they often go together—but they are not
indistinguishable. What most liberals really seek is harmony, which
they believe would be justified on the basis of the principle of comparative advantage. But harmony has never characterized trade politics. There have always been conflicts of interest and real or potential
discord. Throughout the postwar period governments have bargained
for particular advantages. Until the late 1950s this bargaining was
muted by the fact that the United States did not seek to hold its major

trading partners to GATT principles, as the example of the European Payments Union (discussed in chapter 8) illustrates. Tariff negotiations during the 1960s were characterized by a great deal of disagreement, but ultimately by impressive cooperation: mutual adjustment of tariff levels did take place. In the 1970s conflict intensified, but the Tokyo Round led to cuts in tariffs to historically very low and economically almost insignificant levels. Trade therefore provides an example of the point made in chapter 4 that cooperation emerges not from harmony, but from real and potential discord.

In certain perhaps perverse ways, cooperation has increased in world trade as protectionism has risen. Consider, for instance, the international textile and apparel regime, which Vinod Aggarwal has carefully studied (1981, 1983). This is the most important single set of sector-specific rules in world trade. In 1974 over 10 percent of U.S. and European manufacturing sector jobs depended on these industries; and these products accounted for over 20 percent of the manufactured exports of Brazil and Greece and about 40 percent of those of South Korea, Portugal, and India (Aggarwal, 1981, p. 8). During the 1970s this regime became more protectionist, largely under pressure from European governments. It was a weak regime in the 1970s, but the trend in the 1980s seems, according to Aggarwal (1983), to be toward a stronger, tighter regime, whose rules would be more precise as well as more restrictive. This prospect suggests that, in textiles, it would be incorrect to equate the rise in protectionism with a decline in co-operation. On the contrary, mutual adjustment of policies among the major textile and apparel importers continues, and may even become more effective as protectionism against Third World exporters increases. The *purposes* of cooperation have changed more than the fact of cooperation itself. Nothing could better illustrate the point made repeatedly in this book that cooperation is not necessarily benign. Cooperation among importers is as obnoxious to Third World textile producers or cosmopolitan liberals as cooperation among oligopolistic corporations is to their small competitors or to dedicated trust-busters.

The Oil Regime

Although all three regimes changed between the mid-1960s and 1983, the alterations were most pronounced for oil. In oil, an old company-centered regime was destroyed through the exercise of producers' state power in a tightening oil market. Concession arrangements were swept away, operating companies in the oil-producing countries were nationalized, and the companies lost control of their relationships with these countries (Turner, 1978, p. 70). Governments of oil-producing countries, organized since 1960 in the Organization of Petroleum Exporting Countries (OPEC), secured a substantial price rise in negotiations at Teheran in 1971, then virtually quadrupled prices without negotiation after the Yom Kippur War of October 1973. Prices fell in real terms until the beginning of 1979, when the revolution in Iran provided the catalyst for another doubling of prices, to over $30 per barrel in early 1980. By the mid-1980s not only the rules of the old regime had been discarded; different political actors seemed to be dominant. Power relationships had been profoundly transformed.

It would nevertheless be an exaggeration to conclude that the OPEC states had become hegemonic for the oil system—that is, able to make and enforce the rules. The limitations on their power became clear in the wake of the price rises of 1979-80, which could not be maintained in the face of large shifts in world oil demand and supply resulting from the increases in price. The oil consumption of the advanced industrial countries fell by 7 million barrels per day (about 17 percent) between 1979 and 1982. Combined with stock changes and increases in non-OPEC supplies, this decline led to a fall in OPEC production of over 12 million barrels per day (almost 40 percent) and to significant declines in prices. By 1983 international oil relations were more characterized by a market-and-company-mediated international tug-of-war between producers and consumers than by the hegemony of either side. The politics of the issue-area had been transformed, but the outcome of the struggle was not yet clear.

As the regime changed, so did patterns of cooperation and discord within the two major groups of actors—the oil producers and the advanced industrialized countries. In early 1983 OPEC reacted to the decline in prices and production by instituting a new agreement on production quotas, designating Saudi Arabia as the swing producer and accommodating OPEC production as low as 14.5 million barrels per day—about 20 percent lower than 1982 production and as low as the lowest point reached in the winter of 1983 (*World Financial Markets*, April 1983, p. 2). It is important to note that at least until this time OPEC had not functioned as a genuine cartel, since it had not controlled the quantity of production. Indeed, at the beginning of both oil shocks—in 1973 and 1979—the official OPEC price had risen more slowly than prices on the spot market. Rather than OPEC leading prices up, it had followed them up (BIS, 1982, p. 40). Typically, after prices were raised, demand fell and spot prices dropped below the OPEC price. In these relatively slack periods, OPEC may have helped to keep prices high, although in the absence of effective production controls this result would have had to come about through a combination of informal group pressure on individual producers and the beliefs of consumers that OPEC would somehow manage to keep oil prices high in the future.

At the time of writing it was too soon to tell whether OPEC's 1983 production controls would be more effective than its previous efforts at creating a genuine cartel. What was clear, however, was that efforts by members of OPEC to cooperate with each other were continuing, and that mutual adjustments had indeed taken place. Cooperation among producers was certainly greater than it had been in the period of American hegemony.

The first reaction of the advanced industrialized countries to the oil embargo and price rises of 1973 was discordant rather than cooperative. In response to Arab sanctions against Holland in 1973, other EEC governments sought to distance themselves as quickly as possible from their stricken partner and its pro-Israeli policies. Britain and France sought in addition to secure preferential oil supplies for themselves by putting pressure on their own oil companies; Germany relied on its ability to pay high free-market prices to protect itself against shortages. Meanwhile, Japan adopted a pro-Arab declaratory policy, which led the Arabs to put it on their priority list; Japanese officials and firms lobbied the major oil companies for equitable treatment (Stobaugh, 1975, pp. 188-92).

In early 1974 the United States called a conference of the major oil-consuming capitalist countries, and later in the year sixteen of these states (with the significant absence of France) joined together in a new International Energy Agency (IEA) under American leadership. This organization oversaw the development of an emergency sharing system for oil in a future crisis and sought to help governments to limit their dependence on imported petroleum through long-term measures to restrict demand and increase domestic energy supply.

The IEA rested on a set of bargains among its members. The United States regained the diplomatic initiative and the position of leadership that it had lost in the oil crisis. The emergency sharing system, which constituted a major focus of the organization's early work, would benefit the United States if it were the target of a concerted and effective embargo by a producers' cartel. But in the more likely event of a general oil shortage, or an ineffectively targeted embargo leading to a shortage and price rises (as in 1973-74), effective implementation of the sharing system would most directly benefit countries entirely dependent on foreign oil, especially those without sufficient financial resources to bid up the price to secure supplies. In such a contingency, oil-producing IEA members such as the United States, United Kingdom, and Canada could be called upon to share sacrifices, to some extent, with other members of the organization. In return for this insurance policy against catastrophic loss of imports, the oil-poor members of the organization not only accepted U.S. leadership but also agreed in 1976 to a "minimum selling price" of $7 per barrel for oil. In the event of a price collapse, this floor would be established for the benefit of those members of the organization with energy resources that had made investments in the production of domestic petroleum or close substitutes for it (Keohane, 1978).

The IEA performed some useful functions for its members, which will be discussed in more detail in chapter 10. But it did not exercise decisive influence on the pattern of petroleum trade. American notions of using it as a weapon for confronting OPEC soon dissipated in the face of resistance from the other members. The IEA's efforts at energy research and development remained limited in scope (Bobrow and Kudrle, 1979). When a second oil shock occurred in 1979, the IEA was unable to prevent a doubling in prices, even though the overall shortfall of world oil supplies following the Iranian revolution never exceeded 4 percent, and OPEC production for the year reached a record high (OECD *Observer*, July 1980, pp. 10-11). Although the IEA did take some informal measures to facilitate the shipment of oil to countries suffering shortages, it never invoked the emergency sharing system. Yet as we will see in chapter 10, after the outbreak of war between Iran and Iraq in September 1980, informal measures of policy coordination were taken that may have had some dampening effects on speculation and on prices. International cooperation on energy in 1979-80, managed through an international energy organization, did take place, but it was much less effective than hegemonic cooperation had been in 1956-57.

The IEA regime was essentially an insurance regime. That is, rather than being designed to control the oil market, the IEA established internal procedures to share the costs of an oil supply disruption and thereby reduce the risks faced by individual consuming countries. Constructing an insurance regime not only may reduce the vulnerability of its members in the event of a catastrophe, but may also improve the group's strategic position by making it more difficult for their adversaries to divide them through specifically targeted threats. Under conditions of eroding hegemony, one should expect insurance regimes, such as the IEA with its emergency sharing system, to emerge.

Third World oil consumers were left out of both the consumers' and producers' regimes. To be sure, both coalitions sought symbolic support from Third World consumers, and certain limited schemes were developed—for Moslem countries by certain Middle Eastern producers, and in Central America by Venezuela and Mexico—to cushion the effects of price rises. Nevertheless, lacking power to influence events, Third World consumers did not receive significant general price concessions from producers, nor did the IEA wish to reduce its own internal cohesion (already strained on a number of issues) by including less developed countries within its ranks.

Comparing Descriptions of Regime Change

The evidence that we have surveyed indicates that changes in regimes, and the new patterns of cooperation that emerged, were quite different from one issue-area to another. In oil, established rules and principles have been swept away by a new group of countries aspiring to dominant status. Since these countries have not achieved preponderance, no system-wide regime has been reconstituted. Yet the collapse of a hegemonic regime has led to new forms of cooperation, on a bifurcated basis, within OPEC and the IEA. The system as a whole is more discordant, but within it limited areas of institutionalized cooperation have emerged. In the exchange-rate regime, well-defined rules have disappeared, leading to less well-coordinated mutual adjustments of policies. Yet the basic principle of embedded liberalism remains, and the same countries are dominant. Furthermore, there has been a spillover of old patterns of monetary cooperation to cooperation in managing the Third World debt crisis. In trade, even many of the rules persist, although violations have become more frequent and some new discriminatory rules have been instituted. New forms of mutual adjustment, as in the proliferation of voluntary export restraints and the strengthening of the textile regime, have appeared. These qualify as cooperation according to our definition, although they have not contributed to liberalization but rather to the reverse. They represent international cooperation constrained by domestic political and economic pressures; they constitute "second-best" (or third- or fourth-best) policies designed to adapt to protectionist pressures without leading to a total collapse of the GATT system.

In view of the differences that exist among issue-areas, a theory purporting to explain international economic regime change between the 1960s and the 1980s must account for the fact that the oil regime experienced the most serious changes, followed by money and trade. But it must also account for a rather complex general pattern, which

194

seems evident across issue-areas. On the one hand, the old hegemonic international regimes in these areas became weaker, since their rules became in many respects less clear and, where clear, were more often broken. On the other hand, a spiral of collapse was avoided: attempts at policy coordination continued, often on a less-than-global basis and with illiberal intentions. In some cases, these led to new organizations, such as the IEA, or at least nominally stronger regime rules, as exemplified by OPEC's 1983 production controls and by the textile/apparel regime after the mid-1970s. Cooperation persisted, even though its purposes were less likely than before to be applauded by American liberals, and it did not always lead to great success, even in its own terms.

Assessing the Theory of Hegemonic Stability

This section uses historical analysis and comparisons among issue-areas to assess the causal connections between the decline of American hegemony and the deterioration of international cooperation in the world political economy since the mid-1960s. My conclusion is that some causal linkages seem to exist, although they are not as direct and uncomplicated as the theory of hegemonic stability would suggest. Furthermore, the regime-eroding effects of hegemonic decline are to some extent counterbalanced by the value to governments of rules that limit players' legitimate strategies and therefore reduce uncertainty in the world political economy. As hegemony erodes, regimes become more difficult to supply; yet the demand for them, based on their contributions to facilitating mutually beneficial agreements among states, persists. The theory of hegemonic stability draws our attention to an important piece of the puzzle, but it does not provide us with a complete theory. The insights of this power theory must be combined with those of theories that stress the value of cooperation and the functions performed by regimes.

As we saw in chapter 3, only the crude version of the theory of hegemonic stability offers nontautological explanations of changes in international regimes on the basis of changes in the distribution of world power. The refined version of the theory does not make such predictions and should be considered not a theory but merely a framework of ideas that is useful for description and interpretation but not for explanation. As in chapter 3, when I refer simply to the theory of hegemonic stability, I am referring to the crude basic force model, which in its most highly aggregated form attributes recent changes in international regimes to the decline of American power. What U.S.

power created, according to this interpretation, its erosion undermined. This theory is parsimonious. If it were correct and complete, it would be a powerful explanation, since it relies on only one variable—distribution of power among actors—which operates at the level of the system as a whole.

To attribute the decay of the postwar international regimes to the decline of American power requires, first, that one show a correspondence between patterns of regime change and changes in tangible power resources. Second, it must be possible to provide at least a plausible account of how those resource changes could have caused the regime changes that we observe. That is, the investigator must check to see whether the correlation between declining power and regime change is not really accounted for by other forces than those specified in the theory. We will see, for instance, that changes in U.S. domestic politics had important impacts on international monetary regimes in the late 1960s and early 1970s. Trade regimes, meanwhile, changed under the pressure of changing patterns of comparative advantage and international competition (Strange, 1979; Branson, 1980; Cowhey and Long, 1983).

As applied to the period between the mid-1960s and the early 1980s, the crude theory of hegemonic stability begins with the correct assertion that American economic capabilities, relative to those of other major countries, declined. We saw in chapter 3 that a measure of U.S. relative labor productivity fell from almost three times the world average in 1950 to only about one and a half times the world average in 1977 (table 3.1, p. 36). By one reckoning, U.S. national income in 1976 was 31 percent of that of market-economy countries as compared to 45 percent in 1960 (Krasner, 1982, p. 38); by another, it fell between 1960 and 1980 from 25.9 to 21.5 percent of the world total (Oye, 1983a, p. 8).[3] Table 9.1 shows that U.S. gross domestic product (GDP) fell from about 60 to about 40 percent of that of the United States, the EEC, and Japan, combined, between 1960 and 1980. Yet it is also clear that the United States has not become a second-rate power: "In a wide range of activities it continues to be the world's most prominent actor," although "the enormous slack accorded the United States through the 1950s by the absence of any serious threat

---

[3] The discrepancy seems to be accounted for largely by the fact that the first set of figures excludes nonmarket-economy countries. Other discrepancies between series such as these are often attributable to the use of different exchange rates and to different ways of valuing output in nonmarket-economy countries.

Table 9.1. U.S. Gross Domestic Product as a Percentage of the Gross Domestic Products of the United States, the EEC, and Japan Combined

Series:	1	2	3
1950	69.1	—	—
1960	62.4	58.0	61.6
1970	55.1	54.3	—
1980	—	43.3 (1979)	40.5

SOURCE: Percentages in each series were calculated from the following sources: 1) U.S. Council on International Economic Policy series, 1971, cited in Oye et al., 1983, table 1-1, p. 8; 2) *United Nations Yearbook of National Accounts Statistics, 1980* (New York: United Nations, 1982), table 1A, pp. 5-7; 3) World Bank, *World Development Report*, 1982, table 3, p. 115.

to minimalist political goals or specific economic interests was gone in many issue areas by the 1970s" (Krasner, 1982, p. 39).

We must be careful not to leap from these data about the decline in American capabilities between 1950 and 1980 to an inference about future decline, which does not seem inevitable. Nor should we see the correlation between declining capabilities and changes in international regimes as necessarily implying a causal relationship between these two facts. We also need to provide an argument that plausibly links these two sets of events. This, however, is difficult to do on the basis of an *overall* decline in American capabilities, because the patterns of regime change have been so different across our three issue-areas. An aggregate version of the theory of hegemonic stability does not differentiate sufficiently between issue-areas to be very credible as an explanation of events. We therefore need to apply the power-as-resources theory on a differentiated basis by issue-area. If the theory of hegemonic stability is correct, there should be a discernible relationship between the extent to which American capabilities declined in an issue-area and the degree to which the relevant international regime changed.

It is easy enough to get estimates of shifts in capabilities by issue-area: U.S. international financial reserves fell from 49 percent of the world total in 1950 to 21 percent in 1960 and 7 percent in 1976; exports fell from 18 to 16 to 11 percent of the world total for the same years; and the U.S. share of world petroleum production fell from 53 percent in 1950 to 33 percent in 1960 and 14 percent in 1976 (Krasner, 1982, p. 38). But it is more difficult to know what they mean. John Odell has pointed out that using international monetary

197

reserves as indicators of power in the international financial issue-area can be misleading (1982, p. 219):

> By 1972 both Germany and Japan had greater monetary power than the U.S., according to [measures of international reserves]. . . . Yet Japan and Germany did not make more active use of their apparently increased monetary power. . . . This is not surprising, because their monetary power had increased less than their share of world reserves had. Their net influence over monetary policies was diluted by their continuing general dependence on a relatively closed U.S. economy. . . . International monetary policies are inherently macropolicies. Exchange rates cut across all sectors of international transactions in goods, services, and capital. . . . [Therefore,] monetary power should coincide with general power more than is the case in other "issues."[4]

In trade, measures of capability (such as share of world exports or imports) must be augmented by consideration of the relative difficulty to the two partners in a relationship of stopping transactions or altering their terms. Other things being equal, one might expect that the country with the larger market would have more leverage; but whether this is actually so will depend on the opportunity costs to both sides, which will not necessarily be inversely proportionate to their sizes. It may be easier, under certain circumstances, to find other sources of supply for textiles or food than for oil; and it is certainly more convenient to go without peanuts or bananas than to forego supplies of energy or spare parts necessary to make one's economy operate (Hirschman, 1945/1980; Keohane and Nye, 1977, ch. 1).

These caveats should make us cautious about any findings that are claimed to "confirm" the hegemonic stability theory. Yet it may still be worthwhile to ask whether there seems to be any connection, however tenuous, between the rapidity of regime decline in the issues of money, trade, and energy on the one hand and measures of American capabilities in those areas on the other. In each case, I compare U.S. capabilities with those of its major industrialized partners: the European Economic Community (including, for all years, figures for the nine members that belonged during the 1970s) and Japan. For the monetary area, taking into account Odell's criticism, I rely on the figures on gross domestic product in table 9.1, but I also use measures

---

[4] Odell's criticism, which is well taken, was directed at an argument in Keohane and Nye, 1977.

Table 9.2.   U.S. Trade as Percentage of Total Trade of U.S., the
EEC, and Japan Combined (Imports Plus Exports)

1950	33.3	1970	23.5
1960	27.0	1980	22.1

SOURCE: Figures calculated from *UN Yearbook of International Trade Statistics* (New York: United Nations, 1981), vol. 1, special table B, pp. 1080-87.

Table 9.3.   Petroleum Resources in Four Crisis Years

A.   UNITED STATES OIL BALANCE

	U.S. Oil Imports as % of Consumption	U.S. Excess Production Capacity as % of Consumption	Net U.S. Position
1967	19	25	+6
1973	35	10	−25
1979	48	*	(c. −40)
1980	43	*	(c. −40)

* Exact figure not available; but close to zero.
SOURCE: For 1967 and 1973, Darmstadter and Landsberg, 1975, pp. 30-31; for 1979, IEA, 1981, p. 309; for 1980, IEA, 1982a, p. 376.

B.   NET OIL IMPORTS AS PERCENTAGE OF TOTAL ENERGY DEMAND

	U.S.	W. Europe	Japan	Ratio of U.S. to European Dependence	Ratio of U.S. to Japanese Dependence
1967	9	50	62	.18	.15
1973	17	60	80	.28	.20
1979	22	46	75	.48	.29
1980	19	43	69	.44	.28

SOURCE: For 1967 and 1973, Waltz, 1979, appendix X, p. 221; for 1979, calculated from IEA, 1981, pp. 66, 190, 309; for 1980, calculated from IEA, 1982a, pp. 93, 227, 376. Calculations were made by dividing net imports by total primary energy demand (TPE).

199

of the role of the dollar in world capital markets, consistently with the point made in chapter 3 about the importance of capital markets for hegemony. For trade, I use exports plus imports in table 9.2 and, in table 9.4, the relative importance of each of the largest trading areas as markets for the exports of other major trading areas. These figures are relevant to bargaining because the ability to close off one's markets to imports is a major asset in trade negotiations and exports reflect the competitiveness of the economy on the world level. In oil, we need a measure of American power-resources relative to those of the producers, as well as in comparison to its industrialized-country partners. For the former, I use the relationship between U.S. imports and excess U.S. production capacity at home. For the latter, I focus on oil imports as a percentage of energy demand, since this indicates relative U.S., European, and Japanese dependence on imports.

What these figures show is that, like changes in regimes, the patterns of relative U.S. decline in material resources are highly differentiated by issue-area and vary according to the measure used. As table 9.1 indicated, U.S. GDP as a proportion of that of the EEC, Japan, and the United States together fell from about two-thirds of the total in 1950 to under half in 1980. Yet the dollar remained the principal international currency for lending and settlement of transactions, and the United States has been able relatively easily to finance very large current account deficits, as it did in 1983. The percentage of Euro-currency liabilities denominated in dollars remained relatively stable during the decade of the 1970s. In 1970, of Eurocurrency liabilities, 81 percent were denominated in dollars. This fell to a low point of 74 percent in 1973, rose again to 80 percent by 1976, fell to 72 percent in 1979, and rose to about 80 percent in 1982. By a different financial measure, the same conclusion of continued dollar preponderance is reached: in the eight years between 1976 and 1983 inclusive, 55 percent of new international bond issues were denominated in dollars, with the high for that period being reached at a level of 64 percent in 1982.[5]

In trade, the United States never had a dominant position, as table 9.2 indicates. The decline of about a third in its share of trade was similar proportionately to its decline in GDP, but took place from a far lower base.[6] In oil, the United States began from a far stronger

---

[5] *World Financial Markets*, February 1978; July 1983; January 1984.

[6] It would be desirable to have used figures for EEC trade in table 9.2 that netted out intra-EEC trade, since EEC bargaining power vis-à-vis the United States and Japan cannot be expected to be enhanced by increased trade among the EEC members. I was

position, but its relative position fell far more sharply after 1967 than it did in either money or trade. The ratio of U.S. to European or Japanese dependence on oil imports roughly doubled between 1967 and 1980. The decreased U.S. ability to control the oil market, and to use this control as a source of influence over Europe and Japan, reflected this shift in underlying power resources.

In some ways these figures underestimate the changes in trade, since they do not reflect the growing unity of trade policy among the countries of the EEC. Aggarwal (1981) has shown that this made a major difference in the 1977 renegotiation of the Multi-Fiber Agreement, since once the EEC was unified, it controlled more of the relevant power resources (market share) in the textile issue-area than did the United States. The point is relevant not only to textiles but more generally. One way of illustrating it is to compare the exports *to each other* of the United States, EEC, and Japan, as a proportion of their total trade, net of intra-EEC trade. If we consider this measure for 1981, some interesting findings emerge, as table 9.4 indicates.

Japan's well-known dependence on U.S. markets is reflected in table 9.4; what is more surprising is the degree of relative U.S. dependence on European markets. The EEC is larger than the United States in terms of total product, and its exports in 1981 were almost 30 percent greater, but in aggregate terms it is less dependent on the U.S. market than vice versa. Europe is much less dependent on Japan than Japan is on Europe. The asymmetries of interdependence in trade among the three major advanced industrial trading units now run in Europe's favor, as long as it maintains a unified trade policy, although this political advantage may be a result of economic weakness, as reflected in the declining competitiveness of European exports in the markets of other advanced industrialized countries. Indeed, this combination of political strength and economic weakness may help to account for European protectionism, along with the familiar characteristics of European society usually invoked in explanation of this fact.

On the whole, these data lend plausibility to a differentiated hegemonic stability theory. Power shifts have been most evident in the oil area, particularly with respect to U.S. relations with the producers but also with respect to the relationship between the United States and Europe. As the theory would predict, regime change has also been most rapid in oil. In money, the mixed pattern of shifts in power—

unable, however, to find such data in time series, although table 9.4 reports them for 1981. In considering relations between the EEC and the rest of the world on trade issues for which the EEC acts as a bloc, intra-EEC trade should, where possible, be excluded to provide an accurate picture of the EEC's external relations.

Table 9.4. Trade Relations Among the United States, the
EEC, and Japan, 1981

	Billions of Dollars	As % of Exporter's Total Exports	As % of Exporters's Total (1980) Product
U.S. to Japan	21.6	9.2	0.84
Japan to U.S.	39.0	25.7	3.38
U.S. to EEC	52.4	22.4	2.03
EEC to U.S.	38.5	12.8	1.44
Japan to EEC	18.8	12.4	1.63
EEC to Japan	6.3	2.1	0.23

SOURCE: Figures calculated from French Institute for International Relations, 1982, pp. 309, 316-17. Only figures for 1981 are available from this publication.

fairly sharp on GDP measures but muted with respect to the role of the dollar in capital markets—parallels the ambiguous changes in international monetary regimes. The theory of hegemonic stability would have led us to expect a rather steady but moderately paced decline in the postwar trade regime, reflecting the shifts in shares of world trade by the major blocs; and this is indeed what we find.

Yet the evidence does not establish the validity of the issue-differentiated theory of hegemonic stability. Before deciding whether the theory accounts for the observed changes, it is necessary to determine whether plausible causal sequences could be constructed, linking shifts in the international distribution of power to changes in international regimes, and to consider alternative explanations, especially those focusing on variations in policies rather than simply on power. We therefore need to ask whether the causal arguments of hegemonic stability theory help us understand the reasons for the changes that actually took place in oil, money, and trade. The ensuing discussion begins with oil, since it fits the theory so well, and then addresses the more difficult cases.

Explaining the Collapse
of the Old Petroleum Regime

The transformation of oil politics between the mid-1960s and mid-1980s reflected a decline in the ability of the United States, acting in

202

conjunction with Britain and the major oil companies, to make the rules and support the regime. OPEC countries, particularly Saudi Arabia, challenged the Western powers and the companies. OPEC members had previously lacked the ability to capture monopolistic profits by forming a producers' cartel. In part this inability reflected the relative cohesiveness of the oil companies during the 1960s, when seven major companies controlled over 90 percent of international oil trade (Neff, 1981, p. 24). This was changing rapidly by the 1970s: indeed, a crucial strength of the Libyan bargaining position in the early 1970s was its "ability to pick off the smaller companies," inducing them to sign favorable agreements and thus putting pressure on the recalcitrant majors (Turner, 1978, p. 157). Weak self-confidence, poor communications, and a low level of information about one another also played a role, although these deficiencies were already being corrected by greater elite sophistication and more intensive contacts among OPEC members.

Yet OPEC's earlier impotence was also a result of overwhelming U.S. power. Until the huge asymmetry between American power and that of OPEC had been reduced or reversed, massive changes in the regime could not have been expected to occur. Without these changes, neither foolish U.S. tactics nor an Arab–Israeli war could have led to the price rises that began in February 1971 and escalated dramatically in the last quarter of 1973.[7] Support for this assertion may be found in the fact that Saudi Arabia's attempt to organize an oil embargo in 1967, after the Six-Day War in June of that year, was not taken seriously by the OECD countries.

Conceivably, one could try to account for changes in international oil politics by reference to the erosion of American military power vis-à-vis Middle Eastern members of OPEC. This kind of analysis, at any rate, would seem more plausible as applied to oil than to either money or trade. Certainly it had become more difficult by the late 1960s and early 1970s for the United States to intervene in the Middle East than it had been during the 1950s. Arab nationalism, the increasing sophistication of indigenous Middle Eastern armies, and the rise of Soviet political influence and ability to project military power in the area all made a difference. So did British withdrawal from positions east of Suez and diversion of U.S. military forces and attention to Vietnam after 1965. Joseph Nye regards 1971 as a crucial turning point, because

[7] For discussions of U.S. tactics at Teheran in 1971, see Schuler, 1976; Blair, 1976; and Penrose, 1975.

the departure of the British from the Persian Gulf left a power vacuum that the United States, being unwilling to introduce its own force into the region, relied on the Shah of Iran to fill; "the fall of the Shah eventually revealed the true costs to America's energy security policy" (Nye, 1981, p. 8).

Whether reliance on British or American military forces in the Persian Gulf would have altered the course of the Iranian Revolution is difficult to determine, even in hindsight. Indeed, the impact of military power on oil politics is unclear in general, since it is difficult to employ military force effectively to prevent oil embargoes and price increases. During the 1970s the United States government declined to use force, having decided that the "cure would be worse than the disease." Of course, it is possible that the *threat* to use force would have deterred embargoes, or even rapid price increases; but it would be rash to put much confidence in this proposition. Threats whose implementation would have disastrous results for the threatener look like bluffs. The fact that the Shah's Iran was a strong U.S. military ally in the Persian Gulf did not prevent Iran from being the leader in increasing oil prices. Nor was the Saudi regime—an American military and political client— deterred from spearheading the embargo against the United States and Holland. Thus the causal links between American military power and world oil politics remain somewhat elusive and obscure.

The issue-specific hegemonic stability model posits a more direct and traceable linkage between power resources and outcomes in oil. As we saw in table 9.3A, fundamental shifts in U.S. petroleum resources relative to demand took place between 1967 and 1973: the United States went from the position of having greater oil production capacity than demand to one of needing to meet a quarter of normal demand from abroad. In 1967 the United States was "part of the solution," from the European and Japanese point of view, as it had been in 1956-57. In 1973 it was "part of the problem." Its fundamental petroleum resource base had been greatly weakened. As the issue-specific theory of hegemonic stability would predict, this change was followed by a dramatic shift in power relations within the oil area. In contrast to 1956-57 or even 1967, the United States was unable to compensate its allies from its own stocks for an oil shortfall resulting from a disruption in the Middle East. Shifts in the distribution of petroleum resources decisively changed the distribution of power relevant to outcomes (prices and access to supplies) in oil.

According to this interpretation, the Yom Kippur War was more a catalyst for action than a fundamental cause. It made Arab members of OPEC willing to take greater risks. When their actions succeeded in quadrupling the price of oil almost overnight, members of the cartel gained confidence that they could cut back production without being double-crossed by other producers and would benefit from the high prices created by their own actions in conjunction with the similar behavior of others. It appeared that, by cooperating with each other, OPEC members could all gain, without having to take large risks. A self–reinforcing cycle was launched, as increased underlying strength led to increased incentives to take advantage of that strength. Yet as events since 1980 have shown, the erosion of indigenous American oil resources did not give producers limitless power.

The theory of hegemonic stability could not explain why no formal oil regime was established before 1974, since U.S. power in the 1940s and 1950s certainly would have been sufficient to organize a regime had American domestic politics permitted. Yet the theory could help to account for the rise of a new form of consumer cooperation under American leadership in the IEA, after the 1973 debacle. The effect of OPEC's rise was to limit the scope of American dominance to Europe and Japan, whereas it had formerly been worldwide. But, within that circumscribed set of countries, the United States was still preponderant, since its dependence on foreign oil remained much less than that of Europe or Japan. Thus it had the capacity to exert leadership.

A functional theory of international regimes based on common interests would make relatively little contribution to our understanding of changes in the oil regime between 1967 and 1973, although, as we will see in the next chapter, it does help to account for how the IEA was organized and operated after 1973. The old oil regime was based on highly asymmetrical power relations: only in the context of these inequalities was it in the interests of oil producers to accept the U.S.-dominated regime. Shifts in power, giving producer governments viable alternatives to this regime, increased their opportunity costs of failing to challenge it. In view of the relatively low level of benefits that it provided for them, they had little incentive to refrain from destroying it. The old regime was not sufficiently valued to be able to persist.

This example illustrates a point made earlier. A functional theory of cooperation requires, as the condition for its operation, that actors have common interests; otherwise, there will be no mutually advantageous agreements for them to make. If power relations change fundamentally, bargains that were formerly advantageous to both sides (given opportunity costs) may no longer remain so. Agreements that reflect the new distribution of power will have to be very different from the old ones. It is conceivable that both the side whose power was rising and the side whose power was falling would recognize immediately the characteristics of new agreements that would satisfy both, and that they would negotiate such agreements without a rupture of relations. Yet in practice this is very difficult to imagine. New power relationships are not fully appreciated until they are tested. Before 1973 almost everyone underestimated the bargaining power of oil producers; in 1979-80 this power was widely exaggerated. Only after the oil price rise of 1979-80, and the subsequent decline, were both the strengths and weaknesses of producers and consumers clearly in view.

The case of oil therefore indicates why I have no intention of seeking to replace a power theory with a functional one. In world politics, power is always important. Any functional explanation, which deals with the value of a given process or pattern of interaction, must be embedded in an understanding of political structure, especially the distribution of power among actors (Waltz, 1979; Keohane, 1983; Ruggie, 1983a). When structure changes radically, the processes and institutions embedded in it will also be transformed.

Interpreting Changes in
the International Monetary Regime

The breakdown of the Bretton Woods pegged-rate monetary regime is often attributed to the combination of the inherent instability of a gold-exchange standard and the policies of the United States, particularly its monetary policies. With respect to the first point, Benjamin J. Cohen has summarized the issues as follows (1977, p. 99):

A gold-exchange standard is built on the illusion of convertibility of its fiduciary element into gold at a fixed price. The Bretton Woods system, though, was relying on deficits in the U.S. balance of payments to avert a world liquidity shortage. Already, America's "overhang" of overseas liabilities to private and official foreigners was growing larger than its gold stock at home. The progressive deterioration of the U.S. net reserve position, therefore, was bound in time to undermine global confidence in the dollar's continued convertibility. In effect, governments were caught on the horns of a dilemma. To forestall speculation against the dollar, U.S. deficits would have to cease. But this could confront governments with the liquidity problem. To forestall the liquidity problem, U.S. deficits would have to continue. But this would confront governments with the confidence problem. Governments could not have their cake and eat it too.

This situation would have made the international monetary regime of the 1960s quite delicate under the best of circumstances. As a response to the regime's fragility during the 1960s, negotiations took place to create Special Drawing Rights, designed to provide a source of international liquidity to serve in lieu of dollars when the U.S. deficit came to an end. Whether this reform would have been effective, however, is unclear because the conditions that it was meant to deal with never came into being. Rather than eliminating its deficit, the United States let its balance of payments on current account deteriorate sharply in the last half of the 1960s, as a result of a large budgetary deficit, excess demand in the United States, and the consequent inflationary momentum, all of which were linked to the Vietnam War. When U.S. monetary policy eased in 1970 in reaction to a recession, huge capital outflows took place. The U.S. decision of August 1971 to suspend the convertibility of the dollar into gold and thus to force a change in the Bretton Woods regime followed. As we have seen, the Smithsonian Agreement of December 1971 to restore fixed exchange rates at different valuations of currencies and gold collapsed within fifteen months. One reason for this collapse was continued monetary expansion in the United States and abroad.

The theory of hegemonic stability is an unsatisfactory explanation of regime change in international monetary relations. In part its defects would be shared by any systemic theory, since changes in American policies, affected decisively by the nature of U.S. domestic politics, played a major role in the events leading to the collapse of the Bretton Woods par-value system. Combining an institutional theory with the theory of hegemonic stability would not help to correct this fault, which simply reflects the limitations on purely systemic theory in world politics.

Yet the theory of hegemonic stability is deficient in three other respects even as compared with other systemic theories. In the first place, it focuses on changes in tangible resources as the predictor of change. But the resources that were most important to the ability of the United States to maintain the regime were not tangible resources but the symbolic resources that go under the rubric of "confidence" in discussions of international financial affairs. Variations in U.S. gross domestic product were less important than shifts in foreign confidence about U.S. policy: as a reserve-currency country, the United States could generate more international money (dollars) as long as holders of dollars believed that the dollar would retain value compared to alternative assets, such as other currencies or gold. By 1970-71, however, confidence in U.S. economic policy, and hence in the dollar, had become severely undermined. Perceptions of U.S. policy as inflationary translated directly into losses of the most important intangible resource that the United States had commanded: confidence that the dollar would remain a strong currency.

The second crucial problem with the explanation offered by the theory of hegemonic stability is that it fails to capture the *dual* nature of the U.S. power position in 1971. On the one hand, as we have seen, the U.S. position was eroding. Yet to a considerable extent U.S. weakness was an artifact of the rules of the old regime. These rules, written largely by the United States in 1944 to protect interests of creditor countries, now made it impossible for the United States to force Germany and Japan to revalue their currencies within the framework of the existing regime. If the United States wanted to maintain all aspects of the old regime, therefore, it had to defend the dollar through a variety of short-term expedients. Only by breaking the rules explicitly—by suspending convertibility of the dollar into gold—could the United States transform its bargaining position and make its creditors offer concessions of their own. As Henry Aubrey had pointed out in 1969, "surely a creditor's influence over the United States rests on American willingness to play the game according to the old concepts and rules. If the United States ever seriously decided to challenge them, the game would take a very different course" (p. 9). The United States thus had a strong political incentive to smash the specific rules of the old regime, even if it had an equally poweful desire to maintain the essential principles of liberalism. Once the old rules had been destroyed, other governments had to pay more attention to U.S. wishes, insofar as they also wished to retain these principles. For the United States, increased discord was a precondition for cooperation on American terms.

The third deficiency of the hegemonic stability theory in accounting for change in the international monetary system is that insofar as it relies on GDP figures as indices of power resources, it *overpredicts* regime collapse. Although the rules of the Bretton Woods regime were altered in 1971-73, the principles of multilateralism and relatively unfettered capital flows were maintained. After the advent of flexible exchange rates, major capital markets continued to become increasingly open, and elaborate cooperative networks, including private and central banks as well as finance ministries, flourished. By 1983 the Executive Director of the IMF estimated that the *daily* value of foreign exchange transactions in New York was about $30 billion (De La-rosière, 1983). Liberalism, though embedded in the welfare state and limited by state action, persisted.

This persistence is not explained by the theory of hegemonic stability, which leads us to expect discord and even closure. It is partially accounted for by the continued strength of the United States, which had an interest in liberalism. But the persistence of cooperative regimes is also partially explained by the continuation of shared interests in the efficiency and welfare benefits of international economic exchange. Obtaining these benefits, however, requires a continual series of agreements—for instance, to monitor exchange-rate interventions, expand resources at the disposal of the IMF, or lend money to countries in difficulty in conjunction with austerity programs. To facilitate such agreements, an established monetary regime, with the IMF at its center, is of great value to all governments concerned, even if its rules are less explicit than they once were. Thus the institutions of the old par-value regime have been adapted to make them useful in the post-1973 world of flexible exchange rates. The maintenance of international monetary institutions in the tumultuous years since the Nixon Shock of 1971 suggests that governments indeed value international regimes. To focus only on how hegemons supply regimes is onesided; we must also examine the sources of demand for these institutions.

A comparison between U.S. policies in money and oil helps us understand further the value of international regimes. In money, the United States continued to favor a liberal regime, but would neither support pegged exchange rates nor significantly adjust its domestic fiscal and monetary policies to the demands of its partners. Yet mutual interests continued to give all participants incentives to support liberalism. Thus although the post-1971 regime was weaker, with less explicit rules, than the one that prevailed before the Nixon Shock, it remained liberal. In oil, on the other hand, the collapse of the old regime made it necessary for the United States to take decisive action if it were to retain leadership of a relatively coherent group of advanced industrialized countries. It offered to sacrifice some of its control over domestic oil supplies, in a crisis, in exchange for receiving the deference essential to create a regime in which it could exercise leadership. That is, the United States was willing to accept more of the costs of adjustment in oil than it was in the monetary area.

This comparison illustrates, in a subtle way, the value of continuing international regimes to the United States and reinforces a point made in chapter 6 about the greater difficulty of instituting new regimes than maintaining old ones. The interests of the Europeans and Japanese in a liberal international monetary regime, coupled with their belief that maintenance of such a regime was feasible, made them willing to continue to cooperate with the United States despite its demand for a restructuring of the old Bretton Woods arrangements. The United States did not have to persuade its partners not to follow beggar-thy-neighbor policies in response to dilemmas of collective action: in a situation characterized by a relatively small number of actors, a continuing pattern of interaction, and substantial common interests, the persistence of a regime provided reassurance about others' intentions and practices. In oil, by contrast, the old regime had collapsed by 1973. Governments began to resort to competitive self-help strategies. The United States consequently had to make a substantial commitment of its own to create a new consumers' regime. In the absence of ongoing institutions, the American government had to take on new contingent obligations (to share oil in future crises with its partners) in order to reassure its allies about the future and give them incentives to cooperate rather than to defect, as in single-play Prisoners' Dilemma.

There is, however, a darker side to this happy story. This episode suggests that cooperation may be self-limiting in world politics as well as self-reinforcing. As noted above, the existence of a prior international monetary regime made it easier than it would otherwise have been for cooperation to continue. But, by the same token, the regime helped to make it unnecessary for the United States to adjust its own policies to avoid a collapse. Its very stability limited further advances in cooperation. Cooperation often builds on itself, but this process is by no means inevitable. Since cooperation arises from actual or potential discord, serious discord, such as resulted from the oil crisis of 1973-74, may sometimes be necessary to produce a "great leap forward" in international cooperation. International regimes tend to maintain patterns of cooperation, but they do not necessarily facilitate innovative expansions of cooperation in response to crisis and change.

Interpreting Changes in the International Trade Regime

As we have seen, changes in the trade regime between the mid-1960s and the early 1980s were broadly consistent with changes in potential power resources in the issue-area. American power resources (as measured by shares of world trade among the industrialized countries) declined relative to those of U.S. trading partners. But U.S. trade fell less sharply in relative terms than America's share of industrialized countries' gross domestic products. On the basis simply of country data, the theory of hegemonic stability would predict that the regime would deteriorate, but less rapidly than those in money and oil. Furthermore, it would anticipate that the United States, as it became less dominant, would also become less and less willing to bear a disproportionate part of the costs of trade liberalization. Since both of these phenomena are observed (Krasner, 1979; Ruggie, 1983c, pp. 484-85), the evidence for trade may seem at first to support the theory.

The issue, however, is more complicated. As table 9.4 indicates, the emergence of the EEC as a coherent trading bloc has made a much greater difference in relative control over resources than would appear from the country data alone. The distribution of world trade power is no longer hegemonic in any sense: unlike the situation in money and oil, Europe has at least as much potential bargaining power in trade as the United States does. Some of the changes that have taken place—as in the growing restrictiveness of the textile regime—are directly attributable to increased EEC bargaining power (Aggarwal, 1981). Using the EEC rather than individual European countries as the unit of analysis, the theory of hegemonic stability would predict *more* changes in trade than in money, since (despite the European Monetary System) there is no common European monetary policy or currency and the predominance of the dollar relative to individual European currencies has been maintained.

These sources of complexity and confusion are compounded when we look closely at the politics of trade. Pressures for protectionism seem to emanate largely from *within* the major industrialized countries, created by industries and groups of organized workers that are hurt by import competition. In a number of industrial sectors, including textiles, footwear, consumer electronics, steel, shipbuilding, and recently autos, economic distress in the form of surplus production capacity has provided a catalyst for protectionist measures (Strange, 1979; Cowhey and Long, 1983).

Classical and neoclassical economists have seen protectionism as a pathology of group politics, driven by demands of individuals and groups for higher and more stable incomes than they would command in a free market (Olson, 1982). Adam Smith excoriated guilds for protecting the wages of their members at the expense of society, though to the advantage, he thought, of the towns (1776/1976, pp. 132ff.). GATT officials now criticize labor unions and inefficient industries for seeking similar protection and attempt to refute their arguments that such actions would increase national as well as group income. According to this view, low-productivity industries, faced by dynamic, low-cost competitors from abroad, can only remain economically vi-

211

able either by paying lower wages than higher-productivity industries or by reducing employment. Yet the affected workers and their political leaders may resist either measure. This resistance to change leads to pressures for protection: "To maintain both the wage differential and the absolute size of employment in the industry, protection is necessary" (Blackhurst et al., 1977). Thus although most governments of advanced capitalist states have heretofore shown little enthusiasm for protectionist policies, they have been increasingly goaded into them by domestic interests.

Arrayed against these traditional liberals in the policy debate are proponents of active governmental intervention in the form of "industrial policy," although this slogan seems to have almost as many meanings as it has advocates. For our purposes, the important point is not the policy disagreement but the analytical agreement behind it: both liberals and interventionists see the sources of protectionism, and industrial policies, in increased competitiveness and more rapid structural change in the world economy. Policy change results not so much from the decline of American power, as from increased competition among the industrialized countries and between them and newly industrializing countries. Protection is a way of forcing the costs of adjustment onto others (inside one's own country or outside), at least temporarily, and is sought as a shelter from the impact of rapid change with which it is difficult for people to cope.

Most explanations of increased protectionism also emphasize the effects on competition and surplus capacity of the recession of the post-1973 decade and the rise of manufactured exports from less developed countries. Between the end of 1973 and the beginning of 1983 real gross national product in the industrialized market-economy countries grew by barely 2 percent per year, and in Europe the record was significantly worse. Unemployment rates for the seven largest industrialized capitalist countries more than doubled during the same period (IMF, 1983, table 1, p. 170, and table 5, p. 174). Despite the slow aggregate growth of industrial country markets, exports from non-OPEC developing countries increased threefold between 1973 and 1983. Since these exports were highly concentrated in sectors such as clothing, footwear, and consumer electronics, they created alarm among import-competing industries and their work-forces, even though imports by these countries outweighed their exports in the aggregate (Belassa, 1980, table 1; Stein, 1981; OECD, 1979, table 5, p. 24). Some of the restrictive measures of the 1970s, particularly the progressive tightening of export restraints on textiles, reflect these pressures from dynamic developing-country exporters.

Despite the superficial consistency between changes in measures of economic power resources and trade politics, examination of the policy process suggests that pressures of international competition and structural adjustment provide a better explanation of the decline of the trade regime than the theory of hegemonic stability.[8] Certainly the hegemonic stability theory does not explain recent changes in international trade regimes as well as it explains changes in oil. As with the monetary regime, the theory is not disconfirmed by the evidence, but it is also not very helpful in accounting at the level of political process for the changes that we do observe. Many major forces affecting the trade regime have little to do with the decline of U.S. power. For an adequate explanation of changes in patterns of cooperation and discord in trade, other factors—rapid structural changes, domestic political and economic patterns, and the strategies of domestic political actors—would also have to be taken into account.

Even without deviating from our systemic perspective, however, we can improve our understanding of changes in trade regimes by thinking about cooperation in ways suggested by Part II of this book. The theory of hegemonic stability predicts substantial erosion of the trade regime. This has occurred, but as we saw above, what is equally striking is the persistence of cooperation, even if not always addressed to liberal ends. Trade wars have not taken place, despite economic distress. On the contrary, what we see are intensive efforts at cooperation, in response to discord in textiles, steel, electronics, and other areas. The outcomes have not been models of pure liberalism, but even the facts adduced to demonstrate the growth of protection—such as the one mentioned earlier in this chapter that 40 percent of Japanese exports to Europe are covered by restrictive measures—suggest the complexity of what has been happening. If these measures had entailed export prohibitions, the proportion of trade covered by them would be the same as under pure liberalism: namely, zero! That much trade takes place under voluntary export restraints and other such arrangements reveals the loopholes in many of these schemes (Yoffie, 1983) as well as the pattern of "managed trade" that is evolving. Managed trade relies on a mixture of discord and cooperation, whereas truly

[8] See Bressand, 1983, and Cowhey and Long, 1983. In their very interesting article, Cowhey and Long refer to the theory of hegemonic stability as "Keohane's theory," although they briefly note my reservations about it. A review of Keohane, 1980, would make it clear that I was trying to evaluate the theory rather than to propose it as a valid explanation: "We should be cautious," I said, "about putting the hegemonic stability theory forward as a powerful explanation of events" (p. 155).

213

liberal trade depends on harmony. In the contemporary world, bargaining over trade illustrates the dialectical relationship between cooperation and discord that was discussed in chapter 4.

Contemporary trade regimes do not create harmony, but they do facilitate cooperation by reducing transaction costs, limiting the legitimate strategies available to actors, and providing information in a relatively symmetrical fashion. They reduce uncertainty and risk. Precisely because they lessen discord, however, they may create incentives for actors to be exorbitantly demanding in their bargaining strategies, as De Gaulle was in the European community and as others have been since. Such actors may assume that a regime is sufficiently valued that their partners will make concessions to retain it. This puts the latter in a difficult position. As we saw in chapter 5, reciprocity, or "tit for tat," seems to be the most effective strategy for maintaining cooperation among egoists. This strategy threatens increased discord in response to defection from the injunctions of an international regime. Against a myopic partner or a bully, those governments seeking cooperation in the future must be willing to retaliate in the present. Cooperation depends on the prospect of discord in the event of exploitation, as well as on the feasibility of mutually beneficial agreement if the parties involved seek cooperation. The fact that bullying strategies are sometimes followed, however, reminds us that our functional theory of international regimes is no more deterministic than a properly qualified version of the theory of hegemonic stability. Although regimes can facilitate cooperation among governments that seek to make agreements, they do not automatically produce it among those whose interests are in conflict or those that pursue overly demanding bargaining strategies.

CONCLUSIONS

The theory of hegemonic stability, differentiated by issue-area, makes some contribution to understanding recent changes in the international politics of oil, money, and trade. It calls attention to underlying power factors that may be overlooked by apolitical analyses or by those that ignore international political structure. Like Realist theory, to which it is closely related, the theory of hegemonic stability provides a useful, parsimonious basis on which to begin analysis. Yet it hardly constitutes an adequate explanation of the evolution of postwar international economic regimes.

Only in oil is the theory of hegemonic stability consistent not only with overall trends but with the process by which changes took place.

The erosion of American hegemony accounts quite well for the sharp changes in international petroleum regimes over the past twenty years. As American oil production capacity declined, so did its ability to implement the strategy of hegemonic cooperation—supplying its allies with oil when necessary—that it followed so successfully during the 1950s. The oil-sharing provisions of the IEA can be seen as an innovative, more institutionalized way of pursuing that same strategy (since in an emergency American oil would almost certainly be shared with most European countries and Japan rather than vice versa); but in the 1970s this was a defensive, damage-limiting insurance strategy rather than one that could, as in the 1950s, effectively control the situation by deterring deliberate producer embargoes as well as providing effective relief in the event of oil shortages.

The theory of hegemonic stability is less useful in accounting for the disintegration of the specific rules of the Bretton Woods balance-of-payments regime or for the continuing decay of the GATT-based trade regime. One reason for this deficiency is that as a systemic theory it cannot take account of domestic political pressures, some of which arose from changes in the world political economy but which were affected by the nature of domestic belief systems and coalitions (cf. Gourevitch, 1978). Yet even on systemic grounds the theory is inadequate because of its failure to take into account the role of international institutions, such as international economic regimes, in fostering and shaping patterns of cooperation. More cooperation has persisted than the theory of hegemonic stability would have predicted. International regimes perform functions demanded by states having shared interests; when the regimes already exist, they can be maintained even after the original conditions for their creation have disappeared. This argument was made on theoretical grounds in chapter 6, and is reinforced by the evidence about the persistence of international regimes, despite declines in American hegemony, offered in this chapter.

Thus the conceptions of cooperation and discord and the functional theory of international regimes put forth in this book help us understand the persistence of cooperation in the contemporary world political economy. The prospect of discord creates incentives for cooperation; and at least in money and trade, international regimes have been sufficiently well developed to facilitate a good deal of cooperation—certainly more than would have been predicted by the theory of hegemonic stability alone. That cooperation is not always directed to liberal purposes should not surprise us, since cooperation does not imply harmony but rather a highly contentious process of bargaining and mutual policy adjustment. In a period of economic difficulty, governments seek to protect their constituents from the costs of adjustment to change. A feature of the modern world economy is that they have done so as much through illiberal measures of international cooperation, such as the Multi-Fiber Agreement and voluntary export restraints, as through unilateral action leading to escalating discord. They value the rules and principles of international regimes not because they point to a new world "beyond the nation-state," but because they provide a framework that facilitates limited cooperation to serve state purposes, whether liberal or not.

This account of recent developments in the world political economy also illustrates the significance of the legacy of international institutions left to a post-hegemonic world by the era of American dominance. We can only understand the often puzzling mixture of cooperation and discord that we observe today if we recognize the continuing impact of international regimes on the ability of countries with shared interests to cooperate. Whether these regimes will be adapted successfully to a world political economy lacking a hegemon is not foreordained, but depends in substantial part on human choices. Our awareness of the value, as well as the fragility, of these international regimes should lead us to make these choices in a farsighted rather than myopic way.

· 10 ·

THE CONSUMERS' OIL REGIME,
1974-81

In chapter 9 we observed that substantial cooperation in monetary and trade relations continued to take place in the 1970s and 1980s, even though established international regimes were under pressure. Old cooperative arrangements have been undermined in many ways, and the cooperation that remains is not always oriented toward liberal ends; nevertheless, attempts at cooperation persist. Typically, these efforts to cooperate arise, as we would expect, out of discord. For instance, economic summits among the seven largest advanced industrialized countries were instituted in 1975 in reaction to the breakdown of hegemonic cooperation epitomized by the oil crisis and the breakdown of the Bretton Woods monetary regime. The elaborate debt rescheduling arrangements devised by the IMF, central banks, and private banks in 1982-83 constituted responses to the potential discord, and the ruinous financial consequences, that would have arisen had major countries such as Mexico and Brazil defaulted on their outstanding debts.

Neither of these major new international cooperative endeavors began *de novo* at the time of distress or crisis. The practice of summitry grew out of informal meetings of finance ministers that had developed in conjunction with the IMF in the early 1970s—and in which two men who had become leaders of their governments by 1975 (Valery Giscard d'Estaing of France and Helmut Schmidt of Germany) had participated (de Menil, 1983, p. 17; Putnam and Bayne, 1984). The elaborate networks of interbank cooperation that were used to forestall a debt crisis in 1982-83 built on what Charles Lipson (1981) called "the international organization of Third World debt," which had been developed during less severe debt reschedulings in the 1970s. Cooperation, as I have stressed, depends both on real or potential discord and on institutional arrangements that facilitate agreements by reducing transaction costs and providing high-quality information in a relatively symmetrical fashion.

These examples do not, of course, prove the validity of my point about cooperation emerging from discord or my theory about the functions of international regimes. As we saw in chapter 9, it is still difficult to disentangle the residual effects of hegemony and of continued U.S. leadership from the impact of governments' judgments that they need regimes to attain their own objectives multilaterally. Recent efforts to cooperate on issues of Third World debt or on oil have centered on the United States as the leading state, so they could be interpreted as reflecting the persistence of American power.

No decisive test of the independent value of the conceptions of cooperation and regimes put forward in chapters 4-7 is possible at this time, since we are only just entering the post-hegemonic era in the world political economy. The United States remains the most important state in the world political economy, although it is less predominant than before. Hegemony by the standards of the 1950s has disappeared, but the United States is not yet an "ordinary country" (Rosecrance, 1976). To test my theory, one would have to select a range of issue-areas significant in world politics during a period in which no hegemonic power exercises decisive influence over the nature of international regimes; then we would have to explore patterns of international cooperation in each. If my thesis about the decline of American hegemony is correct, the 1980s should provide an appropriate period for such an analysis, but at least when the research for this book was being done, between 1977 and 1983, it was somewhat early to make such an assessment. If we date the close of the period of American hegemony from the late 1960s, the postwar international political economy had only experienced ten to fifteen years of transition toward an anticipated future "after hegemony." As we have seen, this has been a disturbed period, with the old patterns of hegemonic cooperation eroding and with the United States continuing to be the most important actor, yet lacking the ability and sometimes the inclination to make and sustain strong, multilateral liberal rules. We saw in chapter 9 that this period of transition could best be analyzed with a combination of the theory of hegemonic stability and the theories put forward here about cooperation and international regimes.

The implications of my functional theory of international regimes are therefore not tested in this volume. This state of affairs makes my analysis incomplete, but it also has the advantage that my predictions about conditions for nonhegemonic regime formation are made before the evidence for the correctness or falsity of such predictions is available. Thus it is possible to indicate in advance the conditions under which my forecasts about hegemony, or my theory of cooperation, would be falsified.

My forecast about the distribution of power in the world political economy will be falsified if hegemony is restored in the 1980s. The return of hegemony would not contradict my conception of the dialectical relationship between cooperation and discord, nor would it disconfirm a functional theory of international regimes. It would, however, make these contentions less relevant, since the impact of hegemony would, as in the 1950s, outweigh them. We might understand hegemonic leadership better from the account of the 1950s in chapter 8, and our comprehension of the role of international regimes might be improved by the arguments in Part II; but these additions to our knowledge would constitute qualifications to, rather than substitutes for, the basic hegemonic stability model drawn from Realism.

My theory can only be falsified if my estimate of future power realities turns out to be correct—that is, if hegemony is not restored. Thus would the conditions for operation of the theory come into being. The theory would then be disconfirmed if cooperation were not to emerge at all after hegemony. A continual downward spiral into trade and monetary wars and "beggar thy neighbor" policies would constitute support for the Realist position, not for my own. My theory would also be falsified if cooperation were consistently to appear in the "wrong places." For instance, I do not expect much cooperation by large numbers of small countries without the leadership of a few great powers; thus the emergence of a strong United Nations led by small states, or of "collective self-reliance" strategies among Third World countries, would count as strong evidence against my theory. So would a situation in which cooperation did not emerge on issues involving repeated interactions over time, but did appear on single-play issues with Prisoners' Dilemma payoff matrices. Finally, it would count against my theory if most agreements made among governments were constructed not within the framework of international regimes, but on an *ad hoc* basis, either apart from established regimes or in issue-areas that had not experienced prior development of international networks or institutions.

Scholars may later be able to conduct a full evaluation of the theories of cooperation and international regimes put forward in this book. In 1994 they may be able to look back on the post-hegemonic era, as I have looked back on the eras of hegemony and hegemonic decline, and to undertake an analysis, by issue-area, of outcomes relative to the expectations established by theory. But this is not possible now. What is possible, however, is to examine more closely the operation of the international regime centered on the one major new international organization helping the advanced industrialized countries to coordinate policy in any of the issue-areas of money, trade, and oil. This organization is the International Energy Agency (IEA). In money and trade, the old regimes, constructed in the 1940s and 1950s, have experienced continuous existence throughout the last thirty-five years, although they have evolved substantially during that period of time. In oil, by contrast, there was a real break in the early 1970s. The consumers' oil regime built around the IEA therefore constitutes the closest example available of cooperation "after hegemony." Chapter 8 analyzed hegemonic cooperation, and chapter 9 assessed the consequences of the decline of American hegemony for cooperation. This chapter is designed to improve our understanding of the post-hegemonic era, though on a less comprehensive basis, by investigating the IEA-centered regime. We will examine the activities of the IEA as they affected the politics and economics of international oil relations, in order to gain some insights into how contemporary post-hegemonic regimes actually operate. This is a more modest objective than the comprehensive testing of theory, which must be postponed; but it may prove enlightening nonetheless.

THE IEA AND THE OIL REGIME

The International Energy Agency does not limit itself to activities having to do with petroleum, but also undertakes programs in nuclear energy, coal, and unconventional sources of energy. Our focus here, however, is more narrowly on its activities in oil. As we have seen, before 1974 there were no explicit intergovernmental rules governing the behavior of states and multinational oil companies operating in this area, but the advent of the IEA changed that situation. Within the framework of the IEA's founding document, the Agreement on an International Energy Program, extensive rules have been developed by and for the advanced market-economy countries. Some of these rules, especially those governing the operation of the agency's emergency oil-sharing system, are elaborate and detailed. Thus the injunctions of the regime are a great deal clearer than they were during the crises of 1956-57 or 1973-74.

The argument of this book suggests that the IEA regime should turn out to function principally as a facilitator of agreement among states. The IEA itself occupies a critical point in communications networks linking energy ministries with each other, and with oil companies, and could therefore play a significant role in forming coalitions of the like-minded. We expect it to reduce the costs of transactions among these actors and to reduce uncertainty by providing information to governments. It may do so by providing rules that are used as guidelines by governments and complied with because of decentralized incentives;

or it may do so more informally, through coordination on the basis of principles, but without such explicit rules. We do not expect it to be an enforcer of rules.

At the same time that we analyze how the IEA functions, we can explore in a limited way the effectiveness or ineffectiveness of international organizations in the contemporary world political economy. The theory of international regimes presented above does not predict that an international regime such as the one centered on the IEA will be effective. My argument is that cooperation among independent governments in the absence of hegemony, to achieve joint gains, is possible, and that regimes can facilitate such cooperation by reducing transaction costs, providing information, and constructing rules of thumb to guide bureaucracies in making routine decisions. But nothing has been said here to imply that this will necessarily happen, much less that it will take place automatically. If the argument here is correct, cooperation in energy should not be precluded merely by the principle of sovereignty; and insofar as it takes place, it should occur not as a result of successfully enforcing hierarchical rules, but through facilitating agreements among governments, whether by the use of rules as guidelines or through informal coordination.

The IEA provides a particularly convenient focus for a study of regime effectiveness, since its founding after the oil crisis of 1973 and its activities during the crises of 1979 and 1980 provide us fortuitously with a "before and after" research design. It is difficult to make precise comparisons among these three crises, for differences abound; but they are similar enough—all originated with real and prospective cutbacks in Middle Eastern oil production amounting to between 4 and 7 percent of world production during their most severe months—that some tentative inferences about the impact of the IEA-centered energy regime between 1974 and 1981 can be made.[1]

I will begin by briefly reviewing the 1973-74 oil crisis as a way of establishing a comparative baseline for an analysis of the effectiveness of the IEA-centered regime. Then I will consider the 1979 and 1980 crises in turn. For each of the two episodes involving the IEA-centered regime, I will try to determine whether the IEA sought to achieve its purposes principally through enforcement of rules, through manage-

[1] My own research at the IEA was undertaken in 1977 and again in 1981. Since the activities of the agency have been less salient since 1981, in part due to the oil "glut" beginning in that year, and my post-1981 information would be based only on public documents and secondary sources, this account does not go beyond the events of that year.

ment of a decentralized system of rules, or through informal coordination legitimized by regime principles. I will also ask how effective the organization was in dealing with the situations that faced it in 1979 and 1980, as compared with the nonregime conditions of 1973-74. I am interested in regime effectiveness for the light it throws on nonhegemonic cooperation. My conclusions about the functions served by the regime, and how they were performed, will be compared with what we should expect on the basis of the abstract arguments of chapters 5-7.[2]

THE OIL CRISIS OF 1973-74

The essential facts of the 1973-74 oil crisis have been discussed in chapter 9. An Arab-Israeli war, which began in early October, led to a series of decisions by Arab countries to reduce oil production and to impose embargoes on the United States, which was supplying arms to Israel, and the Netherlands, which had adopted a pro-Israeli position in foreign policy and had in various ways supported the Israeli war effort. As a result, available supplies of oil fell about 7 percent on a global scale between October and December 1973 and, by March 1974, were still 5 percent below the October level. The availability of petroleum supplies in Europe in March was also about 5 percent below that in October (Vernon, 1975, pp. 64-65, 101, 181).

The major oil-consuming countries reacted to the crisis in an uncoordinated and competitive way. Britain and France, joined by most other European countries, sought to appease the Arabs even if doing so meant distancing themselves from the Dutch. In early November the European Community adopted a pro-Arab resolution on the Middle East, which led to a loosening of Arab restrictions on oil shipments to Europe. Japan also made pro-Arab pronouncements in the wake of the production cutbacks. Although the OECD secretariat tried to provide information to governments and even to propose an oil-shar-

---

[2] My model here is Alexander George's conception of "structured, focused comparison," in which a number of cases are addressed with a common set of questions. In this book, however, these questions are embedded within a general theory—a functional theory of regimes—that was worked out principally in a deductive manner. For a concise discussion of structured, focused comparison, see George, 1979, and for a study incorporating the method, see George and Smoke, 1974. It should be noted that for the analysis of how regimes operate the IEA constitutes only one case, whereas for the analysis of effectiveness there are three cases as the units of analysis—1973-74, 1979, and 1980.

ing scheme, no effective coordination took place. On the contrary, the major importing countries each adopted a narrowly self-interested approach. France and Britain sought to pressure their oil companies into giving them preferential treatment; Italy, Spain, and Belgium imposed restrictions on exports of petroleum; American, Japanese, and German companies bid up oil prices on the spot market. For each country in its own way, it was *sauve qui peut*. As the new head of the IEA wrote in 1975, the OECD states relied on "uncoordinated national emergency measures that followed different patterns, involving the use of quite different measures and resulting in additional distortions" (Lantzke, 1975, p. 220). The consuming countries were unable to solve the dilemma of collective action: in trying individually to save themselves, they contributed to the quadrupling of official prices (from about $3 per barrel to almost $12) between the beginning of October 1973 and January 1, 1974. During the height of the crisis, spot prices were even higher, reaching $16 to $17 per barrel (Vernon, 1975, pp. 50-51, 68).

Ironically enough, it was the much-maligned international oil companies that saved the OECD countries from the full consequences of their own myopic pursuit of self-interest. The companies generally ignored demands by governments to award preferential treatment, but followed a rule of trying to reduce shipments roughly equally to all of their customers. This practice neither maximized short-term profits nor responded to political pressure, but it provided a rule of thumb that could be justified as equitable in rule-utilitarian terms. A Federal Energy Administration report concluded: "It is difficult to imagine that any allocation plan would have achieved a more equitable allocation of reduced supplies" (Stobaugh, 1975, p. 199). The transnational networks of the companies succeeded where intergovernmental politics had failed.

The 1973-74 crisis illustrates the severity of the dilemma of collective action when uncertainty is high and no institutions for reducing it exist. Each country followed the "defecting" strategy of Prisoners' Dilemma, fearing that if it failed to try to get preferential treatment for itself, it would wind up with the "sucker's payoff" of oil shortages. The Netherlands, which suffered most from the embargo and had to pay premium prices for its oil (Vernon, 1975, p. 99), was the "sucker" this time.

The OECD countries in this crisis had not followed the practice of John Stuart Mill's rule-utilitarian mariner, whom we encountered in chapter 7. Mill's mariner calculated the Nautical Almanack before going out to sea, thus permitting himself to decide on rules of thumb

223

for sailing in the event that a storm should appear. Having no rules established, and with their own severely bounded rationality complicated by the necessity of negotiating collective decisions, the OECD countries foundered in the storm created by the Yom Kippur War. Nothing could better reveal the potential importance of international regimes for cooperation than this indication of the significance of their absence for discord.

THE OIL CRISIS OF 1979

In view of the disastrous events of 1973-74, it is not surprising that the United States called an international energy conference in Washington in early 1974, or that agreement was reached on an International Energy Program, establishing the International Energy Agency, by November of that year. Clearly, some international regime was required to overcome the dilemmas of collective action that had been so starkly revealed during the preceding months. As the leader of several interlocking alliance systems involving most of the advanced market-economy countries, the United States had particular reasons to be concerned about the discord over petroleum, since conflicts over oil had serious implications not only for the world economy but also for America's political influence and the continuation of its most basic security relationships.

By the end of 1978 the International Energy Agency was an operational international organization with a clear orientation toward facilitating cooperation among the advanced consuming countries. All major OECD countries had joined, except for France; and the French maintained close contact with the organization, which was housed at OECD headquarters in Paris. The European members and Japan had successfully resisted turning it into an anti-OPEC organization. Instead, its activities revolved around four working groups, which concentrated on developing an emergency system for sharing oil, establishing an information system to monitor the oil market, facilitating long-term measures to reduce net demand for oil on world markets, and setting up joint energy research and development activities.[3]

The first major task of the IEA was an exercise in rule-making: to construct the emergency sharing system. Complex technical negotia-

---

[3] This account of the IEA as of 1977-78 is based on research done in the IEA files and interviews held with members of the secretariat in Paris during November 1977 and on Keohane, 1978, which reports on that work. Some phrases and sentences in the following paragraphs are drawn directly from that article.

tions led to the drafting of an Emergency Management Manual, which was approved by the Governing Board of the IEA in May 1976. This manual specified the procedures for handling an emergency and, in particular, the relationships among the major international companies involved in the system, the IEA, and governments. It implemented the formal provisions of the International Energy Program, which empower the secretariat of the IEA to make a "finding" that reduction of oil supplies to the group or to a particular member country "has occurred or can reasonably be expected to occur," and "to establish the amount of the reduction for each Participating Country and for the group" (Agreement on an International Energy Program, 1974, Article 19). Such a decision can be reversed by the Governing Board, but only by a special majority constituted on the basis of weighted voting. Unless the secretariat were politically obtuse, it would be almost impossible in practice for its finding to be reversed. Finally, once the emergency provisions of the International Energy Program have been invoked, governments are under obligation to take a variety of mandatory actions.

The formal terms of the International Energy Program thus represent a remarkable delegation of authority to an international organization. Between 1974 and 1976 the IEA used this authority to elaborate a set of rules that were repeatedly tested and modified. A number of simulations of the emergency oil-sharing system, which involves elaborate provisions for reporting by international companies and governments, were conducted beginning in 1976. By 1978 the IEA regime had all the trappings of rules, coupled with the dash of supranationalism provided by the formal authority of the secretariat to declare an oil supply emergency.

The other aspects of the IEA's work that turned out later to be important in the 1979 crisis had to do with monitoring oil markets and conducting long-term planning. By 1978 the Standing Group on the Oil Market had developed an information system to report on the extraordinarily delicate subject of oil pricing, which constituted the focus of some of the IEA's bitterest political struggles in its early years. The Standing Committee on Long-Term Cooperation had spent most of its energy negotiating a "minimum safeguard price," or floor price, for oil, which soon became irrelevant since it was set at $7 per barrel. But in October 1977 the IEA did agree to set an overall group target for oil imports of 26 million barrels per day, up from the 22 to 23 million barrels per day of 1977, yet much less than the 30 million barrels per day projected at the time on the basis of then current policies.[4] This was only a group target, since the organization was unable to secure agreement on specific national targets; thus it had less the character of a set of rules than of a symbolic commitment. Like the other accomplishments of the agency up to this time, the agreement on group targets was largely the result of American leadership, working in conjunction with the IEA secretariat and other influential countries such as Germany and Britain.

The oil crisis of early 1979 was not anticipated by international companies, governments, or the IEA. Companies reduced their stocks of oil during 1978, and when cutbacks in Iranian production occurred in the fall of that year, in response to strikes and revolutionary activity, IEA members were not inclined to take strong formal action. The IEA Executive Director did activate the reporting system on supply and stock positions, so that the emergency sharing system could be put into effect later. The general mood of optimism was reinforced by the fact that, in the last quarter of 1978, noncommunist oil production was 1.4 million barrels per day higher than in the previous quarter, despite a reduction of 2.2 million barrels a day in Iranian output.[5]

Events in the first half of 1979 came as a rude shock. Iranian exports virtually ceased in January and February, leading to a doubling of spot oil prices. For the first quarter as a whole, total production in noncommunist areas fell by about 2 million barrels a day (or 4 percent). Despite the IEA, the response to this shortfall was much the same as it had been in 1973: oil users scrambled to ensure supplies for themselves at whatever price had to be paid. In some respects, indeed, the situation was worse, since the international oil companies controlled only about half of the oil in international trade, rather than the 90 percent or so that they had distributed prior to the 1973-74 crisis, and long-term contracts had become less important (Neff, 1981). Thus it was more difficult for the international companies to allocate supplies as they had in 1973-74; the market was characterized by greater fragmentation, uncertainty, and rigidity. Even a relatively small short-

---

[4] In the wake of the oil price rises of 1979 and the world recession of 1980-82, these forecasts appear extremely high. In 1981 OPEC production had fallen about 30 percent to 22.5 million barrels per day from the peak of 31.4 million barrels in 1977 (IFRI, 1982, p. 31). This was a result of weak demand for oil, not shortages in supply.

[5] Badger and Belgrave, 1982, p. 104. I rely heavily on this work as a reliable published account of the 1979 and 1980 crises. One of the authors is an IEA official, the other closely linked to oil companies and the British government; and its account corresponds well with the information I gained on a visit to the IEA in May of 1981. For other accounts, with much the same message, see Deese and Nye, 1981, and Foreign Policy Research Institute, 1980.

fall of production created a massive problem of collective action, or what Badger and Belgrave call a "chain reaction" (1982, p. 107):

> Some of the majors were deprived at a stroke of an important part of their supplies. . . . Independent refiners feared that they might have to shut down. State refineries, with Iran as their source of supply under government-to-government contracts, did not know where their next cargo of crude was coming from, nor did those independents which had chosen to operate at low marginal prices without contracts. Retailers of oil products, fearing a shortage, placed maximum orders on their suppliers. Final customers, large and small, hurried to fill their tanks.

Governments and the IEA were slow to react to this situation. Different governments adopted divergent stockpiling policies. The United States continued to stockpile large quantities of oil in December and January, ending this practice only at the end of March. Belgium and Sweden permitted companies to draw stocks down below the 90-day compulsory level, but Germany did not. The United States could not have used its stocks in any event because the Department of Energy had not installed pumps to get stockpiled oil out of the ground (Mancke, 1980, p. 39; Badger and Belgrave, 1982, p. 107)! On the whole, both private and official entities were *adding* to their stocks at this time; governments and the IEA secretariat were slow to recognize the importance for oil prices of these uncoordinated actions.[6]

The competitive scramble worsened in the second quarter of 1979. Faced with a choice between paying higher prices or suffering shortages, companies and governments drove oil prices higher by buying petroleum in the spot market. As in 1973-74, governments put pressure on companies to give them preference: Britain restricted North Sea exports, Japan coordinated a program of oil purchasing by its companies, and the United States in effect subsidized increased purchases of heating oil. The most innovative and potentially useful suggestion for dealing with the price problem through coordinated action came, ironically enough, from France, the one major importing country that was not a member of the IEA. This proposal, which called for a maximum frontier price for imports, "foundered on a general skepticism that such a system could be enforced and German (and by the summer) U.S. belief that they could afford to buy their way out of

---

[6] This sentence and much of the rest of this chapter draw heavily, sometimes verbatim, on Keohane, 1982d.

trouble (otherwise known as 'letting the market work')" (Badger and Belgrave, 1982, p. 114).

This combination of speculation and panic drove oil prices much higher even in the absence of a shortfall of supply as compared to demand. Production in the second quarter was equal to the level of the fourth quarter of 1978, and production for the entire year *increased* by more than 2 million barrels per day (4 percent) over 1978 while consumption barely increased at all. Remarkably, production actually *exceeded* consumption during 1979 as a whole (IEA, 1980, p. 12). Yet prices doubled. It is no wonder that sober observers conclude that in 1979 "the industrialized countries of the OECD inflicted on themselves one of the most disastrous events in their economic history" (Badger and Belgrave, 1982, p. 95).

During the crisis the IEA attempted to supply governments with information on the oil markets, especially the spot market. These efforts, however, were relatively ineffective, partly because unanticipated changes in the markets took place with bewildering speed, and partly because companies and governments continued to compete for available supplies. In March of 1979 the IEA attempted to deal with one aspect of the crucial problem of collective action by implementing a policy of demand restraint, seeking to reduce the import demand of its members by 2 million barrels per day. But, like earlier group targets, this resolution created only an overall goal rather than specific objectives for individual countries; it therefore imposed on governments what one representative referred to as a "political not a legal obligation." Since it entailed no real commitments, it provided no assurance to any given member that its partners would reduce their demand for oil, and no incentives to reduce one's own demand in order to preserve a reputation for keeping commitments. It therefore did not alter the structure of the problem of collective action or the dominance of a "defecting" solution for governments whose publics resisted sacrifices. By the end of the year it was clear that the resolution had not been particularly effective. The overall level of IEA imports was about 1 percent higher for 1979 than for 1978, reflecting increases in imports by most members. Consumption did drop in the fourth quarter, but this decline was the result more of a doubling in prices than of effective governmental measures to restrain demand.[7]

---

[7] For the final 1979 figures, see IEA, 1982a, table 6, p. 21. I have compared these with 1978 figures, which are not compiled in a single table but appear in the country tables in IEA, 1980. For a brief discussion of declines in consumption during the last quarter of 1979, see *OECD Observer*, no. 105 (July 1980).

The most remarkable aspect of the IEA's behavior during the 1979 crisis was not what it did, but what it did not do. Despite the effort that had been devoted to establishing an emergency oil-sharing system over the previous years, this arrangement was never activated. No findings were made by the secretariat, and no votes were taken. Despite the nominal importance of the elaborate rules for crisis management, the agency resorted to attempts at informal coordination rather than either enforcing its rules or using them to guide governments' and companies' actions. The relevance of this episode to our theme justifies a rather detailed discussion.

The International Energy Program provides that if any member of the IEA suffers an oil supply shortfall of more than 7 percent, it can request the secretariat to put into effect the emergency sharing system. This provision was included to enable the organization to counteract selective embargoes by oil producers, such as the one that Arab OPEC countries mounted against the United States and the Netherlands in 1973-74. Yet because the meaning of a deficiency is unclear, this selective triggering provision does not necessarily serve the purpose of equalizing burdens among IEA members. Countries with tight price controls, for example, could create the appearance of a deficiency, because such controls would stimulate consumption while turning away sellers. The shortages experienced by any such country, therefore, would be a self-inflicted consequence of national policy. From the market-oriented perspective of dominant members of the IEA and of the secretariat, it did not seem appropriate to use the IEA's emergency procedures to deal with such supply deficiencies; but no caveats regarding price controls are to be found in the language of the International Energy Program.

The issue became relevant in the winter of 1979. In February of that year Sweden, which maintained a system of oil price controls, complained that it was suffering a 17 percent shortfall of supplies for the first quarter. The secretariat's reaction was to argue that a nominal shortfall was normal for Sweden during the winter, owing to seasonal variations. Because ports in northern Europe become blocked by ice, these countries normally build up stocks in the summer and draw them down during the winter. From February to May 1979 the secretariat negotiated with the Swedish government to adjust its calculations of supply patterns, in an attempt to avoid a formal request that the emergency system be triggered.

Finally, in May 1979, Sweden did call for activation of the emergency system, noting a reduction in first-quarter supply of 9.8 percent, after adjusting for seasonal factors. Four days later the governing board declined to accept this request, but called on the secretariat "to examine the case of Sweden further and to consult with oil companies as provided in Article 19.6 of the International Energy Program Agreement in order to obtain their views regarding the situation and the appropriateness of the measures to be taken."[8] The secretariat took the view that there had indeed been a 7.7 percent shortfall in Swedish first-quarter supplies, after a 12 percent seasonal adjustment, and that in strictly statistical terms this should trigger the system. But its "qualitative judgment" was that the situation was improving and that the trigger was therefore not necessary. Informal discussions were taking place with the companies. Clearly, the secretariat engaged in a delicate process of bargaining, with the intention of persuading Sweden to relax its price controls somewhat and the companies to make some compromises on price. During the summer the issue disappeared.

The secretariat subsequently concluded that the governing board of the agency had the legal authority to activate the allocation system. But, from the secretariat's perspective, such action would have been a huge gamble. Hoarding and panic could have been the initial reaction, worsening the situation. In the absence of sufficiently clear rules on prices and costs, it might have been difficult to reach price agreements that would restrain spot markets; some countries might not have had legal authorization to participate in a reallocation system that was activated by an overall shortfall of less than 7 percent, and producers could have been goaded to counteraction. If the system did not work, confidence in the IEA's emergency system as a response to larger-scale disruptions could have been lost, and the IEA itself might have been in danger. Clearly, the less risky course was not to implement the formal rules.

The most powerful members of the agency agreed with the secretariat's conclusion. For the rest of the year the IEA relied on informal consultations with oil companies and governments, persuading holders of oil to make *ad hoc* adjustments, rather than seriously considering

---

[8] This quotation and others that appear in this chapter without citation come from internal IEA documents. I was given access to IEA documents on condition that I would not cite particular documents and that I would submit my notes to the agency for factual review before using them as the basis for published works. No agreement was made giving IEA officials any right to review or challenge any interpretations or arguments that I might make. Access on similar terms has been granted to Professor Peter Cowhey of the University of California, San Diego, and perhaps to other scholars as well. For a more complete statement of the terms under which I operated both in 1977 and 1981, see Keohane, 1978, p. 933.

formal implementation of either the selective or the general sharing arrangements. In light of this experience, there appeared to be little prospect that the sharing system would be formally activated in a crisis involving an overall shortfall of less than 7 percent. *Ad hoc* approaches were seen as more prudent.

Thus the IEA did not hold itself or its members to the letter of its rules, when to do so could have threatened the organization's existence as well as its already limited ability to inspire confidence in the efficacy of its actions and the perspicacity of its judgment. IEA rules served as symbols, used by the custodians of the regime to legitimize their behind-the-scenes attempts to facilitate agreements. As we have seen, in 1979 this informal action led to results that were only marginally, if at all, better than in 1973-74. Spot prices skyrocketed in response to a chain reaction, begun by relatively small and very short-lived supply shortages. OPEC did not act as a strong cartel; on the contrary, its prices simply followed the spot prices upward, with some delay. The inability of the consuming countries to overcome the dilemma of collective action by coordinating their own policies was a decisive cause of the doubling of oil prices during 1979.

THE MINI-CRISIS OF 1980

In the wake of the 1979 disaster the IEA set about "planning for the next war." At the Tokyo summit the United States proposed that demand for oil be restrained through the device of oil import targets agreed upon country by country. The targets for 1980 were formally approved by the IEA in December 1979. Stockpiling issues were also a concern at Tokyo. Not only did stockpiling in a time of shortage raise spot market prices, but it could also lead to increases in the prices contained in longer-term contracts. By the end of the year members of the IEA had apparently reached a consensus that uncoordinated stockpiling actions by the private sector presented a problem with which the agency should deal.

As we have seen, the problems of excessive final demand for oil, and of stockpiling, were both problems of collective action. Individual actors, seeking rationally but in an uncoordinated way to protect themselves, worsened matters for everyone. But the measures adopted by the IEA to deal with these issues diverged. To deal with excess demand, a rule-oriented solution was chosen. Each country was to commit itself publicly to a particular oil import target. Its reputation would therefore be at stake, presumably giving it incentives to comply. The model was not one of centralized but of decentralized enforcement, in which the IEA itself would help negotiate the original targets and monitor compliance with them. For stockpiling, on the other hand, purely informal arrangements were to be relied upon: no formal rules were laid down for secretariat action, which was to take the form of *ad hoc* and informal diplomacy.

A great deal of effort was devoted to the rule-oriented targeting exercise by the IEA secretariat and governing board. Yet even as they were taking final form in December 1979, the targets were recognized by officials as being too high to constitute effective constraints on imports. Most governments were careful to negotiate targets that provided them with a "margin of safety." Two close observers have commented that the targets endorsed by the IEA limited national imports "to levels which even then seemed unlikely to be reached in any case at the new prices and which in the event were never approached" (Badger and Belgrave, 1982, p. 114). This seems to be true for the United States, whose actual 1980 imports were 23 percent below target, and for the eight EEC states that also belong to the IEA, whose imports were 11 percent lower than targeted. It may not, however, be true for Japan, which the secretariat expected as late as early 1981 to exceed its target, and whose final imports were less than 4 percent below it.[9] Demand for oil was restrained not so much by the high targets as by the unwanted 1979 rise in prices.

The governing board of the IEA, prodded by the United States, continued to discuss the targeting issue. In December 1979 the governing board had agreed to monitor national import policies quarterly. During the spring of 1980 the secretariat sought agreement on a set of objective criteria for the determination of country targets, rather than letting them be established through a political process. This proposal was resisted by all important members of the organization except for the United States. It was eventually agreed that the secretariat on its own authority would prepare estimates of the expected oil requirements of each IEA country, but that these would not be regarded as ceilings unless or until ratified by ministerial action. No individual country targets were adopted for 1981 or 1982, despite American pressure. By the end of 1980 the emphasis of the IEA's long-term strategy had shifted away from country targeting to a more general

---

[9] The target figures by country appear in IEA, 1979, table 2, p. 14. Actual 1980 imports are given in IEA, 1981, table 6, p. 21. Putnam and Bayne (1984) discuss the negotiations at Tokyo (June 28-29, 1979) and point out that Japan's target was lower relative to the levels of imports that could be expected in the absence of constraints than were those of the United States or the EEC.

encouragement of structural change through annual reviews of country programs. When the Reagan Administration indicated that it did not care about individual country targets, some members of the IEA secretariat as well as officials of several countries breathed sighs of relief.

The fate of the targeting exercise helps to emphasize the difficulty of constructing and applying meaningful rules in world politics, in the absence of an effective hegemonic power. The United States attempted to exercise leadership, but found itself without followers on the issue. The only significance of the targets that were adopted was symbolic, since they were so high as to be operationally inconsequential.

This does not mean that the targeting exercise was worthless, if we examine it from a more political and less rule-bound perspective. Targets were politically useful because they raised the salience of energy questions in the U.S. government and provided political ammunition for officials who were serious about promoting energy conservation and other measures of import demand restraint. They also helped promote coalitions for oil conservation between U.S. officials and those in other IEA governments. Furthermore, targets provided a highly visible set of international commitments to energy conservation. This helped the Saudis, who had long pressed publicly for importing countries to exercise some demand restraint. Targets indeed constituted symbolic politics; but, in this context, symbolism was important as a way of facilitating cooperation.[10]

This defense of the targeting exercise is quite persuasive. What is most interesting about it for our purposes, however, is that the asserted gains from it have nothing to do with using an international organization to limit governmental autonomy through the imposition and enforcement of rules. The principal political justification for the targeting exercise was not that it established binding controls on national oil imports, but that it provided a rhetorical environment in which transgovernmental and international cooperation could take place. The IEA was used as a facilitator of agreements within and between states rather than as a quasi-government.

At the same meeting at which 1980 import targets were approved, the secretariat secured members' agreement to a proposal that it "seek to develop a system of consultation on stock policies among governments within the IEA and between governments and oil companies, evaluate the 90-day emergency reserve level, and develop other pro-

---

[10] I am indebted to former Undersecretary of State Richard N. Cooper for many of the points in this paragraph.

posals for an effective and flexible stock policy" (IEA/Press, 1979, no. 28, p. 5). This decision led to rather intensive discussions over the next nine months. During the winter of 1980 members of the secretariat developed a wide range of proposals that entailed institution-building and rule-making. Some working papers even suggested that an international buffer stock of oil be managed directly by the IEA, rather than leaving stockpiling solely to national governments.

Reactions by member governments, and apparently by high secretariat officials, to these ambitious proposals were negative. Member governments feared excessive bureaucratic interference with markets and an inordinate increase in power for the IEA secretariat. Instead of endorsing these schemes, the governing board agreed in May 1980 to an informal arrangement, presented in an options paper as the "minimum option." This involved the development of an information system and the scheduling of regular discussions of stocking problems in the Standing Group on the Oil Market, but it did not provide for clear criteria governing the use of national stocks, much less for stocks controlled by the IEA itself. The core of the policy was a complex, informal system in which governments, the secretariat, and the companies would consult one another in order to harmonize IEA and government policies with those of the oil industry. The secretariat tried to encourage companies to maintain their high stock levels in spite of a growing softness in the demand for oil; the idea was to encourage an anticyclical stocks policy—building during slack periods and drawing down during tight markets—rather than the opposite behavior that had been so evident in 1978-79. The governing board was unable to agree on a forthright statement supporting high stock levels, but it did endorse the secretariat's consultative efforts.

Thus the IEA's activities in all three areas of major emphasis—the emergency sharing system, demand restraint, and stockpiling policies—displayed great similarities in outcomes despite different patterns of political activity. In each case, rule-oriented solutions were proposed. As we have seen, such rules were developed in advance for the emergency system and cobbled together hastily in 1979 to achieve demand restraint through targeting. Only on issues of stockpiling were rule-bound proposals consistently rejected. Yet the results in all three areas were, in the end, similar: the rules were never implemented strictly. Where rules had been adopted, they either were not activated or were not very constraining on governments. The principal energies of the secretariat were devoted to informal coordination employing rules symbolically, rather than to rule-enforcement.

In September 1980 hostilities broke out between Iran and Iraq, and by the end of October a full-scale war was clearly under way. By early November oil exports from the belligerents, which had amounted to 4 million barrels per day prior to the fighting, had ceased, contributing to a reduction in noncommunist oil production worldwide of 2.4 million barrels a day for the fourth quarter. This was slightly larger than the production cut sustained in the first quarter of 1979, which sent prices skyrocketing. Yet although spot oil prices rose sharply during the fall of 1980—from $31 per barrel before the war to $40 in early December—they had fallen back to $35.50 by the end of the year, after which they continued to decline gradually. Prices in July 1981 were only 5 percent above the levels prior to the war, which was still continuing (Badger and Belgrave, 1982, pp. 118-25).

What accounts for the dramatic difference between the events of 1979 and those of 1980? In part, the relative calm of 1980 was a result of market conditions. High levels of stocks, general weakness in demand, and the willingness of Saudi Arabia to increase production were of great importance. But this is not the whole story. In 1980 the IEA energy regime seems to have mattered; in several ways, it helped to prevent another disaster of uncoordinated responses to a problem of collective action.

One way in which the IEA contributed to crisis management will be anticipated by readers of this book: it facilitated coordination between governments and companies and reduced uncertainty by providing reliable information to them. In 1978 and the first part of 1979 uncertainty was rife because the IEA's reporting system was not yet working. This uncertainty spread through the industry, leading to panic buying and higher prices. By 1980, however, "a considerable learning process had been completed. Officials were in place who understood the problem; the mechanisms of the IEA or the EEC had been tested and improved; the oil industry had got used to an uncertain supply pattern" (Badger and Belgrave, 1982, p. 130). Furthermore, political leaders had learned that they could not ignore price questions, even if their countries were relatively rich: "Even the apostles of the free market in the German Government feared the effect of further price increases, coming on top of the economic disaster of 1979, and were prepared to take some political risks to prevent such increases" (Badger and Belgrave, 1982, p. 136).

Of the planning that the IEA had done before the Iran–Iraq War, its consultations about stockpiling were most valuable. Although the governing board's decisions on stock policy had been rather vague, the prior discussions of the issue made it easier for the organization to react promptly to the new crisis. Perhaps the fact that no firm rules had been adopted was even an advantage for the secretariat in seeking to negotiate flexibly on this issue. At any rate, in October 1980, IEA member countries agreed on a number of courses of action. They would urge public and private market participants to refrain from "abnormal purchases" on the spot market; they would consult with oil companies to encourage the drawing down of stocks; and they would consult among themselves to ensure that these measures were implemented in a fair and consistent way. In particular, they agreed to "the use of political influence" to convince market participants that they should follow the IEA's advice. No explicit rules were laid down; stress was once again placed on the informal exercise of persuasion by the secretariat and by member governments.

During the next three months the IEA monitored the situation and took action along two sets of distinct but complementary lines. Consultations took place with companies and reassuring public statements were made. At the same time, extensive efforts were undertaken to deal with the supply problems of particular countries and companies, which often revolved around questions of price. The secretariat sought to avoid the enactment of rigid rules about price, strongly emphasizing informal negotiation and voluntary arbitration. In the secretariat's view, rigid price rules would have discouraged companies from cooperating voluntarily with the IEA.[11]

Although it is impossible to specify how much difference the IEA made in the 1980 crisis, it seems clear that it "leaned in the right direction." Stocks were drawn down at double the normal rate in the fourth quarter of 1980. Rather than attempting to control the oil markets, or to persuade companies and governments to act against their own self-interests, the IEA sought to persuade them that it was in their interests to sell oil rather than to stockpile it. This required that market participants believe that oil prices were not going to rise sharply, and that they might even fall. The IEA had to help construct a set of self-fulfilling prophecies that would produce lower rather than higher prices. In the end, "the studied calm displayed by the IEA, the

---

[11] Quiet discussions of stronger measures for dealing with stocks and the spot market did take place during the fall of 1980. It is possible that, had the situation worsened, such measures might have been put into place; but in view of the informal operating style of the IEA, this seems unlikely except as a last resort. For instance, despite the failure of the secretariat effectively to help Turkey (which was very short of oil at the end of the year), the emergency sharing system of the organization was, once again, not invoked. For details, see Badger and Belgrave, 1982, p. 121, and Keohane, 1982d, pp. 477-78.

governments and the industry alike may have done as much to avoid a price rise as any other single measure" (Badger and Belgrave, 1982, p. 136).

Conclusions

In a post-hegemonic world, the rules of international regimes cannot be reliably enforced through centralized organizations. If we view international regimes, and their international organizations, as attempts to construct hierarchies, or quasi-governments, they will appear weak to the point of ineffectiveness. What international regimes can accomplish depends not merely on their legal authority, but on the patterns of informal negotiation that develop within them. Rules can be important as symbols that legitimize cooperation or as guidelines for it. But cooperation, which involves mutual adjustment of the policies of independent actors, is not enforced by hierarchical authority.

The International Energy Agency illustrates these points in an exemplary way. Although it has relatively strong formal powers, as international organizations go, and has developed elaborate rules, it rarely implements these rules in ways that limit the autonomy either of governments or of those powerful transnational actors, the international oil companies. When the agency is pressed to do so, the exercise of rule-making and compliance tends to become symbolic, as in the case of targeting. The IEA's principal value, limited though it may be, is as a facilitator of agreement, both among governments and between governments and companies. It reduces the costs of coordination by providing information and by mobilizing workable coalitions behind political feasible policies. But there is almost no prospect that it will ever make or enforce rules that would require governments to toe the line.

This perspective on international institutions is in sharp contrast to the conception of them that many people seem to carry around in their heads. According to this common view, international organizations are regarded as hierarchies—quasi-governments that seek to perform governmental functions, albeit in a limited manner. It is imagined that international organizations serve as devices for limiting governmental autonomy. Even Realists often adopt this view of international organizations, asserting that there are "hierarchic elements within international structures," which "limit and restrain the exercise of sovereignty" (Waltz, 1979, pp. 115-16). Some writers in the Institutionalist tradition have sought to glorify international institutions, similarly conceived as hierarchies, as the leading edges of a better organized

237

new world; and postwar internationalists dreamt of supranational organizations that would subordinate governments to the collective will.

Even the most highly institutionalized international regimes do not rely on centralized rule-enforcement against their most important members. The IMF under the Bretton Woods regime and GATT both elaborated rules for national conduct, to which sanctions could be attached. Yet even during the early years of GATT such enforcement of its rules as took place was highly decentralized, relying principally on informal sanctions involving reputation, and only secondarily on retaliation by members against offenders. The IMF could enforce rules on small countries, but not on the United States. In the end it relied for enforcement of its rules on the incentives for compliance provided by its members, particularly by the United States. Centralized rule-enforcement by international organizations is a pipe-dream as long as the nation-state remains more "obstinate" than "obsolete" (Hoffmann, 1966).

Realists, seizing on the deficiencies that international organizations and regimes appear to display when conceived as rule-enforcing institutions, emphasize that these supposed hierarchies only operate "in ways strongly conditioned by the anarchy of the larger system" (Waltz, 1979, pp. 115-16). Many Realists can hardly conceal their pleasure at demonstrating the ineffectiveness of international organizations as centralized rule-enforcers. The ease with which international regimes can be shown to have only weak centralized enforcement powers is taken by Realists as demonstrating the irrelevance of these institutions to crucial issues of world politics. Yet what regimes' lack of enforcement powers suggests, on the contrary, is the shallowness of this conception of international institutions. Indeed, the dichotomy between "anarchy" and "hierarchy" upon which the conception rests is itself fundamentally misleading. Adherents of this view overlook non-hierarchic coordination in world politics and misinterpret international organizations and regimes as feeble hierarchies. As this book stresses, regimes are less important as centralized enforcers of rules than as facilitators of agreement among governments.

Yet rules can still play a role even if the principle of sovereignty ensures the futility of trying to establish hierarchies above the state. As we saw in chapters 5-6, rational actors may have incentives to obey rules, particularly if cooperation by others in future situations depends on their own compliance in the present. The incentives may come from patterns of behavior within the issue-area that lead actors to react to rule-violations, as in the retaliatory provisions of GATT; or they may arise from fear that violations would lead to greater discord in other issue-areas or damage to one's reputation. Even if rules of international regimes are not enforceable by centralized institutions, they may serve as "standards" or "guidelines" for governments. In such regimes the actions of international organizations may be significant. If an international organization can activate a system of rules, it may provide incentives for governments, aware of the importance of reputation if not fearful of retaliation, to behave differently than they otherwise would have done.

The GATT trade regime and the Bretton Woods monetary regime both functioned in this way for some time. In chapter 7 we emphasized the value of rules, as in such a regime, for governments laboring under constraints of bounded rationality. In general, this remains the model for international organizations: strong regimes are those with clear rules and effective incentives to comply with them. But our examination of the IEA leads us to qualify this conclusion somewhat, since its rules remained in the background, unused, while more informal means of policy coordination were pursued. In the IEA regime, rules are little more than symbolic. The consumers' energy regime contains injunctions—rules and principles—for state behavior; but its more specific injunctions (the "rules") are rarely implemented. What actually happens is that the less specific injunctions of the regime (the "principles") are used to guide and to legitimate informal attempts at mutual adjustment of policies, in which the secretariats of international organizations are intimately involved.

In conclusion, let us look again at the question of the effectiveness of post-hegemonic international regimes as compared to hegemony in the oil issue-area. An enlightening contrast can be drawn by recalling briefly the discussion in chapter 8 of the petroleum supply crisis of 1956-57. Reaction to this crisis constituted virtually the epitome of hegemonic cooperation. The United States orchestrated the consumers' response to the closure of the Suez Canal, through reallocation of tanker routes and increases in oil production at home. Although it gave little more than a passing nod to the OEEC and acted without a formal regime, the United States adopted measures that were highly effective. America supplied Europe with oil, thus averting feared economic and political collapse, but only after Britain and France had been forced to withdraw from Egypt and fall into line behind U.S. policy in the Middle East.

If the 1956-57 case reflects the significance of hegemony for cooperation, the 1980 episode suggests the potential value of international regimes and the international organizations associated with them.

239

The IEA played an important role in that crisis, although policy co-ordination through its efforts was less elaborate and effective than the hegemonic cooperation of 1956-57. Furthermore, the IEA was aided by an unusually favorable conjunction of other conditions. As the events of 1980 indicate, cooperation is most likely to occur not only when there are shared interests but when international institutions exist that facilitate cooperation on behalf of those interests. But, to be successful, these institutions require not just a pattern of underlying common interests but a sufficiently favorable environment that the marginal contributions of international institutions—to minimizing transaction costs, reducing uncertainty, and providing rules of thumb for government action—can make a crucial difference. International regimes cannot create order as well as a strong hegemon can, but regimes sometimes tip the balance toward self-fulfilling expectations of success and away from panic and failure.

Hegemony and international regimes can both contribute to cooperation. Neither is necessary: cooperation took place without a regime in 1956-57 and without hegemony in 1980. Neither is sufficient: U.S. dominance in the interwar period did not lead automatically to cooperation, and the IEA regime, despite its extensive rules and nominal authority, did not avoid discord in 1979. But as the oil crisis of 1973-74 suggests, if there is neither a hegemonic leader nor an international regime, prospects for cooperation are bleak indeed, and dilemmas of collective action are likely to be severe. It is not surprising that, after hegemony, governments persist in trying to build viable international regimes.

PART IV

Conclusion

·11·

THE VALUE OF INSTITUTIONS
AND THE COSTS OF FLEXIBILITY

Three tasks remain for this concluding chapter. The first is to restate my principal themes, linking my argument about international regimes to the question about cooperation after hegemony and the dialogue between Institutionalist and Realist writers discussed in chapter 1. What are the implications of this book for understanding the prospects for international cooperation during the coming decades and for theories of world politics? Second, I will return to the question of ethics and cooperation, introduced in chapter 1 but not subjected to sustained analysis there. Finally, I will show how my analysis of international regimes, despite its highly theoretical and systemic orientation, has implications for how we think about foreign policy. Indeed, it suggests caution about accepting the conventional view that foreign policy-makers should seek, except when known and specific interests mandate otherwise, to maintain flexibility in policy, maximizing the scope for choice. Foreign policies that seek to "keep options open" may carry substantial hidden costs.

INTERDEPENDENCE, INSTITUTIONS, AND REGIMES

Interdependence in the world political economy generates conflict. People who are hurt by unexpected changes emanating from abroad, such as increases in the prices that producers charge for oil or that banks charge for the use of money, turn to their governments for aid. So do workers, unemployed because of competition from more efficient or lower-wage foreign production. Governments, in turn, seek to shift the costs of these adjustments onto others, or at least to avoid having them shifted onto themselves. This strategy leads them to pursue incompatible policies and creates discord.

If discord is to be limited, and severe conflict avoided, governments' policies must be adjusted to one another. That is, cooperation is necessary. One way of achieving such mutual policy adjustment is through the activities of a hegemonic power, either through *ad hoc* measures or by establishing and maintaining international regimes that serve its own interests while managing to be sufficiently compatible with the interests of others to be widely accepted. As we saw in chapter 8, the

243

United States played this role during the first fifteen or twenty years after World War II; hegemonic cooperation was a reality. Chapters 9 and 10 indicated that the United States is still the most important country in the world political economy and that it remains an essential participant in international regimes. Indeed, U.S. involvement is usually necessary if cooperation is to be fostered successfully.

Nevertheless, chapter 9 also demonstrated that the ability and willingness of the United States to devote substantial resources to maintaining international economic regimes have both declined since the mid-1960s. As noted earlier, it seems unlikely that the United States will reassume the dominant position that it had during the 1950s, or that any other country will come to occupy such a position, in the absence of a wrenching upheaval such as occurred in the past as a result of major wars. Since war in the nuclear age would have altogether different and more catastrophic effects than the world wars of the past, it is probably safe to assume that hegemony will not be restored during our lifetimes. If we are to have cooperation, therefore, it will be cooperation without hegemony.

Nonhegemonic cooperation is difficult, since it must take place among independent states that are motivated more by their own conceptions of self-interest than by a devotion to the common good. Nothing in this book denies this difficulty, nor do I forecast a marvelous new era of smooth mutual policy adjustment, much less one of harmony. But, despite the persistence of discord, world politics is not a state of war. States do have complementary interests, which make certain forms of cooperation potentially beneficial. As hegemony erodes, the demand for international regimes may even increase, as the lack of a formal intergovernmental oil regime in the 1950s, and the institution of one in 1974, suggest. Furthermore, the legacy of American hegemony persists, in the form of a number of international regimes. These regimes create a more favorable institutional environment for cooperation than would otherwise exist; it is easier to maintain them than it would be to create new ones. Such regimes are important not because they constitute centralized quasi-governments, but because they can facilitate agreements, and decentralized enforcement of agreements, among governments. They enhance the likelihood of cooperation by reducing the costs of making transactions that are consistent with the principles of the regime. They create the conditions for orderly multilateral negotiations, legitimate and delegitimate different types of state action, and facilitate linkages among issues within regimes and between regimes. They increase the symmetry and improve the quality of the information that governments receive. By clustering issues together in the same forums over a long period of time, they help to bring governments into continuing interaction with one another, reducing incentives to cheat and enhancing the value of reputation. By establishing legitimate standards of behavior for states to follow and by providing ways to monitor compliance, they create the basis for decentralized enforcement founded on the principle of reciprocity. The network of international regimes bequeathed to the contemporary international political economy by American hegemony provides a valuable foundation for constructing post-hegemonic patterns of cooperation, which can be used by policymakers interested in achieving their objectives through multilateral action.

The importance of regimes for cooperation supports the Institutionalist claim, discussed in chapter 1, that international institutions help to realize common interests in world politics. An argument for this view has been made here not by smuggling in cosmopolitan preferences under the rubric of "world welfare" or "global interests," but by relying on Realist assumptions that states are egoistic, rational actors operating on the basis of their own conceptions of self-interest. Institutions are necessary, even on these restrictive premises, in order to achieve *state* purposes.

Realism provides a good starting-point for the analysis of cooperation and discord, since its taut logical structure and its pessimistic assumptions about individual and state behavior serve as barriers against wishful thinking. Furthermore, it suggests valuable insights that help us interpret the evolution of the world political economy since the end of World War II. Yet it is in need of revision, because it fails to take into account that states' conceptions of their interests, and of how their objectives should be pursued, depend not merely on national interests and the distribution of world power, but on the quantity, quality, and distribution of information. Agreements that are impossible to make under conditions of high uncertainty may become feasible when uncertainty has been reduced. Human beings, and governments, behave differently in information-rich environments than in information-poor ones. Information, as well as power, is a significant systemic variable in world politics. International systems containing institutions that generate a great deal of high-quality information and make it available on a reasonably even basis to the major actors are likely to experience more cooperation than systems that do not contain such institutions, even if fundamental state interests and the distribution of power are the same in each system. Realism should not be discarded, since its insights are fundamental to an understanding of world politics (Keohane, 1983), but it does need to be reformulated to reflect the impact of information-providing institutions on state behavior, even when rational egoism persists.

Thus when we think about cooperation after hegemony, we need to think about institutions. Theories that dismiss international institutions as insignificant fail to help us understand the conditions under which states' attempts at cooperation, *in their own interests*, will be successful. This is especially true in the contemporary world political economy, since it is endowed with a number of important international regimes, created under conditions of American hegemony but facilitating cooperation even after the erosion of U.S. dominance. We seem now to be in a period of potential transition between the hegemonic cooperation of the two decades after World War II and a new state of affairs, either one of prevailing discord or of post-hegemonic cooperation. Whether discord or cooperation prevails will depend in considerable measure on how well governments take advantage of established international regimes to make new agreements and ensure compliance with old ones.

Yet an awareness of the importance of institutions—defined broadly as sets of practices and expectations rather than in terms of formal organizations with imposing headquarters buildings—must not lead us to lapse into old habits of thought. It is not particularly helpful to think about institutions in terms of "peace through law" or world government. Institutions that facilitate cooperation do not mandate what governments must do; rather, they help governments pursue their own interests through cooperation. Regimes provide information and reduce the costs of transactions that are consistent with their injunctions, thus facilitating interstate agreements and their decentralized enforcement. It is misleading, therefore, to evaluate regimes on the basis of whether they effectively centralize authority. Nor do institutions that promote cooperation need to be universal. Indeed, since regimes depend on shared interests, and on conditions that permit problems of collective action to be overcome, they are often most useful when relatively few like-minded countries are responsible for both making the essential rules and maintaining them. Finally, international institutions do not need to be integrated into one coherent network. Cooperation is almost always fragmentary in world politics: not all the pieces of the puzzle will fit together.

Building institutions in world politics is a frustrating and difficult business. Common interests are often hard to discover or to maintain. Furthermore, collective action invites myopic behavior: as in Rousseau's well-known tale, the hunters may chase individually after rabbits rather than cooperate to capture the deer (1755/1950, p. 238). Yet institutions are often worth constructing, because their presence or absence may determine whether governments can cooperate effectively for common ends. It is even more important to seek to maintain the valuable international institutions that continue to exist, since the effort required to maintain them is less than would be needed to construct new ones, and if they did not exist, many of them would have to be invented. Information-rich institutions that reduce uncertainty may make agreement possible in a future crisis. Since they may facilitate cooperation on issues that were not thought about at the time of their creation, international regimes have potential value beyond their concrete purposes. Such institutions cannot, therefore, be evaluated merely on the basis of how well they serve the perceived national interest at a given time; on the contrary, an adequate judgment of their worth depends on an estimate of the contribution they are likely to make, in the future, to the solution of problems that cannot yet be precisely defined. Such estimates should reflect an awareness that, in world politics, unexpected events—whether assassinations, coups, or defaults on debts—are likely, and that we need to insure against them.

The significance of information and institutions is not limited to political-economic relations among the advanced industrialized countries, although that is the substantive focus of this book. The theory presented here is relevant to any situation in world politics in which states have common or complementary interests that can only be realized through mutual agreement. As we have seen, there are almost always conflictual elements in these relationships as well. Like Prisoners' Dilemma, most of these situations will be "mixed-motive games," characterized by a combination of conflicting and complementary interests (Schelling, 1960/1980). Building information-rich institutions is as important in relations among the superpowers, where confidence is a key variable, and in arms control negotiations, in which monitoring and verification are of great importance, as in managing political-economic relations among the advanced industrialized countries. Institution-building may be more difficult where security issues are concerned, but is equally essential if cooperation is to be achieved.

THE ETHICAL VALUE OF COOPERATION

The introduction to this book raised the question of ethical evaluation. What is the moral value of the patterns of cooperation discussed here? Can they be justified on the grounds of a defensible moral theory?

Attempting to answer this question requires careful evaluation of criteria for ethical judgment.

Either of two competing doctrines could form the basis for our evaluation. We could rely on the "morality of states" or on a "cosmopolitan" view. The doctrine of the morality of states holds that "states, not persons, are the subjects of international morality." Major features of this view are its emphasis on state autonomy and the absence of any principle of distributive justice: "there are no moral rules regarding the structure and conduct of economic relations between states" (Beitz, 1979b, pp. 65-66; Walzer, 1977, Nye, 1983). A cosmopolitan perspective, by contrast, denies that state boundaries have deep moral significance, holding that "there are no reasons of basic principle for exempting the internal affairs of states from external moral scrutiny, and it is possible that members of some states might have obligations of justice with respect to persons elsewhere" (Beitz, 1979b, p. 182; see also Beitz, 1979a).

On the basis of the morality of states, genuinely voluntary cooperation among states is easy to justify. The primary value from the standpoint of this doctrine is state autonomy. Since international regimes help states to pursue their interests through cooperation, but without centralized enforcement of rules, an adherent of the doctrine of the morality of states would hold a strong presumption in their favor. The only serious issue would be to establish that a given regime was indeed formed on the basis of voluntary agreement and maintained through voluntary compliance. Yet as we saw in our discussion of Hobbes's arguments for the Leviathan in chapter 5, it is difficult to distinguish clearly voluntary from involuntary political action. Is my decision to give a robber my money, or a government my allegiance, "voluntary" if I make this choice at the point of a gun? To apply the morality of states doctrine, we would have to establish a threshold of constraint above which we would not consider actions to be voluntary, or autonomous. Once having found that the level of constraint in a given cooperative relationship fell below that threshold, we would be able to justify cooperation as promoting state purposes without violating state autonomy.

I believe that the international regimes discussed in this book would be regarded by an adherent of the doctrine of the morality of states as, on the whole, morally justifiable. It is true that different states face different constraints, or opportunity costs, in deciding whether to join or remain in regimes, so effective equality is not achieved. But equality is not a requirement of the morality-of-states doctrine, which is based on a keen awareness of the prevalence of inequality in world politics.

In any case, most international regimes seem to be less constraining of the autonomy of weak states than politically feasible alternatives, which would presumably involve bilateral bargaining on the basis of power rather than of general rules. The International Monetary Fund may be an exception to this judgment, since IMF practices for dealing with debtor countries involve considerable constraint on the autonomy of these countries' governments. But a hard-nosed proponent of the morality of states doctrine would reject even this criticism, since she would deny that rich lenders have any obligation to provide resources to poor borrowers in the first place. Such an observer could regard loans as properly conditional on the voluntary acceptance by borrowers of obligations to repay them, implying that the constraints imposed by the IMF on a borrower's autonomy would not constitute moral wrongs but simply consequences of the latter's earlier voluntary acts.

Critics of the morality of states doctrine, such as Charles Beitz, have pointed out that since ethical theory normally takes the individual person as the moral subject, special justification must be offered for abandoning this principle where international relations is involved. Beitz argues for a cosmopolitan conception, which "is concerned with the moral relations of members of a universal community in which state boundaries have a merely derivative significance" (1979b, p. 182). As Beitz suggests, the burden of argument should be on those who would ascribe rights to what E. H. Carr, in attempting to provide such a justification, referred to as "the fiction of the group-person" (1946/1962, p. 149). Even those who argue that there is justification for the morality of states doctrine must admit that "there is a relation between the rights of individuals and the rights of states. The latter are not unlimited and unconditional. States are artificial constructs" (Hoffmann, 1981, p. 39). That is, states cannot be considered independent subjects of moral theory; a justification of the morality of states doctrine must ultimately be made in terms of the rights or interests of individual human beings.

No effort will be made here to resolve the argument between advocates of the morality of states and cosmopolitanism, although I have a great deal of sympathy for the cosmopolitan view. It is important to note, however, that the closer we come to this view the more demanding must our criteria be for the evaluation of cooperation. If individuals in different societies have moral obligations toward one another, even a voluntary agreement that was beneficial for all citizens of the states entering into it could be considered immoral if it damaged people elsewhere in the world. To the extent that we accept a cosmopolitan morality, we have to examine the system-wide consequences of action, rather than narrowly focusing on the autonomy of the states involved in cooperative activity.

Such a cosmopolitan morality could rest either on utilitarianism or on a conception of rights. Cosmopolitan utilitarianism is attractive in many ways, since the criterion of attaining the greatest happiness of the greatest number worldwide seems consistent with the individualist orientation of cosmopolitanism. But utilitarianism encounters serious philosophical problems. In one respect, it seems *too demanding*, since it appears to imply an almost unlimited moral obligation to help anyone, anywhere, who is less well-off than oneself (Singer, 1972). This requires a high level of altruism. It also encounters difficulty in dealing with cross-cultural disparities in standards of living and social customs. A citizen of the United States who retained only enough income to live at the subsistence level of an Indian peasant would actually be more deprived than that peasant, since the American would be virtually cut off from her own culture and society, whereas the peasant would not. Yet if cultural standards were introduced into the utilitarian comparison, huge economic inequalities would again be sanctioned. In other respects, however, utilitarianism seems *insufficiently strict*, since it can be used to justify the view that innocent people can legitimately be sacrificed in the interests of the "greatest happiness of the greatest number." This may well seem intuitively unjust, and is so subject to abuse or manipulation that many reflective people find it repugnant (Rawls, 1971; Taurek, 1977; Sandel, 1983).

The principal alternative to utilitarianism is a theory of rights. According to John Rawls's influential formulation of this view, one begins such an analysis by asking how certain features of society would be evaluated "behind the veil of ignorance." That is, how would we regard particular institutions or rules if we had to evaluate them without knowing our place in society and therefore how they would affect us? Rawls's principles of justice emphasize liberty and equity. Of particular importance for a moral evaluation of international economic regimes is his "difference principle," which requires that "social and economic inequalities are to be arranged so that they are . . . to the greatest benefit of the least advantaged" (Rawls, 1971; Beitz, 1979b, p. 151).

Although Rawls has resisted doing so, Charles Beitz (1979b) has extended this reasoning to international relations. A follower of Beitz's argument would ask whether she would approve of international regimes and the cooperation they entail even without knowing her nationality or her position within the structure of her society. "Behind the veil of ignorance," with only one chance in six or seven of being a citizen of an industrialized market-economy country, would she approve of these institutions and the policy coordination that they facilitate?

Notice that this rights-based argument depends in practice on estimates of the consequences of action. Like utilitarianism, it focuses on the act rather than the intentions—whether pure or not—of the actor. This emphasis makes sense for both practical and conceptual reasons. It is often impossible to know the motivation of political leaders; and even if they could be reliably discovered, it would be odd to use our judgments about the moral worth of individuals as a basis for evaluating their actions as statesmen (Hoffmann, 1981, pp. 10-27). Cooperation that has benign effects should be praised even if we do not extend our blessings to its architects; and cooperation that leads to bad outcomes is subject to criticism even if the intentions of those who engage in it are pure. Students of international relations do not praise the appeasement in which the British government engaged at Munich in 1938 because Neville Chamberlain genuinely desired peace; nor do they condemn Richard Nixon's rapprochement with China on the grounds that Nixon took this step largely for selfish reasons.

Since both a consequentialist rights-based evaluation relying on the difference principle and a utilitarian standard focusing on aggregate welfare depend on an analysis of consequences, the distinction between intentions and consequences does not differentiate them from one another. The major difference between these two views is found in the willingness of utilitarians, and the refusal of rights-oriented thinkers, to justify losses of small increments of welfare by disadvantaged people in exchange for larger gains for more favored individuals. In practice, however, this distinction may be blurred, since utilitarians can use the principle of diminishing marginal utility to argue that a small gain in monetary terms for a poor person is really worth much more, in utility, than a much larger gain for someone who is already rich. The distinction between rights-oriented and utilitarian theories has fewer implications, therefore, for our evaluation of international regimes than the distinction between the doctrine of the morality of states and cosmopolitanism.

How would the international regimes discussed in this book fare when evaluated on cosmopolitan grounds, whether according to principles of utilitarianism or Rawls's difference principle? In sketching out possible answers to this question, I will focus first on the impact of these regimes on residents of the advanced industrialized countries, before evaluating their effects on a worldwide basis.

Evaluating Effects of Regimes on
People in Rich Countries

It is not clear that any of the international regimes discussed in this book would be regarded as good on the basis of either utilitarianism or Rawls's difference principle, even if only effects on people in advanced industrialized countries were considered. Utilitarians could argue that aggregate human welfare gains would be made by using these regimes to transfer resources from advantaged to disadvantaged people within these societies. Likewise, adherents of the difference principle would demand to know whether these regimes really help the least well-off people in the advanced industrialized countries as much as they could. Would it not be possible for the IMF to demand greater contribution from banks and less from taxpayers of the advanced countries? Could greater efforts not be devoted under GATT to alleviating the human costs to workers of adjustment to new international economic conditions? Why should the IEA not press for national policies to subsidize the fuel bills of the poor?

These moral deficiencies are, of course, not specific to international regimes, but reflect the inequalities inherent in the political and social systems of the advanced industrialized countries. They by no means suggest that matters would be improved for citizens of these countries by discarding these regimes and trying to start over. On the contrary, it seems more likely that a collapse of contemporary international economic regimes, imperfect as they are, would reduce overall welfare without benefiting the worst-off members of these societies. This judgment is reinforced by remembering the point made earlier in this chapter that international institutions such as international regimes may have favorable unintended consequences. Crises arise more suddenly than cooperative international regimes can be created. International institutions constructed for one purpose may be very helpful for another, as the example of the IMF—created principally to deal with exchange rates but relied on heavily in 1982-83 to prevent a world banking crisis—illustrates. The value of an international regime is not limited by the purposes of its founders.

A cosmopolitan evaluation of the effects of international regimes on people in the advanced industrialized countries would have to be mixed. The principles of the regimes are deficient on either the basis of Rawls's difference principle or the utilitarian premise of the equal value of individuals. But, given these defects, the institutions themselves nevertheless perform the valuable function of promoting cooperation. Furthermore, this cooperation, however imperfect, appears likely to have positive overall effects on the stability of the world political economy and the welfare of individuals within the advanced industrialized countries. It is hard to believe that these people would be better-off if the regimes were to disappear but the inegalitarian principles on which they are based remained.

Nevertheless, some caveats are in order. Writers of a variety of political persuasions have pointed out that liberal international regimes improve the bargaining power of private investors vis-à-vis governments and other groups in society. In an open world economy, the mobility of capital creates a double bias in favor of pro-capitalist governments. Economically, capital flows tend to move toward areas perceived by investors as "islands of stability," benefiting economies run by conservatives as opposed to those governed by leftists. Politically, capital mobility also helps the forces of the right, since the "exit" possibilities open to capitalists are likely to increase the efficacy of their attempts at "voice"—that is, their ability to influence policy through the political process at home (Hirschman, 1970).[1] Once an open capitalist world system has been established, as we saw in chapter 7, it is therefore likely to favor pro-capitalist governments and disadvantage socialist ones. When Thatcher or Reagan induces a recession through tight monetary policies, the pound or dollar appreciates and funds flow into Britain or the United States. This result may be inconvenient for a country seeking to control its money supply or expand exports; but it does not lead to a loss of confidence in the government, and it expands rather than contracts the resources at its disposal. When Mitterand tries to stimulate demand and to nationalize industries, by contrast, the franc declines, France's foreign reserves are jeopardized, and assistance may be needed from the IMF or selected governments of wealthy countries. Both the prestige of the government and the material resources at its disposal fall.

Fred Block argues that "the openness of an economy provides a means to combat the demands of the working class for higher wages and for economic and social reforms" (1977, p. 3). Thus it is not surprising that Block and other socialists cheerfully regard conflict within capitalism as a sign of decay, perhaps even of collapse, and gloomily view effective cooperation as indicating capitalism's unwelcome adaptability (Block, 1977; Mandel, 1974; Wallerstein, 1979).

---

[1] Hirschman points out, however, that the availability of exit may also reduce the incentives to use voice—that is, to act politically. This can be a counterbalancing factor to the one discussed in the text.

Conservatives use different language, regarding the constraints of the world economy as salutary antidotes to misguided policies based on political pressure or ideology; but they also view left-wing governments of advanced industrialized countries as constrained by the world capitalist system. "Countries pursuing equality strenuously with an inadequate growth rate" may, according to the McCracken Report, face "capital flight and a brain drain" (OECD, 1977a, pp. 136-37).

To portray socialist governments as paralyzed by world capitalism would be highly oversimplified, since this contention fails to take into account strategies that can be followed by clever leaders, backed by strong domestic institutions, popular support, and coherent policies. Austria is often pointed to as an example of such success (Katzenstein, 1984). Nevertheless, this argument suggests a possible basis for denying that the international regimes discussed in this book are morally justified on cosmopolitan grounds. One could argue that democratic socialism is preferable to capitalism but that its realization is thwarted by the existence of liberal international economic regimes. In this case, one might want to reject these regimes, on the grounds that their demise would lead to a new and benign socialism.

Such a rejection, however, not only assumes the beneficial consequences of socialism but also depends on the proposition that international regimes constitute a crucial barrier to the creation of better societies. It would be hard to accept this. Were liberal, cooperative international regimes to be destroyed without fundamental changes in the domestic politics of modern capitalism, it seems likely that the result would be worse rather than better: political xenophobia and economic inefficiency appear more probable than a dramatic advance toward more egalitarian societies in relationships of concord with one another. The collapse of international regimes as frameworks for cooperation is not likely to be the thunderclap ushering in a better world.

It would also be possible to mount a protectionist critique of liberal international regimes. To avoid the objection that protectionism leads to discord and conflict, a proponent of this view could draw on the finding of chapter 9 that cooperation can serve illiberal purposes. Thus a cooperative protectionist policy would not be a contradiction in terms. Indeed, some of the mutual policy adjustment that has taken place among the advanced countries in the 1970s and early 1980s, such as the promotion and acceptance of voluntary export restraints, has been designed to accommodate political demands to protect people against the costs of adjustment. Promoting cooperation without liberalism could serve the interests of many people who are disadvantaged by an open world economy. Citizens of advanced industrialized countries employed in industries facing strong foreign competition could therefore benefit. Since many of these people hold relatively low-wage jobs, as in the shoe and textile industries, one could attempt to make a moral argument for protectionist patterns of cooperation on the basis of concern for their welfare.

Despite the ingenuity of such an argument, it would be difficult to defend even if we only considered the effects of such a policy in the advanced countries. Whether cooperative or not, protectionism would lead to economic inefficiency and therefore to aggregate economic losses. Furthermore, the distribution of the benefits of protectionism would tend to favor well-organized and politically powerful groups within the advanced industrialized countries. Thus many of these benefits would flow to industries, such as automobiles and steel in the United States, whose workers receive relatively high wages. It would be even harder to endorse this position if we took worldwide effects into account, since the counterpart of jobs gained as a result of protection in Detroit and Düsseldorf would be jobs lost—by much more disadvantaged people—in Mexico City and Seoul.

Evaluating Effects of Regimes on a Global Basis

Mention of less developed countries brings us to the final aspect of our evaluative task: how to judge international regimes on cosmopolitan grounds if we consider their effects on the world as a whole, not just the advanced industrialized countries. When poor countries are taken into account, it seems even more clear that the principles of contemporary international economic regimes would be found morally deficient by the standards of cosmopolitan moral theory. These principles would fail an egalitarian utilitarian test because the benefits in terms of human welfare of redistributing resources to poorer countries would be greater than the costs of doing so (Russett, 1978). They would fail the test implied by the difference principle because any of them could be changed to benefit poor and weak individuals more. It is debatable whether the liberal principles of GATT and the IMF help the advanced industrialized countries more than the less developed ones; but it certainly is clear that changes in both regimes to reallocate more resources to poorer countries, and to direct those resources toward some of the world's least advantaged people, would be morally desirable either on utilitarian grounds or on the basis of Rawls's difference principle. The moral status of these regimes would be improved if the IMF were to devote more attention to helping poor people in debtor countries, if GATT were to give more generous preferences to the export of developing countries' manufactured goods insofar as doing so would have positive effects on employment and income redistribution, and if the IEA were to enact and implement provisions for subsidizing use of oil by people at the margin of subsistence in the Third World.

Thus it is compelling to argue that the principles on which present patterns of cooperation are based show insufficient sensitivity to the interests of disadvantaged people in the Third World. This suggests, however, not that there is too much cooperation, but that its orientation towards the interests of the rich is morally questionable. Contemporary monetary, trade, and oil regimes help the advanced industrialized countries to cooperate with each other, serving their interests. They create some benefits for poor countries, but these are small compared to what would be needed to correct gross violations of basic human rights that take place when people die of hunger or are continually miserable because of lack of clean water, adequate health care, or decent shelter. Greater empathy between rich and poor people—across national borders as well as within them—would not only be desirable; sharing more generously with poor people abroad is arguably the moral duty of affluent citizens of Europe, Japan, and North America, as well as of other countries.

Like the argument made above about the advanced industrialized countries, this argument suggests the moral inadequacy of the principles on which international regimes rely. Yet it does not imply that contemporary international regimes themselves should be abandoned or overturned. The principles underlying the rules and practices of the IMF, GATT, or the IEA reflect the interests and ideologies of the most powerful states in the international system. The cooperation that the institutions themselves foster, however, probably works to mitigate some of the harsher inequities inherent in the principles. Exchange of information and personal contacts between northern and southern elites, and the creation of organizations such as the World Bank and some of the United Nations specialized agencies, which are charged with promoting development, may marginally divert resources from North to South and slightly limit the tendency of advanced industrialized countries toward selfishness and exploitation. On consequentialist grounds, therefore, contemporary international economic regimes may be superior to politically feasible alternatives, although the principles on which they are based are morally deficient. This conditional acceptability of international economic regimes, however, does not relieve citizens of the advanced industrialized countries of the obligation to seek to modify the principles on which these institutions are based.[2]

Improvements (as judged by cosmopolitan moral standards) are more likely to be incremental than sudden, building on the knowledge of one another created by successful cooperation. The trick is not to ignore self-interest but to redefine it, to make it less myopic and more empathetic. Empathy by the advantaged may be more likely to develop in the context of well-functioning international institutions than in an international state of nature that approximates Hobbes's "war of all against all." Closer approximation to the ideals of cosmopolitan morality is therefore more likely to be promoted by modifying current international regimes than by abandoning them and attempting to start all over. Abstract plans for morally worthy international regimes, which do not take into account the reality of self-interest, are like castles constructed in the air, or—if implemented in a fit of absent-mindedness by governments—on sand.

FOREIGN POLICY AND THE COSTS OF FLEXIBILITY

It is often assumed that makers of foreign policy should maintain flexibility of action as much as possible. They are urged to "keep their options open." At first glance, this appears to be good advice, since the unpredictability of events in world politics makes it prudent to be able to change policy in response to new information. Yet governments are continually making commitments of one sort or another. For some reason they seem unable to follow the prescriptions of those who emphasize the value of retaining maximum room for maneuver.

The argument of this book helps to account for this discrepancy between the conventional wisdom of foreign policy analysis and the practices of states. Uncertainty pervades world politics. International regimes reduce this uncertainty by providing information, but they can only do this insofar as governments commit themselves to known rules and procedures and maintain these commitments even under pressure to renege. As we have seen, the fact that governments anticipate a future need for agreements with the same countries to which

---

[2] My formulation of the conditional acceptability of international economic institutions, despite the deficiency of the principles on which they are based, has been influenced by a paper by my colleague, Susan Moller Okin (1984), on the American Catholic bishops' pastoral letter on nuclear war. The bishops hold deterrence, though evil, to be conditionally acceptable because it is better than politically feasible alternatives; but they impose the condition that people relying on it must seek to find a better way to manage their relations.

they currently have commitments gives them incentives to fulfill those commitments even when it is painful to do so. Furthermore, theories of bounded rationality make us aware that, even apart from their adherence to international regimes, governments do not have the capability to maintain as high a degree of flexibility as would purely rational actors. They need rules of thumb to guide their actions.

If there were an infinitely large number of equally small actors in world politics, the general desirability of reducing uncertainty through the formation of international regimes would not lead to the creation of such institutions. International conditions would more closely approximate the Hobbesian model in which life is "nasty, brutish, and short." But as we have seen, the fact that the number of key actors in the international political economy of the advanced industrialized countries is typically small gives each state incentives to make and keep commitments so that others may be persuaded to do so.

Committing oneself to an international regime implies a decision to restrict one's own pursuit of advantage on specific issues in the future. Certain alternatives that might otherwise appear desirable—imposing quotas, manipulating exchange rates, hoarding one's own oil in a crisis—become unacceptable by the standards of the regime. Members of a regime that violate these norms and rules will find that their reputations suffer more than if they had never joined at all. A reputation as an unreliable partner may prevent a government from being able to make beneficial agreements in the future.

Reputation is important, but may not provide a sufficient basis for others to estimate the value of one's commitments. As we saw in chapters 5 and 6, diplomats have to deal with "quality uncertainty," much like buyers of used cars. That is, they need information about the real intentions and capabilities of their prospective partners: they may be prepared to enter into agreements only if they can gather convincing evidence that intentions are benign and capabilities sufficient to carry them out, and that the information at their disposal is not significantly worse than that possessed by their partners. Admittedly, governments such as that of the United States—whose bureaucratic struggles take place in public, and whose legislatures often fail to do the bidding of their executives—may earn reputations for unreliability, and their leaders may be viewed abroad as not having the capability to implement their agreements. Yet, as pointed out in chapter 6, there is another side to this question. Governments that close off their decisionmaking processes to outsiders, restricting the flow of information about their true preferences or their likely future actions, will have more difficulty providing high-quality evidence about their intentions than their less tightly organized counterparts, and will therefore find it harder to make mutually beneficial agreements.

These arguments suggest that governments should seek to combine reliability of action with the provision of high-quality information to their partners. International regimes facilitate both of these objectives, by providing rules that constitute standards for evaluating state behavior and by facilitating the establishment of contacts among governments that help to provide information not merely about policies but about intentions and values. Both the value of a reputation for reliability and the gains to be made from providing high-quality information to others challenge the traditional *Realpolitik* ideal of the autonomous, hierarchical state that keeps its options open and its decisionmaking processes closed. Maintaining unrestrained flexibility can be costly, if insistence on it makes a government an undesirable partner for others. Admittedly, there are tactical gains to be made from concealing preferences and "keeping others guessing." But such a policy can undermine one's ability to make beneficial agreements in the future. Being unpredictable not only disconcerts one's partners but reduces one's own ability to make credible promises. Where there are substantial common interests to be realized through agreement, the value of a reputation for faithfully carrying out agreements may outweigh the costs of consistently accepting the constraints of international rules. To pursue self-interest does not require maximizing freedom of action. On the contrary, intelligent and farsighted leaders understand that attainment of their objectives may depend on their commitment to the institutions that make cooperation possible.

259

BIBLIOGRAPHY

All references in the text are included below, as well as other works relied on in writing this book. Where a date is given for an original as well as a later edition, the latter was used; page references in the text refer to it.

Aggarwal, Vinod, 1981. Hanging by a Thread: International Regime Change in the Textile/Apparel System, 1950-1979 (Ph.D. dissertation. Stanford University).

Aggarwal, Vinod, 1983. The unraveling of the Multi-Fiber Arrangement, 1981: an examination of regime change. *International Organization*, vol. 37, no. 4 (Autumn), pp. 617-46.

Agreement on an International Energy Program (1974). TIAS no. 8278, 14 ILM 1 (1975); or in Committee Print, Committee on Interior and Insular Affairs, United States Senate, 93rd Congress, 2nd session, November 1974.

Aivazian, Varouj A., and Jeffrey L. Callen, 1981. The Coase theorem and the empty core. *Journal of Law and Economics*, vol. 24, no. 1 (April), pp. 175-81.

Akerlof, George A., 1970. The market for "lemons." *Quarterly Journal of Economics*, vol. 84, no. 3 (August), pp. 488-500.

Alchian, Armen A., 1968. Cost. *International Encyclopedia of the Social Sciences* (New York: Macmillan), pp. 404-15.

Allison, Graham, 1971. *Essence of Decision: Explaining the Cuban Missile Crisis* (Boston: Little, Brown).

Alt, James E., 1979. *The Politics of Economic Decline* (Cambridge: Cambridge University Press).

Anderson, Irvine H., 1981. *Aramco, the United States, and Saudi Arabia: A Study of the Dynamics of Foreign Oil Policy, 1933-1950* (Princeton: Princeton University Press).

Anderson, Perry, 1974. *Lineages of the Absolutist State* (London: New Left Books).

Arrighi, Giovanni, 1982. A crisis of hegemony. In Samir Amin, Giovanni Arrighi, Andre Gunder Frank, and Immanuel Wallerstein, *Dynamics of Global Crisis* (New York: Monthly Review Press), pp. 55-108.

Arrow, Kenneth J., 1974. *Essays in the Theory of Risk-Bearing* (New York: North-Holland/American Elsevier).

Aubrey, Henry, 1969. Behind the veil of international money. *Princeton Essays in International Finance*, no. 71 (January).

Avery, William P., and David P. Rapkin, eds., 1982. *America in a Changing World Political Economy* (New York: Longman).

Avineri, Shlomo, ed., 1969. *Karl Marx on Colonialism and Modernization* (Garden City, N.Y.: Anchor Books).

260

Axelrod, Robert, 1981. The emergence of cooperation among egoists. *American Political Science Review*, vol. 75, no. 2 (June), pp. 306-18.

Axelrod, Robert, 1984. *The Evolution of Cooperation* (New York: Basic Books).

Badger, Daniel, and Robert Belgrave, 1982. *Oil Supply and Price: What Went Right in 1980?* (London: Royal Institute of International Affairs, Energy Paper no. 2).

Bagehot, Walter, 1873/1962. *Lombard Street* (Homewood, Ill.: Richard D. Irwin, Inc.).

Baldwin, David A., 1979. Power analysis and world politics: new trends versus old tendencies. *World Politics*, vol. 31, no. 2 (January), pp. 161-94.

Barber, William J., 1981. The Eisenhower energy policy: reluctant intervention. In Craufurd D. Goodwin, ed., *Energy Policy in Perspective: Today's Problems, Yesterday's Solutions* (Washington, D.C.: Brookings Institution), pp. 205-86.

Barkun, Michael, 1968. *Law without Sanctions: Order in Primitive Societies and the World Community* (New Haven: Yale University Press).

Bauer, Raymond A., Ithiel de Sola Pool, and Lewis Anthony Dexter, 1963/1968. *American Business and Public Policy: The Politics of Foreign Trade* (New York: Atherton).

Beitz, Charles, 1979a. Bounded morality: justice and the state in world politics. *International Organization*, vol. 33, no. 3 (Summer), pp. 405-24.

Beitz, Charles, 1979b. *Political Theory and International Relations* (Princeton: Princeton University Press).

Belassa, Bela, 1980. Structural Change in Trade in Manufactured Goods Between Industrial and Developing Countries (Washington, D.C., World Bank Staff Working Paper no. 396, June).

Bergsten, C. Fred, 1975a. *Dilemmas of the Dollar* (New York: New York University Press).

Bergsten, C. Fred, 1975b. On the non-equivalence of import quotas and "voluntary" export restraints. In C. Fred Bergsten, ed., *Towards a New World Trade Policy: The Maidenhead Papers* (Lexington, Mass.: D.C. Heath), pp. 239-71.

Bernstein, Karen, 1983. The International Monetary Fund and Debtor Countries: The Case of Britain (Ph.D. dissertation, Stanford University).

Bhagwati, Jagdish, ed., 1982. *Import Competition and Response* (Chicago: University of Chicago Press).

BIS (Bank for International Settlements), 1982. 52nd Annual Report (Basle).

Blackhurst, Richard, Nicolas Marian, and Jan Tumlir, 1977. *Trade Liberalization, Protectionism and Interdependence* (Geneva: GATT Studies in International Trade no. 5, November).

Blair, John M., 1976. *The Control of Oil* (New York: Vintage Books).

Block, Fred L., 1977. *The Origins of International Economic Disorder* (Berkeley: University of California Press).

Bloomfield, Arthur I., 1959. *Monetary Policy Under the International Gold Standard* (New York: Federal Reserve Bank of New York).

Bobrow, Davis W., and Robert Kudrle, 1979. Energy R & D: in tepid pursuit of collective goods. *International Organization*, vol. 33, no. 2 (Spring), pp. 149-76.

Bohi, Douglas R., and Milton Russell, 1978. *Limiting Oil Imports: An Economic History and Analysis* (Baltimore: The Johns Hopkins University Press for Resources for the Future).

Branson, William H., 1980. Trends in United States international trade and investment since World War II. In Feldstein, 1980, pp. 183-257.

Brenner, Robert, 1977. The origins of capitalist development: a critique of neo-Smithian Marxism. *New Left Review*, no. 104 (July), pp. 25-81.

Bressand, Albert, 1983. Mastering the "worldeconomy." *Foreign Affairs*, vol. 61, no. 4 (Spring), pp. 745-72.

Brown, A. J., 1955. *The Great Inflation, 1939-1955* (London: Oxford University Press).

Brown, Seyom, 1983. *The Faces of Power: Constancy and Change in United States Foreign Policy from Truman to Reagan* (New York: Columbia University Press).

Brown, William Adams, Jr., 1950. *The United States and the Restoration of World Trade* (Washington, D.C.: Brookings Institution).

Brown, William Adams, Jr., and Redvers Opie, 1953. *American Foreign Assistance* (Washington, D.C.: Brookings Institution).

Cahn, Linda, 1980. National power and International Regimes: The United States and International Commodity Markets (Ph.D. dissertation, Stanford University).

Calleo, David P., and Benjamin M. Rowland, 1973. *America and the World Political Economy: Atlantic Dreams and National Realities* (Bloomington: Indiana University Press).

Calleo, David P., 1982. *The Imperious Economy* (Cambridge: Harvard University Press).

Cameron, David R., 1978. The expansion of the public economy: a comparative analysis. *American Political Science Review*, vol. 72, no. 4 (December), pp. 1243-61.

Campen, James T., and Arthur MacEwan, 1982. Crises, contradictions, and conservative controversies in contemporary U.S. capitalism. *Review of Radical Political Economics*, vol. 14, no. 3, pp. 1-22.

Carr, E. H., 1946/1962. *The Twenty Years' Crisis* (London: St. Martin's).

Chase-Dunn, Christopher K., 1981. Interstate system and capitalist world-economy: one logic or two? *International Studies Quarterly*, vol. 25, no. 1 (March), pp. 19-42.

Chase-Dunn, Christopher K., 1982. International economic policy in a declining core state. In Avery and Rapkin, 1982, pp. 77-96.

Cipolla, Carlo, ed., 1970. *The Economic Decline of Empires* (London: Methuen).

Cipolla, Carlo, ed., 1976. *The Fontana Economic History of Europe: The Twentieth Century*, 2 vols. (London: Fontana).

Coase, Ronald, 1960. The problem of social cost. *Journal of Law and Economics*, vol. 3, pp. 1-44.

Cohen, Benjamin J., 1977. *Organizing the World's Money: The Political Economy of International Monetary Relations* (New York: Basic Books).

Cohen, Benjamin J., 1983. Balance of payments financing: evolution of a regime. In Krasner, 1983, pp. 315-36.

Cohen, G. A., 1978. *Karl Marx's Theory of History: A Defense* (Princeton: Princeton University Press).

Colson, Elizabeth, 1974. *Tradition and Contract: The Problem of Order* (Chicago: Aldine Publishing Company).

Conybeare, John A.C., 1980. International organization and the theory of property rights. *International Organization*, vol. 34, no. 3 (Summer), pp. 307-34.

Cooper, Richard N., 1968. *The Economics of Interdependence* (New York: McGraw Hill for the Council on Foreign Relations).

Cooper, Richard N., 1972-73. Trade policy is foreign policy. *Foreign Policy*, no. 9, pp. 18-36.

Cooper, Richard N., 1982. The gold standard: historical facts and future prospects. *Brookings Papers on Economic Activity*, no. 1, pp. 1-56.

Cooper, Richard N., 1983. Economic interdependence and the coordination of economic policies (Cambridge: Harvard Institute of Economic Research, Harvard University, Discussion Paper no. 1003, August).

Corden, W. N., 1977. *Inflation, Exchange Rates and the World Economy: Lectures on International Monetary Economics* (Chicago: University of Chicago Press).

Corden, W. N., 1981. The logic of the international monetary non-system (Canberra: Centre for Economic Policy Research, Australian National University, Discussion Paper no. 24, March).

Cowhey, Peter F., and Edward Long, 1983. Testing theories of regime change: hegemonic decline or surplus capacity? *International Organization*, vol. 37, no. 2 (Spring), pp. 157-83.

Cox, Robert W., 1977. Labor and hegemony. *International Organization*, vol. 31, no. 3 (Summer), pp. 385-424.

Cox, Robert W., 1981. Social forces, states and world orders: beyond international relations theory. *Journal of International Studies, Millennium*, vol. 10, no. 2 (Summer), pp. 126-55.

Cyert, Richard, and James G. March, 1963. *The Behavioral Theory of the Firm* (Englewood Cliffs, N.J.: Prentice-Hall).

Dam, Kenneth W., 1970. *The GATT: Law and International Economic Organization* (Chicago: University of Chicago Press).

Darmstadter, Joel, and Hans H. Landsberg, 1975. The economic background. In Vernon, 1975, pp. 15-38.

Davis, Lance, and Douglass C. North, 1971. *Institutional Change and American Economic Growth* (Cambridge University Press).

De Cecco, Marcello, 1975. *Money and Empire: The International Gold Standard, 1890-1914* (Totowa, N.J.: Rowman and Littlefield).

Deese, David A., and Joseph S. Nye, eds., 1981. *Energy and Security* (Cambridge, Mass.: Ballinger).

De Larosière, J., 1983. The domestic economy and the International economy—their interactions. *IMF Survey*, December 5.

De Menil, George, and Anthony Solomon, 1983. *Economic Summitry* (New York: Council on Foreign Relations).

Diebold, William, Jr., 1952. *Trade and Payments in Western Europe* (New York: Harper).

Diebold, William, Jr., 1983. The United States in the world economy: a fifty-year view. Paper prepared for a meeting of the Council on Foreign Relations, New York, May 16.

Eckes, Alfred E., Jr., 1975. *A Search for Solvency: Bretton Woods and the international Monetary System, 1941-1971* (Austin: University of Texas Press).

Economist (London), various issues.

Ehrenberg, Richard, 1928. *Capital and Finance in the Age of the Renaissance: A Study of the Fuggers and Their Connections*, translated from the German by H. M. Lucas (New York: Harcourt, Brace).

Eklund, Klas, 1980. Long waves in the development of capitalism? *Kyklos*, vol. 33, fasc. 3, pp. 383-419.

Engler, Robert, 1961. *The Politics of Oil* (Chicago: University of Chicago Press).

Feis, Herbert, 1930. *Europe, The World's Banker* (New Haven, Yale University Press).

Feis, Herbert, 1966. *1933: Characters in Crisis* (Boston: Little, Brown).

Feldstein, Martin, ed., 1980. *The American Economy in Transition* (Chicago: University of Chicago Press).

Fellner, William, 1949. *Competition among the Few* (New York: Knopf).

Field, Alexander J., 1981. The problem with neoclassical institutional economics: a critique with special reference to the North/Thomas model of pre-1500 Europe. *Explorations in Economic History*, vol. 18. no. 2 (April), pp. 174-98.

Fine, Ben, and Laurence Harris, 1979. *Rereading Capital* (New York: Columbia University Press).

Finifter, Ada W., ed., 1983. *Political Science: The State of the Discipline* (Washington, D.C.: American Political Science Association).

Finlayson, Jock A., and Mark Zacher, 1983. The GATT and the regulation of trade barriers: regime dynamics and functions. In Krasner, 1983, pp. 273-314.

Ford, A. G., 1962. *The Gold Standard, 1880-1914* (Oxford: The Clarendon Press).

Foreign Policy Research Institute, 1980. *Oil Diplomacy: The Atlantic Nations in the Oil Crisis of 1978-79* (Philadelphia).

Frankel, P. H. 1966. *Mattei: Oil and Power Politics* (London: Faber and Faber).

French Institute for International Relations, 1982. *RAMSES 1982: The State of the World Economy* (Cambridge, Mass.: Ballinger).

Gardner, Richard, 1956/1980. *Sterling-Dollar Diplomacy in Current Perspective* (New York: Columbia University Press, 1980). This is an expanded edition of *Sterling-Dollar Diplomacy* (New York: Oxford University Press, 1956).

Gardner, Richard, 1983. Comments on a paper by Raymond Vernon, Twenty-Fifth Anniversary Conference of the Center for International Affairs, Harvard University, Cambridge, June 11.

GATT (General Agreement on Tariffs and Trade), *Focus* (Geneva), bimonthly.

Geertz, Clifford, 1973. *The Interpretation of Cultures* (New York: Basic Books).

George, Alexander L., 1979. Case studies and theory development: the method of structured, focused comparison. In Paul Gordon Lauren, ed., *Diplomacy: New Approaches in History, Theory and Policy* (New York: The Free Press).

George, Alexander L., and Richard Smoke, 1974. *Deterrence in American Foreign Policy* (New York: Columbia University Press).

Gerth, H. H., and C. Wright Mills, eds., 1946. *From Max Weber: Essays in Sociology* (New York: Oxford University Press).

Gilpin, Robert, 1972. The politics of transnational economic relations. In Keohane and Nye, 1972, pp. 48-69.

Gilpin, Robert, 1975, *U.S. Power and the Multinational Corporation* (New York: Basic Books).

Gilpin, Robert, 1981. *War and Change in World Politics* (Cambridge: Cambridge University Press).

Goldstein, Judith, 1983. A Re-examination of American Trade Policy: An Inquiry into the Causes of Protectionism (Ph.D. dissertation, UCLA).

Gouldner, Alvin, 1960. The norm of reciprocity. *American Sociological Review*, vol. 25, no. 2 (April), pp. 161-78.

Gourevitch, Peter Alexis, 1978. The second image reversed. *International Organization*, vol. 32, no. 4 (Autumn), pp. 881-912.

Graham, Richard, 1968. *Britain and the Modernization of Brazil, 1850-1914* (Cambridge: Cambridge University Press).

Haas, Ernst B., 1958. *The Uniting of Europe* (Stanford: Stanford University Press).

Haas, Ernst B., 1964. *Beyond the Nation-State* (Stanford: Stanford Unversity Press).

Haas, Ernst B., 1980. Why collaborate? Issue-linkage and international regimes. *World Politics*, vol. 32, no. 3 (April), pp. 357-405.

Haas, Ernst B., 1983. Words can hurt you; or, who said what to whom about regimes. In Krasner, 1983, pp. 23-60.

Haas, Ernst B., Mary Pat Williams, and Don Babai, 1977. *Scientists and World Order: The Uses of Technical Knowledge in International Organizations* (Berkeley: University of California Press).

Habermas, Jurgen, 1973/1976. *Legitimation Crisis* (London: Heinemann), translated from the German edition, published in 1973.

Hardin, Russell, 1982. *Collective Action* (Baltimore: The Johns Hopkins University Press for Resources for the Future).

Harsanyi, John, 1962/1971. Measurement of social power, opportunity costs and the theory of two-person bargaining games, *Behavioral Science*, vol. 7, no. 1, pp. 67-80. Much of this article also appears as Harsanyi, The dimension and measurement of social power, in K. W. Rothchild, ed., *Power in Economics* (Baltimore: Penguin Books), pp. 77-96.

Hart, H.L.A., 1961. *The Concept of Law* (Oxford: The Clarendon Press).

Henkin, Louis, 1979. *How Nations Behave: Law and Foreign Policy*, 2nd edition (New York: Columbia University Press for the Council on Foreign Relations).

Heymann, Philip B., 1973. The problem of coordination: bargaining and rules. *Harvard Law Review*, vol. 86, no. 5 (March), pp. 797-877.

Hibbs, Douglas, and Heino Fassbinder, eds., 1981. *Contemporary Political Economy: Studies on the Interdependence of Politics and Economics* (Amsterdam: North-Holland).

Hickman, Bert G., 1977. Comment on Salant, in Krause and Salant, 1977, pp. 227-32.

Hirsch, Fred, 1967. *Money International* (London: Penguin Books).

Hirsch, Fred, 1976. *Social Limits to Growth* (Cambridge: Harvard University Press).

Hirsch, Fred, 1977. The Bagehot problem. *The Manchester School*, vol. 45, no. 3 (September), pp. 241-57.

Hirsch, Fred, 1978. The ideological underlay of inflation. In Hirsch and Goldthorpe, 1978, pp. 263-84.

Hirsch, Fred, and Peter Oppenheimer, 1976. The trial of managed money: currency, credit and prices 1920-1970. In Cipolla, 1976, vol. 2, pp. 603-98.

Hirsch, Fred, and Michael Doyle, 1977. Politicization in the world economy: necessary conditions for an international economic order. In Hirsch and Doyle et al., *Alternatives to Monetary Disorder* (New York: McGraw-Hill for the Council on Foreign Relations).

Hirsch, Fred, and John Goldthorpe, eds., 1978. *The Political Economy of Inflation* (London: Martin Robertson).

Hirschman, Albert O., 1945/1980. *National Power and the Structure of Foreign Trade* (Berkeley: University of California Press).

Hirschman, Albert O., 1970. *Exit, Voice and Loyalty* (Cambridge: Harvard University Press).

Hirschman, Albert O., 1981. The social and political matrix of inflation: elaborations on the Latin American experience. In Hirschman, *Essays in*

Trespassing: Economics to Politics and Beyond (Cambridge: Cambridge University Press), pp. 177-207.

Hobbes, Thomas, 1651/1958. *Leviathan.* (Indianapolis: Bobbs-Merrill).

Hobsbawm, E. J., 1968. *Industry and Empire* (New York: Pantheon Books).

Hobson, John A., 1902/1938. *Imperialism: A Study* (London: George Allen & Unwin).

Hoffmann, Stanley, 1960. *Contemporary Theory in International Relations* (Englewood Cliffs, N.J.: Prentice-Hall).

Hoffmann, Stanley, 1965. *The State of War: Essays on the Theory and Practice of International Politics* (New York: Praeger).

Hoffmann, Stanley, 1966. Obstinate or obsolete? The fate of the nation-state and the case of Western Europe. *Daedalus*, vol. 95 (Summer), pp. 862-915.

Hoffmann, Stanley, 1981. *Duties Beyond Borders* (Syracuse: Syracuse University Press).

Hudec, Robert E., 1975. *The GATT Legal System and World Trade Diplomacy* (New York: Praeger).

Hutton, Nicholas, 1975. The salience of linkage in international economic negotiations. *Journal of Common Market Studies*, vol. 13, nos. 1-2, pp. 136-60.

Hymer, Stephen, 1972. The internationalization of capital. *Journal of Economic Issues*, vol. 6, no. 1 (March), pp. 91-111.

IEA (International Energy Agency), 1980. *Energy Policies and Programmes of IEA Countries, 1979 Review* (Paris: OECD/IEA).

IEA, 1981. *Energy Policies and Programmes of IEA Countries, 1980 Review* (Paris: OECD/IEA).

IEA, 1982a. *Energy Policies and Programmes of IEA Countries, 1981 Review* (Paris: OECD/IEA).

IEA, 1982b. *World Energy Outlook* (Paris: OECD/IEA).

IEA/Press (Paris). Press releases.

IMF (International Monetary Fund), 1983. *World Economic Outlook* (Washington, D.C.).

Inglehart, Ronald, and Jacques-René Rubier, 1978. Economic uncertainty and European solidarity: public opinion trends. *Annals of the American Academy of Political and Social Science*, no. 440 (November), pp. 66-97.

Jackson, John, 1983. Seminar on international trade bargaining, Harvard University, December 1.

Jervis, Robert, 1978. Cooperation under the security dilemma. *World Politics*, vol. 30, no. 2 (January), pp. 167-214.

Jervis, Robert, 1983. Security regimes. In Krasner, 1983, pp. 357-78.

Johnson, Paul, 1957. *The Suez War* (New York: Greenberg Press).

Jönsson, Christer, 1981. Sphere of flying: the politics of international aviation. *International Organization*, vol. 35, no. 2 (Spring), pp. 273-302.

Kalt, Joseph P., 1981. *The Economics and Politics of Oil Price Regulation: Federal Policy in the Post-Embargo Era* (Cambridge: MIT Press).

267

Kapstein, Ethan Barnaby, 1983. The sterling-dollar oil problem (unpublished manuscript).

Katzenstein, Peter J., 1975. International interdependence: some long-term trends and recent changes. *International Organization*, vol. 29, no. 4 (Autumn), pp. 1021-34.

Katzenstein, Peter J., ed., 1978. *Between Power and Plenty: Foreign Economic Policies of Advanced Industrial States* (Madison: University of Wisconsin Press).

Katzenstein, Peter J., 1984. *Corporatism and Change.* (Ithaca: Cornell University Press).

Keohane, Nannerl O., 1980. *Philosophy and the State in France: The Renaissance to the Enlightenment* (Princeton: Princeton University Press).

Keohane, Robert O., 1978. The International Energy Agency: state power and transgovernmental politics. *International Organization*, vol. 32, no. 4 (Autumn), pp. 929-52.

Keohane, Robert O., 1980. The theory of hegemonic stability and changes in international economic regimes, 1967-1977. In Ole Holsti et al., *Change in the International System* (Boulder: Westview Press), pp. 131-62.

Keohane, Robert O., 1982a. The demand for international regimes. *International Organization*, vol. 36, no. 2 (Spring), pp. 325-55. Also in Krasner, 1983.

Keohane, Robert O., 1982b. Hegemonic leadership and U.S. foreign economic policy in the "Long Decade" of the 1950s. In Avery and Rapkin, 1982, pp. 49-76.

Keohane, Robert O., 1982c. State power and industry influence: American foreign oil policy in the 1940s. *International Organization*, vol. 36, no. 1 (Winter), pp. 165-83.

Keohane, Robert O., 1982d. International agencies and the art of the possible: the case of the IEA, *Journal of Policy Analysis and Management*, vol. 1, no. 4 (Summer), pp. 469-81.

Keohane, Robert O., 1983. Theory of world politics: structural Realism and beyond. In Finifter, 1983, pp. 503-40.

Keohane, Robert O., forthcoming. The international politics of the great inflation. In Leon Lindberg and Charles Maier, eds., *The Politics of Inflation and Recession* (Washington, D.C.: Brookings Institution).

Keohane, Robert O., and Joseph S. Nye, eds., 1972. *Transnational Relations and World Politics* (Cambridge: Harvard University Press).

Keohane, Robert O., and Joseph S. Nye, 1974. Transgovernmental relations and international organizations. *World Politics*, vol. 27, no. 1 (October), pp. 39-62.

Keohane, Robert O., and Joseph S. Nye, 1977. *Power and Interdependence: World Politics in Transition* (Boston: Little, Brown).

Kindleberger, Charles P., 1972. The international monetary politics of a near-great power: two French episodes, 1926-1936 and 1960-1970. *Economic Notes* (Siena), vol. 1, nos. 2-3, pp. 30-44.

Kindleberger, Charles P., 1973. *The World in Depression, 1929-1939* (Berkeley: University of California Press).

Kindleberger, Charles P., 1978a. The aging economy (lecture given at the Institut für Welfwirtschaft, Kiel, July 5; published in Weltwirtschaftliches Archv Bd. CXIV).

Kindleberger, Charles P., 1978b. *Economic Response: Comparative Studies in Trade, Finance and Growth* (Cambridge: Harvard University Press).

Kindleberger, Charles P., 1978c. *Manias, Panics and Crashes* (New York: Basic Books).

Kindleberger, Charles P., 1981. Dominance and leadership in the international economy. *International Studies Quarterly*, vol. 25, no. 3 (June), pp. 242-54.

Kindleberger, Charles P., 1983. On the rise and decline of nations. *International Studies Quarterly*, vol. 27, no. 1 (March), pp. 5-10.

Klebanoff, Shoshana, 1974. *Middle East Oil and U.S. Foreign Policy* (New York: Praeger).

Knorr, Klaus, 1975. *The Power of Nations: The Political Economy of International Relations* (New York: Basic Books).

Kolko, Gabriel, 1968. *The Politics of War: The World and United States Foreign Policy, 1943-1945* (New York: Vintage Books).

Kolko, Joyce and Gabriel, 1972. *The Limits of Power* (New York: Harper & Row, 1972).

Krasner, Stephen D., 1976. State power and the structure of international trade. *World Politics*, vol. 28, no. 3 (April), pp. 317-43.

Krasner, Stephen D., 1978a. *Defending the National Interest: Raw Materials Investments and U.S. Foreign Policy* (Princeton: Princeton University Press).

Krasner, Stephen D., 1978b. United States commercial and monetary policy: unravelling the paradox of external strength and internal weakness. In Katzenstein, 1978, pp. 51-88.

Krasner, Stephen D., 1979. The Tokyo round: particularistic interests and prospects for stability in the global trading system. *International Studies Quarterly*, vol. 23, no. 4 (December), pp. 491-531.

Krasner, Stephen D., 1982. American policy and global economic stability. In Avery and Rapkin, 1982, pp. 29-48.

Krasner, Stephen D., 1983. Structural causes and regime consequences: regimes as intervening variables. In Krasner, 1983, pp. 1-22.

Krasner, Stephen D., ed., 1983. *International Regimes* (Ithaca: Cornell University Press).

Krause, Lawrence, and Walter Salant, eds., 1977. *Worldwide Inflation* (Washington, D.C.: Brookings Institution).

LaFeber, Walter, 1972. *America, Russia and the Cold War, 1945-71* (New York: John Wiley & Sons).

Laidler, D.E.W., 1975. *Essays on Money and Inflation* (Chicago: University of Chicago Press).

Laidler, D.E.W., 1977. *The Demand for Money: Theories and Evidence* (New York: Harper & Row).

Laitin, David, D., 1982. Capitalism and hegemony: Yorubaland and the international economy. *International Organization*, vol. 36, no. 4 (Autumn), pp. 687-713.

Lakatos, Imre, 1970. Falsification and the methodology of scientific research programmes. In Imre Lakatos and Alan Musgrave, eds., *Criticism and the Growth of Knowledge* (Cambridge: Cambridge University Press).

Lake, David A., 1983. International economic structures and American foreign economic policy, 1887-1934. *World Politics*, vol. 35, no. 4 (July), pp. 517-43.

Lantske, Ulf, 1975. The OECD and its International Energy Agency. In Vernon, ed., 1975, pp. 217-28.

Larson, Henrietta M., Evelyn H. Knowlton, and Charles S. Popple, 1971. *New Horizons, 1927-1950*, vol. 3 of *History of Standard Oil Company (New Jersey)* (New York: Harper & Row).

Latsis, Spiro J., 1976. A research programme in economics. In Latsis, ed., 1976, pp. 1-41.

Latsis, Spiro J., ed., 1976. *Method and Appraisal in Economics* (Cambridge: Cambridge University Press).

Lawson, Fred, 1983. Hegemony and the structure of international trade reassessed: a view from Arabia. *International Organization*, vol. 37, no. 2 (Spring), 317-38.

Lebow, Richard Ned, 1981. *Between Peace and War: The Nature of International Crisis* (Baltimore: The Johns Hopkins University Press).

Lenin, V. I., 1917/1939. *Imperialism: The Highest Stage of Capitalism* (New York: International Publishers).

Lewis, David K., 1969. *Convention: A Philosophical Study* (Cambridge: Harvard University Press).

Lewis, W. Arthur, 1978. *Growth and Fluctuation, 1870-1913* (London: George Allen & Unwin).

Lindblom, Charles E., 1965. *The Intelligence of Democracy* (New York: The Free Press).

Lindert, Peter H., 1969. *Key Currencies and Gold, 1900-1913*. Princeton Studies in International Finance no. 24 (Princeton: Princeton University Finance Section).

Lipson, Charles, 1981. The international organization of Third World debt. *International Organization*, vol. 35, no. 4 (Autumn), pp. 603-32.

Lipson, Charles, 1983. The transformation of trade: the sources and effects of regime change. In Krasner, 1983, pp. 233-72.

Locke, John, 1690/1960. *Two Treatises of Government*, edited by Peter Laslett (Cambridge: Cambridge University Press).

Lombra, Raymond, and Willard Witte, eds., 1982. *Political Economy of International and Domestic Monetary Relations* (Ames: Iowa State University Press).

Lowry, S. Todd. 1979. Bargain and contract theory in law and economics. In Samuels, 1979, pp. 261-82.

Mackie, J. L., 1977. *Ethics: Inventing Right and Wrong* (Harmondsworth, England: Penguin Books).

Macpherson, C. B., 1962. *The Political Theory of Possessive Individualism* (New York: Oxford University Press).

Mancke, Richard B., 1980. The American response: "on the job training?" In Foreign Policy Research Institute, 1980, pp. 27-43.

Mandel, Ernest, 1970. *Europe vs. America: Contradictions of Imperialism* (New York: Monthly Review Press).

Mandel, Ernest, 1974. *Late Capitalism* (London: Verso).

March, James G., 1966. The power of power. In David Easton, ed., *Varieties of Political Theory* (Englewood Cliffs, N.J.: Prentice-Hall), pp. 39-70.

March, James G., 1978. Bounded rationality, ambiguity, and the engineering of choice. *Bell Journal of Economics*, vol. 9, no. 2 (Autumn), pp. 587-608.

March, James G., and Herbert Simon, 1958. *Organizations* (New York: John Wiley & Sons).

Marx, Karl, 1852/1972. *The Eighteenth Brumaire of Louis Bonaparte*, in Robert C. Tucker, ed., *The Marx-Engels Reader* (New York: W. W. Norton), pp. 436-525.

Maull, Hans, 1980. *Europe and World Energy* (London: Butterworth).

McKeown, Timothy J., 1983a. Hegemonic stability theory and 19th century tariff levels in Europe. *International Organization*, vol. 37, no. 1 (Winter), pp. 73-92.

McKeown, Timothy J., 1983b. Orthodox microeconomics and theories of international politics (Pittsburgh: Carnegie-Mellon University, Department of Social Sciences, June).

Mikesell, Raymond, 1954. *Foreign Exchange in the Postwar World* (New York: Twentieth Century Fund).

Mill, John Stuart, 1861/1951. *Utilitarianism* (New York: E. P. Dutton).

Miller, Aaron David, 1980. *Search for Security: Saudi Arabian Oil and American Foreign Policy, 1939-1949* (Chapel Hill: University of North Carolina Press).

Mitrany, David, 1975. *The Functional Theory of Politics* (London: St. Martin's Press for the London School of Economics and Political Science).

Modelski, George, 1978. The long cycle of global politics and the nation-state. *Comparative Studies in Society and History*, vol. 20, no. 2 (April), pp. 214-38.

Modelski, George, 1982. Long cycles and the strategy of U.S. international economic policy. In Avery and Rapkin, 1982, pp. 97-118.

Morgenthau, Hans J., 1948/1966. *Politics Among Nations*, 4th edition (New York: Knopf).

Mork, Knut Anton, and Robert E. Hall, 1979. Energy prices, inflation and recession, 1974-75 (National Bureau of Economic Research, Working Paper no. 369, July).

Morse, Edward L., 1976. *Modernization and the Transformation of International Relations* (New York: The Free Press).

Murray, Robin, 1971. The internationalization of capital and the nation state. *New Left Review*, no. 67 (May-June), pp. 84-109.

Nagel, Ernest, 1961. *The Structure of Scientific Explanation* (New York: Harcourt Brace).

Nau, Henry, 1974-75. U.S. foreign policy in the energy crisis. *Atlantic Community Quarterly*, vol. 12, no. 4 (Winter), pp. 426-39.

Neff, Thomas, 1981. The changing world oil market. In Deese and Nye, 1981, pp. 23-48.

Neustadt, Richard E., 1970. *Alliance Politics* (New York: Columbia University Press).

North, Douglass C., 1981. *Structure and Change in Economic History* (New York: W. W. Norton).

North, Douglass C., and Robert Paul Thomas, 1973. *The Rise of the Western World: A New Economic History* (Cambridge: Cambridge University Press).

Nye, Joseph S., 1981. Energy and security. In Deese & Nye, 1981, pp. 3-22.

Nye, Joseph S., 1983. Ethics and foreign policy (unpublished paper).

Odell, John S., 1980. Latin American trade negotiations with the United States. *International Organization*, vol. 34, no. 2 (Spring), pp. 207-28.

Odell, John S., 1982. *U.S. International Monetary Policy: Markets, Power, and Ideas as Sources of Change* (Princeton: Princeton University Press).

OECD (Organization for Economic Cooperation and Development), 1977a. *Towards Full Employment and Price Stability* (McCracken Report, Paris).

OECD, 1977b. *World Energy Outlook* (Paris).

OECD, 1979. *The Impact of the Newly Industrializing Countries on Production and Trade in Manufactures* (Report by the Secretary-General, Paris).

OECD, 1980. *Main Economic Indicators: Historical Statistics, 1960-1979* (Paris).

OECD, 1982. *Economic Outlook: Occasional Studies* (Paris), June.

OECD, 1983. *Economic Outlook* (Paris), no. 33 (July).

OECD, *Observer* (Paris), bimonthly.

OEEC (Organization for European Economic Cooperation), 1958. *Europe's Need for Oil: Implications and Lessons of the Suez Crisis* (Paris).

Okin, Susan Moller, 1984. Taking the bishops seriously. *World Politics*, vol. 36, no. 4 (July).

Olson, Mancur, 1965, *The Logic of Collective Action* (Cambridge: Harvard University Press).

Olson, Mancur, 1982. *The Rise and Decline of Nations: Economic Growth, Stagflation, and Social Rigidities* (New Haven: Yale University Press).

Olson, Mancur, and Richard Zeckhauser, 1966. An economic theory of alliances. *Review of Economics and Statistics*, vol. 48, no. 3 (August), pp. 266-79. Reprinted in Bruce Russett, ed., *Economic Theories of International Politics* (Chicago: Markham, 1968), pp. 25-49.

Osgood, Robert E., 1953. *Ideals and Self-Interest in American Foreign Relations* (Chicago: University of Chicago Press).

Oye, Kenneth A., 1979. The domain of choice. In Oye et al., 1979, pp. 3-33.

Oye, Kenneth A., 1983a. International system structure and American foreign policy. In Oye et al., 1983, pp. 3-32.

Oye, Kenneth A., 1983b. Belief Systems, Bargaining and Breakdown: International Political Economy 1929-1934 (Ph.D. dissertation, Harvard University).

Oye, Kenneth A., Donald Rothchild, and Robert J. Lieber, eds., 1979. *Eagle Entangled: U.S. Foreign Policy in a Complex World* (New York: Longman).

Oye, Kenneth A., Robert J. Lieber, and Donald Rothchild, eds., 1983. *Eagle Defiant: United States Foreign Policy in the 1980s* (Boston: Little, Brown).

Page, S.A.B., 1981. The revival of protectionism and its consequences for Europe. *Journal of Common Market Studies*, vol. 20, no. 1 (September), pp. 17-40.

Panitch, Leo, 1976. *Social Democracy and Industrial Militancy: the Labour Party, the Trade Unions and Incomes Policy, 1945-1974* (Cambridge: Cambridge University Press).

Patterson, Gardner, 1966. *Discrimination in International Trade, The Policy Issues* (Princeton: Princeton University Press).

Penrose, Edith T., 1975. The development of crisis. In Vernon, 1975, pp. 39-57.

Polanyi, Karl, 1957/1971. The economy as instituted process. In Polanyi et al., *Trade and Market in the Early Empires* (Chicago: Henry Regnery), pp. 243-70.

Puchala, Donald J., 1975. Domestic politics and regional harmonization in the European Communities. *World Politics*, vol. 27, no. 4 (July), pp. 496-520.

Puchala, Donald J., and Raymond F. Hopkins, 1983. International regimes: lessons from inductive analysis. In Krasner, 1983, pp. 61-92.

Putnam, Robert D., 1978. Interdependence and the Italian Communists. *International Organization*, vol. 32, no. 2 (Spring), pp. 301-49.

Putnam, Robert D., and Nicholas Bayne, 1984. *Hanging Together: The Seven-Power Summits* (Cambridge: Harvard University Press).

Radner, C. B. and R., 1972. *Decision and Organization* (Amsterdam: North-Holland).

Rawls, John, 1971. *A Theory of Justice* (Cambridge: Harvard University Press).

Reich, Robert B., 1983. Beyond free trade. *Foreign Affairs*, vol. 61, no. 4 (Spring), pp. 773-804.

Robbins, Lionel, 1932. *An Essay on the Nature and Significance of Economic Science* (London: Macmillan).

Rosecrance, Richard, ed., 1976. *America as an Ordinary Country* (Ithaca: Cornell University Press).

Rosecrance, Richard, and Arthur Stein, 1973. Interdependence: myth or reality? *World Politics*, vol. 26, no. 1 (October), pp. 1-27.

Rostow, W. W., 1975. Kondratieff, Schumpeter and Kuznets: trend periods revisited. *Journal of Economic History*, vol. 25, no. 4 (December), pp. 719-53.

Rousseau, Jean-Jacques, 1755/1950. *A Discourse on the Origin of Inequality* (New York: E.P. Dutton).

Rubin, Barry, 1980. *Paved with Good Intentions: The American Experience in Iran* (New York: Oxford University Press).

Ruggie, John Gerard, 1975. International responses to technology: concepts and trends. *International Organization*, vol. 29, no. 3 (Summer), pp. 557-84.

Ruggie, John Gerard, 1983a. Continuity and transformation in the world polity: toward a neorealist synthesis. *World Politics*, vol. 35, no. 2 (January), pp. 261-86.

Ruggie, John Gerard, 1983b. International regimes, transactions, and change: embedded liberalism in the postwar economic order. In Krasner, 1983, pp. 195-232.

Ruggie, John Gerard, 1983c. Political structure and change in the international economic order: the north-south dimension. In Ruggie, 1983, pp. 423-88.

Ruggie, John Gerard, ed., 1983. *The Antinomies of Interdependence: National Welfare and the Division of Labor* (New York: Columbia University Press).

Russell, Robert W., 1973. Transgovernmental interaction in the international monetary system, 1960-1972. *International Organization*, vol. 27, no. 4 (Autumn), pp. 431-64.

Russett, Bruce, 1978. The marginal utility of income transfers to the Third World. *International Organization*, vol. 32, no. 4 (Autumn), pp. 913-28.

Sahlins, Marshall, 1972. *Stone Age Economics* (Chicago: Aldine-Atherton).

Salant, Walter, 1977a. International transmission of inflation. In Krause and Salant, 1977, pp. 167-227.

Salant, Walter, 1977b. A supranational approach to the analysis of worldwide inflation. In Krause and Salant, 1977, pp. 633-50.

Samuels, Warren J., 1979. *The Economy as a System of Power* (New Brunswick, N.J. Transaction Books).

Samuelson, Paul A., 1967. The monopolistic competition revolution. In R. E. Kuenne, ed., *Monopolistic Competition Theory* (New York: John Wiley & Sons).

Sandel, Michael J., 1982. *Liberalism and the Limits of Justice* (Cambridge: Cambridge University Press).

Saxonhouse, Gary, 1982. Cyclical and macrostructural issues in U.S.–Japan economic relations. In Daniel I. Okimoto, ed., *Japan's Economy: Coping with Change in the International Environment* (Boulder: Westview Press). pp. 123-48.

Schelling, Thomas C., 1960/1980. *The Strategy of Conflict* (Cambridge: Harvard University Press).

Schelling, Thomas C., 1978. *Micromotives and Macrobehavior* (New York: W. W. Norton).

Schieffelin, Edward L., 1980. Reciprocity and the construction of reality. *Man*, vol. 15, no. 3 (September), pp. 502-17.

Schroeder, Paul W., 1958. *The Axis Alliance and Japanese-American Relations* (Ithaca: Cornell University Press).

Schuler, Henry M., 1976. The international oil negotiations. In Zartman, 1976, pp. 124-207.

Schumpeter, Joseph A., 1934/1951. *The Theory of Economic Development: An Inquiry into Profits, Capital, Credit, Interest and the Business Cycle*, translated from the German by Redvers Opie (Cambridge: Harvard University Press).

Scitovsky, Tibor, 1978. Market power and inflation. *Economica*, vol. 45, no. 179 (August), pp. 221-33.

Shwadran, Benjamin, 1955. *The Middle East, Oil, and the Great Powers* (New York: Praeger).

Simon, Herbert A., 1955. A behavioral model of rational choice. *Quarterly Journal of Economics*, vol. 69, no. 1 (February), pp. 99-118. Reprinted in Simon, 1979a, pp. 7-19.

Simon, Herbert A., 1972. Theories of bounded rationality. In Radner and Radner, 1972, pp. 161-76. Reprinted in Simon, 1982, pp. 408-23.

Simon, Herbert A., 1976. From substantive to procedural rationality. In Latsis, 1976, pp. 129-48. Reprinted in Simon, 1982, pp. 424-43.

Simon, Herbert A., 1978. Rationality as process and as product of thought. *American Economic Review*, vol. 68, no. 2 (May), pp. 1-16. Reprinted in Simon, 1982, pp. 444-59.

Simon, Herbert A., 1979a. *Models of Thought* (New Haven: Yale University Press).

Simon, Herbert A., 1979b. Rational decision making in business organizations. *American Economic Review*, vol. 69, no. 4 (September), pp. 493-513. Reprinted in Simon, 1982, pp. 474-94.

Simon, Herbert A., 1982. *Models of Bounded Rationality*, 2 vols. (Cambridge: MIT Press).

Singer, Peter, 1972. Famine, affluence, and morality. *Philosophy & Public Affairs*, vol. 1, no. 3 (Spring), pp. 229-43.

Skocpol, Theda, 1977. Wallerstein's world capitalist system: a theoretical and historical critique. *American Journal of Sociology*, vol. 82, no. 5 (March), pp. 1075-90.

Smith, Adam, 1776/1976. *The Wealth of Nations* (Chicago: University of Chicago Press).

Snidal, Duncan, 1979. Public goods, property rights, and political organization. *International Studies Quarterly*, vol. 23, no. 4 (December), pp. 532-66.

Snidal, Duncan, 1981. Interdependence, Regimes and International Cooperation (unpublished manuscript).

Snyder, Glenn H., and Paul Diesing, 1977. *Conflict among Nations: Bargaining, Decision making, and System Structure in International Crises* (Princeton: Princeton University Press).

Solomon, Robert, 1977. *The International Monetary System, 1945-1976: An Insider's View* (New York: Harper & Row).

Stein, Arthur A., 1980. The politics of linkage. *World Politics*, vol. 33, no. 1 (October), pp. 62-81.

Stein, Arthur A., 1983. Coordination and collaboration: regimes in an anarchic world. In Krasner, ed., 1983, pp. 115-40.

Stein, Leslie, 1981. The growth and implications of LDC manufactured exports to advanced countries. *Kyklos*, vol. 34, fasc. 1, pp. 36-59.

Steinbruner, John D., 1974. *The Cybernetic Theory of Decision: New Dimensions of Political Analysis* (Princeton: Princeton University Press).

Stigler, George J., and Gary S. Becker, 1977. *De Gustibus Non Est Disputandem. American Economic Review*, vol. 67, no. 1 (March), pp. 76-90.

Stinchcombe, Arthur L., 1968. *Constructing Social Theories.* (New York: Harcourt, Brace & World).

Stobaugh, Robert B., 1975. The oil companies in the crisis. In Vernon, 1975, pp. 179-202.

Stocking, George W., 1970. *Middle East Oil: A Study in Political and Economic Controversy* (Nashville: Vanderbilt University Press).

Stoff, Michael B., 1980. *Oil, War, and American Security: The Search for a National Policy on Foreign Oil, 1941-1947* (New Haven: Yale University Press).

Stone, Jeremy J., 1983. Saga of the MIRV flight-test ban. *F.A.S. Public Interest Report*, vol. 36, no. 7 (September), pp. 1-3.

Strange, Susan, 1976. The study of transnational relations. *International Affairs* (London), vol. 52, no. 3 (July), pp. 333-45.

Strange, Susan, 1979. The management of surplus capacity: or how does theory stand up to protectionism 1970s style? *International Organization*, vol. 33, no. 3 (Summer), pp. 303-34.

Strange, Susan, 1982. Still an extraordinary power: America's role in a global monetary system. In Lombra and Witte, 1982, pp. 73-93.

Strange, Susan, 1983. *Cave! hic dragones*: a critique of regime analysis. In Krasner, 1983, pp. 337-54.

Sweezy, Paul M., and Harry Magdoff, 1972. *The Dynamics of U.S. Capitalism: Corporate Structure, Inflation, Credit, Gold and the Dollar* (New York: Monthly Review Press).

Swoboda, Alexander, 1977. Monetary approaches to worldwide inflation. In Krause and Salant, 1977, pp. 9-62.

Sylvan, David, 1981. The newest mercantilism. *International Organization*, vol 35, no. 2 (Spring), pp. 375-94.

Taurek, John M., 1977. Should the numbers count? *Philosophy & Public Affairs*, vol. 6, no. 4 (Summer), pp. 293-316.

Taylor, Michael, 1976. *Anarchy and Cooperation* (New York: John Wiley & Sons).

Taylor, Paul, 1980. Interdependence and autonomy in the European Communities: the case of the European monetary system. *Journal of Common Market Studies*, vol. 18, no. 4 (June), pp. 370-87.

Tollison, Robert D., and Thomas D. Willett, 1979. An economic theory of mutually advantageous issue linkages in international negotiations. *International Organization*, vol. 33, no. 4 (Autumn), pp. 425-49.

Toplin, Robert, 1971. *The Abolition of Slavery in Brazil* (New York: Atheneum).

Triffin, Robert, 1957. *Europe and the Money Muddle* (New Haven: Yale University Press).

Tucker, Robert W., 1977. *The Inequality of Nations* (New York: Basic Books).

Tufte, Edward R., 1978. *Political Control of the Economy* (Princeton, Princeton University Press).

Turner, Louis, 1978. *Oil Companies in the International System* (London: George Allen & Unwin for the Royal Institute of International Affairs).

Turner, Louis et al., 1982. *The Newly Industrializing Countries: Trade and Adjustment* (London: George Allen & Unwin).

U.S. House of Representatives, 1957. Hearings before the Committee on Interstate and Foreign Commerce, *Petroleum Survey, 1957 Outlook*, 85th Congress, 1st session, February-March 1957.

U.S. Senate, 1952. Select Committee on Small Business, Subcommittee on Monopoly, *The International Petroleum Cartel* (Staff Report by the Federal Trade Commission), 94th Congress, 1st session, reprint April 1975.

U.S. Senate, 1957. Joint Hearings Before Subcommittees of the Committee on the Judiciary and Committee on Interior and Insular Affairs, *Emergency Oil Lift Program and Related Oil Problems*, 85th Congress, 2nd session, February 5-21.

U.S. Senate, 1974a. Committee on Foreign Relations, Subcommittee on Multinational Corporations, *The International Petroleum Cartel, the Iranian Consortium, and U.S. National Security*, Committee Print, 93rd Congress, 2nd session, February 21, 1974.

U.S. Senate, 1974b. Committee on Foreign Relations, Subcommittee on Multinational Corporations, *Multinational Oil Corporations and U.S. Foreign Policy: Hearings of the Subcommittee on Multinational Corporations*, 93rd Congress, 2nd session.

U.S. Senate, 1975. Committee on Foreign Relations, Subcommittee on Multinational Corporations, *Multinational Oil Corporations and U.S. Foreign Policy, Report*, Committee Print, 93rd Congress, 2nd session, January 1975.

277

Urmson, J. O., 1968. Utilitarianism. *International Encyclopedia of the Social Sciences* (New York: Macmillan), pp. 224-29.

Veljanovski, Cento G., 1982. The Coase theorems and the economic theory of markets and law. *Kyklos*, vol. 35, fasc. 1, pp. 53-74.

Vernon, Raymond, 1971. *Sovereignty at Bay: The Multinational Spread of U.S. Enterprises* (New York: Basic Books).

Vernon, Raymond, ed., 1975. *The Oil Crisis*, special issue of *Daedalus*, Fall 1975.

Vernon, Raymond, 1982. International trade policy in the 1980's: prospects and problems. *International Studies Quarterly*, vol. 26, no. 4 (December), pp. 483-510.

Vernon, Raymond, 1983. Old rules and new players: GATT in the world trading system. Paper presented at the Twenty-Fifth Anniversary Conference of the Center for International Affairs, Harvard University, Cambridge, June 11.

Verreydt, Eric, and Jean Waelbroeck, 1982. European community protection against manufactured imports from developing countries: a case study in the political economy of protection. In Bhagwati, 1982, pp. 369-92.

Viner, Jacob, 1948. Power versus plenty as objectives of foreign policy in the seventeenth and eighteenth Centuries. *World Politics*, vol. 1, no. 1 (October), pp. 1-29.

Wagner, R. Harrison, 1983. The theory of games and the problem of international cooperation. *American Political Science Review*, vol. 77, no. 2 (June), pp. 330-46.

Wallerstein, Immanuel, 1974. *The Modern World-System: Capitalist Agriculture and the Origins of the European World-Economy in the Sixteenth Century* (New York: Academic Press).

Wallerstein, Immanuel, 1979. *The Capitalist World Economy* (Cambridge: Cambridge University Press).

Wallerstein, Immanuel, 1980. *The Modern World-System II: Mercantilism and the Consolidation of the European World-Economy, 1600-1750* (New York: Academic Press).

Waltz, Kenneth, 1959. *Man, the State and War* (New York: Columbia University Press).

Waltz, Kenneth, 1979. *Theory of World Politics* (Reading, Mass.: Addison-Wesley).

Walzer, Michael, 1977. *Just and Unjust Wars: A Moral Argument with Historical Illustrations* (New York: Basic Books).

Warren, Bill, 1971. The internationalization of capital and the nation state: a comment. *New Left Review*, no. 68 (July-August), pp. 83-88.

Weber, Max, 1904/1949. Objectivity in social science and social policy. In Weber, *The Methodology of the Social Sciences*, translated and edited by Edward A. Shils and Henry A. Finch (New York: The Free Press).

Weber, Max, 1905/1949. Critical studies in the logic of the cultural sciences.

In Weber, *The Methodology of the Social Sciences*, translated and edited by Edward A. Shils and Henry A. Finch (New York: The Free Press).

Weber, Max, 1918/1946. Politics as a vocation. In Gerth and Mills, 1946, pp. 77-128.

Whitman, Maria v.N., 1979. *Reflections of Interdependence: Issues for Economic Theory and U.S. Policy* (Pittsburgh: University of Pittsburgh Press).

Wilcox, Clair, 1949. *A Charter for World Trade* (New York: Macmillan).

Willett, Thomas D., and John Mullen, 1982. The effects of alternative international monetary systems on macroeconomic discipline and inflationary biases. In Lombra and Witte, 1982, pp. 143-55.

Williamson, Oliver, 1965. A dynamic theory of interfirm behavior. *Quarterly Journal of Economics*, vol. 79, no. 4 (November), pp. 579-607.

Williamson, Oliver, 1975. *Markets and Hierarchies: Analysis and Anti-Trust Implications* (New York: The Free Press).

Williamson, Oliver, 1983. Credible commitments: using hostages to support exchange. *American Economic Review*, vol. 73, no. 4 (September), pp. 519-40.

Wilson, Charles, 1957. *Profit and Power. A Study of England and the Dutch Wars* (Cambridge: Cambridge University Press).

Wolfers, Arnold, 1962. *Discord and Collaboration: Essays on International Politics* (Baltimore: Johns Hopkins University Press).

Wolfers, Arnold, and Laurence Martin, eds., 1956. *The Anglo-American Tradition in Foreign Affairs* (New Haven: Yale University Press).

Woolcock, Stephen, 1982. Adjustment in Western Europe. In Turner et al., 1982, pp. 220-37.

World Financial Markets, published monthly by Morgan Guaranty Trust Company of New York.

Yeager, Leland B., 1976. *International Monetary Relations: Theory, History, Policy*, 2nd edition (New York: Harper & Row).

Yoffie, David B., 1983. *Power and Protectionism: Strategies of the Newly Industrializing Countries* (New York: Columbia University Press).

Young, Oran R., ed., 1975. *Bargaining: Formal Theories of Negotiation* (Urbana: University of Illinois Press).

Young, Oran R., 1979. *Compliance and Public Authority* (Washington, D.C.: Resources for the Future).

Young, Oran R., 1980. International regimes: problems of concept formation. *World Politics*, vol. 32, no. 3 (April), pp. 331-56.

Young, Oran R., 1983. Regime dynamics: the rise and fall of international regimes. In Krasner, 1983, pp. 93-114.

Zartman, I. William, ed., 1976. *The 50% Solution* (New York: Doubleday).

Zysman, John, and Laura Tyson, 1983. *American Industry in International Competition: Government Policies and Corporate Strategies* (Ithaca: Cornell University Press).

INDEX

'Abd al-'Aziz, King of Saudi Arabia, 152, 157
ABM (anti-ballistic missile), 118n
Achnacarry agreement, 60
act-utilitarians, 113n
adjustment costs, 6, 161, 163, 166, 209, 216, 243
Aggarwal, Vinod, 33n, 61, 91n, 190, 201, 211
Agreement on an International Energy Program, 220
Aivazian, Varouj A., 87
Akerlof, George A., 82, 83, 93, 95n, 96
Alchian, Armen A., 80n
Algeria, 129
Allison, Graham, 114
altruism, 122; "putative," 130
"American Century," 15, 138
American hegemony (post-World War II), 8, 16, 23-24, 31, 36, 37, 41, 42, 49n, 139, 179, 182, 194, 195-216 passim, 243-44
Anderson, Irvine H., 151, 152, 153, 154, 155n, 156n, 157, 157n, 159n, 160, 161n
Anglo-American Petroleum Agreement (1943-45), 60, 118, 141, 150, 153-54, 163, 164
Anglo-Iranian Oil Company (AIOC), 156, 156n, 167, 168, 169
anomie, 73
antitrust enforcement, 169
Arab nationalism, 203
Aramco (Arabian American Oil Company), 151, 155, 156-57, 161
arms control agreements, 118n
arms races, 123n
Arrighi, Giovanni, 42, 43
Arrow, Kenneth J., 83, 96
aspiration levels, 112
Aswan Dam, 169
asymmetrical information, 93-94
Aubrey, Henry, 208
Austin, John, 113
Austria, 259

automobiles, 211, 255
Avery, William P., xxi
Axelrod, Robert, 13, 53, 76, 104, 127

Babai, Don, 132
Badger, Daniel, 226n, 227, 228, 232, 235, 236n, 237
Bagehot, Walter, 130
balanced reciprocity, 129
balance-of-payments regime, 59
balancing of accounts, bilateral vs. multilateral, 144-45
Baldwin, David A., 121
Barber, William J., 175
Barkun, Michael, 91n
basic force models, 20, 34, 195. See also force activation models
Bauer, Raymond A., 175
Bayne, Nicholas, 101n, 217, 232n
behavior, 26, 64, 73, 238; egoism and empathy as competing explanations of, 125-31 passim
behavioral models, 21-22
Beitz, Charles, 120, 124, 248, 249, 250-51
Belgium, 223, 227
Belgrave, Robert, 226n, 227, 228, 232, 235, 236n, 237
benefits, 123n; distribution of, 18, 86
Bergsten, C. Fred, 99, 185
Blackhurst, Richard, 212
Blair, John, 156n, 203n
Bliss, Don C., 162n
Block, Fred L., 42, 73, 120n, 137, 143, 145, 253
Bobrow, Davis W., 96n, 193
Bohi, Douglas R., 174, 175
bomber, B-1, 118
bounded rationality, 13, 108, 110, 111-16, 131, 224, 258
Bourses (medieval Europe), 129, 130n
Branson, William H., 196
Brazil, 123, 190, 217
Brenner, Robert, 43
Bressand, Albert, 188, 213n

281

285